1963

The Year of Hope and Hostility

Byron Williams

Byronspeaks

1963 © 2013 Byronspeaks

Byronspeaks is a nonprofit organization and commercial publishing company, committed to bringing meaningful commentary into the public discourse through the lens of public morality; and it actively participates in the creation of the next generation of writers and thinkers.

"I Have a Dream" and the "Letter from Birmingham Jail" were reprinted by arrangement with the Heirs to the Estate of Dr. Martin Luther King, Jr., c/o Writers House Inc. as agent for the proprietor, New York City.

ISBN: 978-0-9896620-0-0

First Edition 2013

This book is dedicated to Jack O'Dell, who faced unbridled absurdity from his own government as he fought for equal protection under the law 50 years ago, and remains today an unwavering prisoner of hope.

Contents

ACKNOWLEDGEMENTS

There are so many people I need to thank for the fruition of this project. I will undoubtedly omit someone, and for this I offer my apologies in advance.

In addition to being a writer and columnist, I also have the privilege of serving as pastor of the Resurrection Community Church in Berkeley, California. I must therefore begin by acknowledging my congregation for their love and support. Week after week, they amaze me with their courage, conviction, and embrace of inconvenient love.

Writing a book that chronicles events that occurred fifty years ago means that it is likely that many of the key players are no longer living. I was fortunate to speak with several survivors. There are four in particular: without their invaluable input, I don't know if I would have been able to effectively capture this year that was intertwined with hope and hostility.

I am deeply indebted to the late Ted Sorensen. At the time of his death there was no greater source to offer insight on "President Kennedy," especially on events related to 1963. He was the first person to grant me an interview for this project. He was gracious with his time, and his willingness to sit down with me four years ago only bolstered my belief in this book.

During an interview on my BlogTalkRadio show, Clarence Jones, personal counsel and advisor to Martin Luther King Jr., illuminated for me Dr. King's mindset as he was incarcerated in Birmingham, which led to his penning his "Letter from Birmingham Jail."

I want to also thank Rev. James Lawson for writing the foreword. Rev. Lawson is one of this country's prophetic giants. His unwavering commitment to the Gandhian tactics of nonviolent direct action is one of the great gifts bestowed to this nation as it wandered through the wilderness in search of its demagnetized moral compass for fairness and human dignity. Anyone who views the 1963 clips of innocent children taking on Bull Connor's police dogs and high-powered fire hoses should thank Rev. Lawson for his patriotic service.

This book is dedicated to Jack O'Dell, one of the true unsung heroes of the Civil Rights Movement. O'Dell served as director of voter registration and direct mail campaigns for the Southern Christian Leadership Conference. FBI Director J. Edgar Hoover portrayed O'Dell, along with Stanley Levison, as members of the Communist Party. Their removal from the SCLC was the price that the Kennedy Administration exacted from Martin Luther King in order for the president to support civil rights legislation. This unfortunate set of events did not deter O'Dell, who remains committed to justice and equality. We would all benefit should he decide to write a book about his wonderful and rich life.

I want to give a shout-out to Barrett Briske, my copy editor, Cole Print and Marketing for the cover design, and Maureen McNabb for her endurance while proofreading the initial manuscript.

To my friend, colleague, and brother Rev. Robert Wilkins, I am beholden to his sage counsel during the most challenging times of this project. And to Rev. Michael Smith, whose friendship is beyond measure, I am thankful for his authentic love and support.

I owe a special debt to my friends at Casa Belicoso Cigar Lounge for their willingness to engage in myriad stories about 1963, asking probing questions, and never appearing to grow weary as I managed to divert every conversation into something about this year of hope and hostility.

The seeds were sowed for this project many years ago through the love of Henry Cheatham, the man that I refer to as my father. He was my first glimpse at unconditional love. He gave me the confidence to follow my dreams and to not fear the possibility of failure.

I wish to thank my wife, Gabrielle, for her support, wisdom, and keen insight. To her I say only, "Je t'aime"!

Finally, I must acknowledge the one who sat through every word composed without complaint: my precocious boxer, Zeus. I miss him terribly, but at least this way I don't have to give him any writing credits or any share of royalties.

Byron Williams
May 2013

FOREWARD

When I think back on the year 1963, I do so with a great deal of pride. The source of my satisfaction is not rooted in any individual accomplishment, but rather the privilege to participate in the second American Revolution.

The first American Revolution, which originated on July 4, 1776, advanced the lofty ideal for the human race that all were created equal. Too often this concept is buried in antiquity in terms of its radical nature. Oppression, subjugation, and conquest—not equality—were the universal concepts that the eighteenth century embraced. One would be hard-pressed to journey to any part of the world in the eighteenth century and not find the oppression in some form that was not part of the systematic policy of that land.

The Founders courageously pledged to one another their lives, fortunes, and sacred honor to ensure that governments are instituted among the people, deriving their just powers from the consent of the governed.

But history has tragically reminded us that the immortal words taken from the preamble to the Constitution, "We the People of the United States, in Order to form a more perfect Union," came with hidden qualifiers that were not printed on the document that is proudly encased in the rotunda of the National Archives, as it managed to leave many of America's citizens, and as it continues to do today, on the sidelines of fairness and human dignity.

There seems to be some misunderstanding of who exactly comprised the "we" in the vaunted phrase "We the People." This was the basis for the second American Revolution, more commonly known as the Civil Rights Movement.

But to discuss my participation in the Birmingham campaign in 1963, it is important to underscore that my involvement in the movement unofficially began on December 6, 1955. That was the day I picked up my copy of the *Nagpur Times*—I was living in Nagpur, India serving as a Methodist missionary at Nagpur University—and the headline read: "70,000 Negroes Boycott in Montgomery, Alabama." I can't begin to convey my excitement.

While in Nagpur I also studied Satyagraha, the principles of nonviolent resistance developed by Mohandas K. Gandhi to win India's independence from Great Britain. I had been convinced this was what the Negro needed to help America realize the moral commitment it made back in 1776.

I officially met Martin Luther King on February 6, 1957. I told him that once my theological studies at Oberlin College concluded, I was ready and willing to join his efforts. But King said to me, "Come now. We don't have anyone like you down there." As a result of this gentle but persuasive request, I found myself later that year training the "Little Rock Nine" in nonviolent direct-action concepts.

By the time the decades of the 1960s began, there was a nonviolent direct-action campaign occurring annually. In 1960, there was the sit-in movement in Greensboro, North Carolina; in 1961, there were the Freedom Riders, who rode interstate buses into the segregated South; in 1962, there was the campaign in Albany, Georgia; and in 1963, there was Birmingham. The Birmingham campaign was part of a watershed moment for the movement in that it fueled the momentum for the March on Washington, ultimately the civil rights legislation enacted in 1964 and '65.

We expected opposition from the city government of Birmingham, led by Public Safety Commissioner Eugene "Bull" Connor, and ostensibly the state of Alabama, led by Governor George Wallace. And we received tepid support from the Kennedy Administration.

My use of the term "tepid" is based on the realities of 1963 politics. John F. Kennedy did not run on a civil rights platform in 1960. He really didn't know that much about the country in relationship to structural poverty, Jim Crow laws, and segregation. But he came as a person eager to be president and eager to learn—one who was willing to talk to different types of people.

But the administration was shackled by the bipartisan agreement that the Cold War was the most critical issue for the United States, not the welfare of all the people. Nor supporting the values of a movement that had the audacity to place the Fourteenth Amendment's equal protection under the law clause at its epicenter.

In addition to the administration's tepid support, the movement received opposition from the federal government in the form of FBI Director J. Edgar Hoover, who was placing his own form of pressure on the administration.

But we were so convinced that nonviolent direct action was the transformative method whereby love could indeed overcome hate. For all its well-documented hatred, Birmingham possessed the fertile soil that produced King's famous "Letter from Birmingham Jail." It was in Birmingham where thousands of high school and elementary students left the Sixteenth Street Baptist Church to show the world that they possessed a fire that burned within—one that no high-pressured water hose could deter, and one that was equally impervious to ferocious dogs.

We persevered in what on the surface appeared to be a David versus Goliath struggle, but we saw Birmingham as having the opportunity to do the nation a favor by making it uphold to the values it had committed on paper for all its citizens.

For it was the events in Birmingham beginning in April 1963 that not only paved the way to landmark civil rights legislation in 1964 and 1965, but also allowed King to tell America about his dream on August 28.

As Byron Williams writes persuasively, 1963 was undeniably a year of hope and hostility that has taken fifty years to begin to comprehend it's influence on the ongoing battle for justice.

James Lawson
Los Angeles

INTRODUCTION

On June 11, 2008, I was having one of my musing conversations with my good friend Mark Brown from Atlanta, who was preparing to attend the Democratic Convention. Mark shared with me that the convention coincided with the fortieth anniversary of one of the most memorable Democratic Conventions in the summer of 1968. That was the year Martin Luther King Jr. and Robert Kennedy were assassinated, Vietnam had become an untenable situation, and the convention itself was marred by violence that seemed to define the year.

I said to Mark, "You know 1963 was really the year that changed things." In addition to the assassination of President John F. Kennedy, it was the year that King wrote his "Letter from Birmingham Jail" and gave the keynote address at the March on Washington; four girls were killed at the Sixteenth Street Baptist Church; and George Wallace stood in front of the schoolhouse doors symbolically blocking two Negro students from admittance.

Mark then asked, "When was [NAACP Field Secretary] Medgar Evers assassinated?"

I responded, "Tonight is actually the anniversary of Medgar's death!" Mark and I were speaking on June 11, the forty-fifth anniversary of one of the most remarkable twenty-four-hour periods in American history. I then told Mark that 1963 would be the topic of my forthcoming Sunday column.

As a twice-weekly columnist, once a column is written, I seldom dwell on the subject matter after it is written—unless it is part of a series. And my column on 1963 was no exception. But after the column was published, I received the following comment:

"This piece merits use in a textbook for those who were not adults in 1963. It's a concise, complete, fair and balanced recap of 1963 in politics, which changed America."

There it was, the invitation to take the journey into one of the most remarkable years in the twentieth century. Without the aforementioned comment, it is quite possible that my 1963 column would have been one of myriad columns that I write annually, possessing a shelf life of no more than seven days. Instead it has been part of my life for the past five years.

Like many others, I was aware, largely on the periphery, of the events chronicled in this project. There are a plethora of books that discuss them either in detail or in passing. But none have approached them through the lens of a 365-day odyssey. Moreover, it was learning of the circuitous route that led to the transformative moments in 1963 where I was able to see who we were fifty years ago and its impact on who we are today.

There are three individuals who stand out in 1963: President John F. Kennedy, Rev. Martin Luther King Jr., and George Wallace. Each of the events that I chronicle features at least one, in some cases all, of the protagonists in a significant way.

John F. Kennedy

In Kennedy, 1963 reveals a remarkable transformation of leadership. In 1961, Kennedy had in my view the worst inaugural foreign policy year of any first-term president in the twentieth century, marred by the Bay of Pigs, an unsuccessful conference in Vienna with Soviet Premier Nikita Khrushchev, and the building of the Berlin Wall.

Domestically, his tepid response to civil rights caused frustration within the Negro community, who had provided overwhelming support in his close election against Vice President Richard Nixon in 1960. During the campaign, Kennedy naively promised changes in civil rights with a "stroke of his presidential pen," but politics and desires for reelection in 1964 would leave many supporters of civil rights wanting throughout majority of his term.

By 1963, we see how Kennedy emerges as a world leader, evident in his famous "Ich bin ein Berliner" speech in West Berlin.

On June 10, 1963, his speech at American University set the stage for a Limited Nuclear Test Ban Treaty with the Soviet Union, becoming the first U.S. president to humanize his Cold War adversaries. As he stated at American University: "Our most basic common link is that we all inhabit this planet. We all breathe the same air. We all cherish our children's future. And we are all mortal."

After signing the last embargo against Cuba, maintaining Operation Mongoose, a CIA plan that included the assassination of Fidel Castro, Kennedy also made overtures toward normalizing relations with Cuba.

The confidence that Kennedy demonstrated internationally was not present domestically, at least not at the onset of 1963. However, the commitment of civil rights workers in Birmingham, the political ambition of Wallace, and the overt hatred exhibited by Public Safety Commissioner Eugene "Bull" Connor forced a politically reluctant Kennedy by June 1963 to give a nationally televised address on civil rights. Though Kennedy's growth as a leader in 1963 is undeniable, there would be one area where decisions made that year would have a lasting impact negatively on future generations.

Martin Luther King

For King, 1963 was his "coming out" party onto the world stage. He was already nationally known, but 1963 would be the year King used the warring factions of hope and hostility to place civil rights on the nation's conscience. On the heels of his perceived defeat in Albany, Georgia in 1962, King embarked on what many viewed at the time to be a suicide mission to desegregate Birmingham, the citadel of Jim Crow segregation. But history shows that King had an unwitting ally in "Bull" Connor. In 1963, King would produce his most significant work ("Letter from Birmingham Jail") and his most memorable work (the keynote address at the March on Washington).

It was during the speech at the March on Washington that America heard King for the first time speak beyond sound bites. It prompted Kennedy, who was watching on television, to reply, "He's good. He's damn good." Nationally televised before a curious audience, many of whom questioned whether a large assembly of Negroes could remain nonviolent for the duration of the rally, witnessed King officially become what A. Phillip Randolph offered in his introduction as "the moral leader of our nation."

George Wallace

The systematic mythologizing of Kennedy and King in the aftermath of their deaths has somewhat blurred the lines between reality and idealism. Yet, I submit Wallace's tangible influence on our national public discourse and its praxis may have been the most significant of the three.

The key to understanding Wallace circa 1963 is to understand a statement he made following his 1958 gubernatorial loss. There was common agreement among his aides that his opponent John Patterson's stance on segregation was stronger. Moreover, Patterson enjoyed the support of the Ku Klux Klan. In 1958, Wallace was viewed as a moderate on segregation, having received the endorsement of the NAACP. In the aftermath of his election defeat, Wallace reportedly said, "Well, boys, no other son-of-a-bitch is ever going to out-nigger me again." It is through this statement that we see the political ambition of Wallace 1963 take shape. Wallace hardly stands alone as an overly ambitious political animal, but what he accomplished beginning in 1963 became a trademark for future politicians, in particular the Republican Party.

Why 1963?

Invariably, two questions are raised when the topic of my writing a book on 1963 comes up. The first: "I know Kennedy was assassinated, but what else happened?" The short answer is, "A lot!" It was a year simultaneously entangled in Cold War ideology that would span to Cuba, the Soviet Union, Germany, and Vietnam. Civil rights, with the help of television, would force the nation to be self-reflective about its stated democratic values. Both would unveil high and low moments for the nation.

The second question: "Are you suggesting that 1963 is more important than 1968?" The short answer is no. That is, in my view, a shortcut through history. Could one provide a cogent analysis of the women's suffrage movement in the United States that culminated with passage of the Nineteenth Amendment in 1920 without considering the influence of the passage of the Fourteenth Amendment in 1868? No year stands in isolation. Many of the transformative events of 1963 were dependent upon actions in previous years. Sometime it was decades in the making. The reader will discover that what occurred in 1963 influenced 1968.

This project does demonstrate that fifty years ago America was a much different place. It was a hundred years from the Emancipation Proclamation, but the Negro population still struggled to enjoy the fruit provided from equal protection under the law. The domino theory blinded our political leaders to the glaring unexamined assumption that would contribute to the Vietnam quagmire.

But the uniqueness lies in a conversation I had with Jack O'Dell, a key player in the Civil Rights Movement. According to O'Dell, Martin Luther King would often share with him that facts alone do not reveal truth—it is within the interrelated nature of facts where truth often is realized. The events I have selected from 1963, though they have been presented for fifty years as unrelated, are a collection of interrelated facts that tell a truth about who we were then, paving a methodical trail that leads to who we are today.

Chapter One:

Segregation Now, Segregation Tomorrow, and Segregation Forever

January 1963 began with two seemingly innocuous events, concerning a Broadway play and a famous poet, and one significant commemoration, that of a U.S. law celebrating its hundredth birthday. But all three would later serve as inauspicious metaphors of the defining moments in the year of hope and hostility.

Five days into the year, *Camelot*, a musical by Alan Jay Lerner and Frederick Loewe, starring Richard Burton and Julie Andrews, closed after 873 performances and four Tony Awards at New York's Majestic Theater to embark on its U.S. tour. Though *Camelot* managed to secure an unprecedented $3 million in sales before its Broadway opening, its initial tryout at Toronto's O'Keefe Centre in 1960 was met with mixed reviews, but when the curtain came down at 12:40 AM, Lerner noted that "only Wagner's *Tristan and Isolde* equaled it as a bladder endurance contest."[1] Camelot's U.S. tour would continue with success until its scheduled close in 1964.

By the end of 1963, however, *Camelot* would no longer refer to the long-running Broadway hit, but rather would serve as a poignant pronoun for the presidency of John F. Kennedy, as his albeit brief term offered possibility and hope. Jacqueline Kennedy, in her first interview after Kennedy's assassination, compared his presidency to the fall of King Arthur. In her interview with Theodore White, she said, "There'll be great presidents again," and she added, "but there'll never be another Camelot again . . . it will never be that way again."[2]

The other disheartening event was the death of poet Robert Frost. It wasn't Frost's passing per se, but a poem he'd composed two years earlier, which was left unread, that in hindsight would shine through a metaphorical lens. Kennedy requested the eighty-six-year-old Frost, one of America's preeminent poets, who won four Pulitzer Prizes during his lifetime, to speak at his inauguration on January 20, 1961.

Frost had written a poem for the occasion called "Dedication." As he approached the microphone, blinded by the sun's glare on the snow-covered Capitol grounds and chilled by the twenty-degree weather, Frost found it impossible to read his newly penned poem. He instead recited "The Gift Outright," a poem he had written in 1942 that he knew quite well:

> The land was ours before we were the land's.
> She was our land more than a hundred years
> Before we were her people. She was ours
> In Massachusetts, in Virginia.
> But we were England's, still colonials,
> Possessing what we still were unpossessed by,
> Possessed by what we now no more possessed.

---

[1] Alan Jay Lerner, *The Street Where I Live* (New York: W.W. Norton & Company, 1978), 214.

[2] Jacqueline Kennedy, interview by Theodore H. White, *Life*, December 6, 1963.

Something we were withholding made us weak.
Until we found out that it was ourselves
We were withholding from our land of living,
And forthwith found salvation in surrender.
Such as we were we gave ourselves outright
(The deed of gift was many deeds of war)
To the land vaguely realizing westward,
But still unstoried, artless, unenhanced,
Such as she was, such as she would become."[3]

Though the crowd on that chilly Washington, D.C., day was treated to the greatness of Frost, the undelivered "Dedication" would prove in hindsight to better capture both the tragic events that would unfold and the unfilled promise of the Kennedy Administration:

The glory of a next Augustan age
Of a power leading from its strength and pride,
Of young ambition eager to be tried,
Firm in our free beliefs without dismay,
In any game the nations want to play.
A golden age of poetry and power
Of which this noonday's the beginning hour."[4]

Just as the sun set on Frost's long and rich life on January 29, 1963, it would also set on the promise held within that poem undelivered on January 20, 1961. The significance of *Camelot* closing on Broadway and the passing of Robert Frost was not immediately felt. That would not be the case with the third event, which actually occurred before the first two. January 1, 1963, marked the centennial of the Emancipation Proclamation becoming law.

---

[3] Robert Frost, "The Gift Outright," in *The Poetry of Robert Frost,* ed. Edward C. Lathem (New York: Henry Holt and Company, 1969), 348.

[4] Ibid. 348.

4

The Emancipation Proclamation and JFK

Abraham Lincoln signed the Emancipation Proclamation on September 22, 1862, and it went into effect on January 1 of the following year. Abolitionist Frederick Douglass considered the Proclamation a "worthy celebration of the first step on the part of the nation in its departure from the thralldom of the ages."[5] The Emancipation Proclamation did not free all slaves in the United States. Rather, it declared free only those slaves living in states not under Union control. Furthermore, there were slave-holding states that were not in rebellion, such as Kentucky, Missouri, Maryland, and Delaware, where the Proclamation did not apply. But the Proclamation was nevertheless a seminal moment in the country because it was the first time the federal government sent an unwavering message to at least some states that slavery would no longer be tolerated. But as Douglass had prophetically opined, it was only a first step. For if the initial step meant freedom for slaves of African descent, historical events would suggest the second step—that of equality—was still in its infancy one hundred years later.

The significance of the anniversary and the work left undone throughout the previous century was not lost on the civil rights community in the 1960s. Since the bus boycott in Montgomery, Alabama, in 1955, the Civil Rights Movement had been captivating the nation and the world with its use of nonviolent civil disobedience.[6] Though not as systematic in its approach as it is often portrayed in popular culture, the underpinnings of the movement were guided by

[5] John Hope Franklin, "The Emancipation Proclamation: An Act of Justice," *National Geographic*, http://news.nationalgeographic.com/news/2003/02/0206_030206_jubilee5.html (February 6, 2003).

[6] The Civil Rights Movement usually refers to a set of social movements from 1955 to 1968 aimed at abolishing public and private acts of racial discrimination in the United States, especially in the South. It is also referred to as the Second Reconstruction era.

two overarching principles: a private morality rooted in the teachings of Jesus and a God that sided with the oppressed, along with a public morality rooted in the Declaration of Independence and the Constitution. This public—and political—element of the movement called for advocacy from the president, but in early 1963, the movement still found in Kennedy someone who offered, at best, tepid support for its cause.

For several months leading up to 1963, the National Association for the Advancement of Colored People had coined the phrase "Free by '63." In commemorating the signing of the Proclamation, Martin Luther King Jr., addressing the New York Centennial Commission, stated:

The somber picture [of the condition of the American Negro today] may induce the sober thought that there is nothing to commemorate about the centennial of the Emancipation Proclamation. But tragic disappointments and undeserved defeats do not put an end to life, nor do they wipe out the positive, however submerged it may have become beneath floods of negative experience."[7]

King concluded his remarks by lobbying for that second unrealized step of equality:

There is but one way to commemorate the Emancipation Proclamation. That is to make its declarations of freedom real; to reach back to the origins of our nation when our message of equality electrified an unfree world, and reaffirm democracy by deeds as bold and daring as the issuance of the Emancipation Proclamation.[8]

During the latter part of 1962, Kennedy had been under increasing pressure to play an active role in the Emancipation Proclamation celebrations. With racial tension spilling out onto the

---

[7] Martin Luther King Jr., speech at the New York Civil War Centennial, September 12, 1962.

[8] Ibid.

streets and into the national spotlight for several years, Kennedy was indeed reluctant to be seen visibly participating in any Proclamation events in January 1963. The winds of change that were propelling participants within the Civil Rights Movement to put their lives on the line had yet to reach the Kennedy Administration, which was bogged down by internal warring factions—some pushed to do what was morally right and some pushed for what was politically possible, while everyone operated under the amoral construct of governing.

On the heels of his successful handling of the Cuban Missile Crisis in October 1962, Kennedy had an approval rating of 73 percent in January 1963. Moreover, the South was key to Kennedy's reelection hopes in 1964. From Kennedy's perspective, to involve himself overtly with the growing civil rights struggle would have meant risking support in the South as well as damaging his meteoric approval ratings.

During the 1960 campaign, Kennedy promised that, if elected, he would end racial discrimination in federally aided housing "by a stroke of the presidential pen." But the campaign promise can often serve as the most overrated aspect of the election process because a gap invariably exists between the campaign and governing, and this is not realized until one assumes office. Kennedy's "stroke of the presidential pen" campaign promise provided hope and unrealistic expectations to disenfranchised Negro voters. [9] What candidate Kennedy did not understand when he made the campaign promise was that the depth of the problem ran much deeper than a mere pen stroke.

Kennedy was at times deft and at other times clumsy in avoiding the overtures of the civil rights community urging him to play an active and visible role in the Proclamation celebrations, but there was one whose actions in 1963 would leave Kennedy no alternative but to involve himself in the civil rights struggle in ways he had not anticipated nor wanted.

---

[9] American President: John F. Kennedy (1917-1963),
http://millercenter.org/president/kennedy

George Wallace

George Corley Wallace was one of the most complicated, controversial, and politically ambitious individuals of the twentieth century. He was born to George C. and Mozell Smith Wallace in Clio, Alabama, on August 25, 1919. Wallace, a farmer's son, would embark on one of the most unlikely of political odysseys that would take him from populist on the side of injustice to poster child for segregation to Governor of Alabama, being swept into office by the overwhelming support of African Americans.

In 1936, while attending Barbour County High School, Wallace won the state Golden Gloves bantamweight championship and held the title the following year. He was also a member of the high school football team. Wallace's father died the year Wallace graduated high school, leaving the family with limited financial resources, but despite the monetary challenges, Wallace enrolled in the University of Alabama Law School that fall. Wallace worked his way through law school by boxing professionally, waiting tables, serving as a kitchen helper, and driving a taxi. Somehow still finding time to take part in school activities, he was president of his freshman class, captain of the university boxing team and the freshman baseball team, and a member of the highly regarded law school honor court.[10] He received his law degree in 1942. Wallace's tenacity and ambition were on display early in life, and they would serve him well in his meteoric political rise, but his path was not as direct as one might expect. After receiving his law degree in 1942, Wallace entered pilot cadet training in the United States Army Air Corps, but he failed to complete the course. He did serve as a staff sergeant and flew B-29 combat missions over Japan in 1945.[11] While in the Army, he nearly died as the result of contracting spinal meningitis. He left the Army, receiving a medical discharge, with partial hearing loss and permanent nerve damage.

[10] Alabama Governors: George C. Wallace,
http://www.archives.state.al.us/govs_list/g_wallac.html
[11] Stephen Lesher, *George Wallace: American Populist* (Reading, Mass: Da Capo Press, 1995), xi.

8

Progressive Beginnings

In 1946, Wallace served as assistant attorney general, after which he was elected to two terms in the state legislature. As a young state legislator, Wallace quickly garnered the attention of Alabama Governor "Big" Jim Folsom. Folsom, who stood six foot eight, was often referred to as the "little man's big friend." Running for governor in 1946, Folsom took his populist campaign to rural areas of the state, entertaining folk with a country band called The Strawberry Pickers while he carried a mop and bucket to demonstrate his commitment to clean state government. Folsom advocated reapportionment, increased and expanded benefits for elderly citizens, increased funding in education, the repeal of the poll tax, and better roads and highways. Unfortunately, Alabama's conservative legislature and Folsom's political naïveté and personal missteps derailed much of his populist agenda. Folsom's first term in office was marred by accusations of misconduct, corruption, and a paternity case. Despite the drama, Folsom did manage to increase funding to aid education and the elderly as well as to fund road improvements. But Folsom failed in the most controversial parts of his agenda—the changes in state government that would extend voting rights and other components of a democratic society to blacks, poor whites, and women. But at the height of Folsom's popularity, he was a populist star with which Wallace wanted to be associated.

From 1950 to 1952, Wallace requested and was appointed by Folsom to the board of trustees of the all-black Tuskegee Institute founded by Booker T. Washington. He also endorsed and campaigned for Democratic presidential candidate Adlai Stevenson in 1956. And when Wallace ran for governor the first time in 1958, he ran as an anti–Ku Klux Klan candidate, going as far as refusing their endorsement. Though it developed over the first few years of his career, Wallace's political progressivism, which began with his relationship with Folsom, would eventually wane under the weight of Wallace's ambition and Alabama's political climate.

Wallace's initial experience on the national stage was during the 1948 Democratic Convention. Though he was part of the Southern delegation, he did not join the other members that walked out in protest with South Carolina Governor Strom Thurmond. Thurmond was running as a third-party presidential candidate—under the Dixiecrat Party—mainly in opposition to President Truman's desegregating the U.S. Army and proposing the creation of a Fair Employment Practices Commission. By not Walking out, Wallace was making a courageous stand to side with the weakened Truman, who would go on to be reelected despite losing four traditionally held Democratic Southern states, including Alabama.

In 1954 the U.S. Supreme Court unanimously overturned *Plessy v. Ferguson* in its *Brown v. Board of Education of Topeka* decision. As a result, de jure segregation was ruled to be in violation of the Fourteenth Amendment. For fifty-eight years the South had had the Supreme Court on its side. Though *Brown* did not end segregation, it was the first sign that the tide had shifted.

In the immediate aftermath of the *Brown* decision, Wallace was hardly leading the segregationist charge. But *Brown* gave rise to a more boisterous Southern populism led by politicians, The White Citizens' Council, and the Ku Klux Klan that could hardly go unnoticed by the politically ambitious Wallace. In 1956, largely in response to *Brown*, the Southern Manifesto was drafted by Strom Thurmond, now in his first term as Senator of South Carolina. Thurmond's Southern Manifesto accused the Supreme Court of "clear abuse of judicial power."[12] The manifesto vowed to use "all lawful means to bring about a reversal of this decision which is contrary to the Constitution and to prevent the use of force in its implementation."[13] It was signed by 101 members of Congress, all from the southern region of the country, and based its legitimacy on two erroneous assumptions: one, that the Civil War did not occur, and

---

[12] Southern Manifesto (1956),
http://www.milestonedocuments.com/documents/view/southern-manifesto/text
[13] Ibid.

two, that the Supreme Court had no jurisdiction to rule on matters involving the U.S. Constitution. Since the manifesto was supported primarily by southern Democrats (two of the 101 signatories were southern Republicans), it created a problem for Adlai Stevenson's 1956 presidential bid against President Eisenhower. Stevenson had based a portion of his strategy for victory on his presumed support from southern moderates, which was exactly the same way Wallace had been positioning himself at the time in his preparations to run for Governor of Alabama in 1958. But the southern moderates that Stevenson was hoping for were diminishing in number. The southern coalition that swept Franklin D. Roosevelt into office and kept him there for three additional elections was fragmenting because of race. Many southern elected officials who may have opposed the Manifesto privately remained publicly silent.

Wallace's public silence hardly qualified him as liberal on race. Being a southern moderate circa 1956 did not make one a de facto friend of the Negro; it simply meant that one was less vitriolic in one's public opinion on black inequality. Wallace did, however, receive the endorsement of the NAACP in his 1958 gubernatorial bid. But at the same time, Wallace's television commercials boasted of his ability to defeat the NAACP based on his 1956 convention battles, ensuring a moderate—rather than extreme—civil rights plank in the Democratic platform. In that commercial he referred to the NAACP as "enemies of the South."[14] Wallace's moderate view on race was evident by his own words from a 1958 campaign commercial:

I want to tell the good people of this state as a judge of the third judicial circuit if I didn't have what it took to treat a man fair regardless of his color then I don't have what it takes to be the governor of your great state.[15]

---

[14] Dan T. Carter, interview, "George Wallace Settin' the Woods on Fire," PBS (2000), transcript.
[15] George Wallace, "The Contenders: George Wallace," C-SPAN, November 27, 2011.

Nevertheless, Wallace lost the 1958 governor's race by 64,000 votes, marking a turning point in Wallace's political career.

Wallace Never To Be "Out-Niggered" Again

According to Wallace, at age fourteen while working as a statehouse page in Alabama, he stood on the spot where Jefferson Davis had taken the oath of office as President of the Confederacy and vowed to himself, "I am going to be governor someday."[16] It has been argued by a number of historians that George Wallace was primarily committed to his own political ambitions rather than the good of the people. John Kohn, a former Wallace advisor, noted in a 1988 interview, "If George had parachuted into the Albanian countryside in 1962, he would have been head of a collective farm by the fall, a member of the Communist Party by mid-winter, on his way to the district party meeting by the following year, and a member of the Comintern in two to three years."[17] This was a remarkable statement, given that Wallace was a staunch anti-Communist throughout his political career. But what Kohn said next summed up Wallace's infamous ambition. "Hell, George could believe whatever he needed to believe."[18]

Dan T. Carter, who wrote a biography on Wallace, said in a PBS interview in 2000 that, when George Wallace lost in 1958, it was the first defeat he had ever suffered in anything he had ever run for. And those around him, newspaper people who covered him, his friends, noticed a real change in his personality. He drank for the first time. He was never a serious drinker, so it didn't take but a couple of drinks to throw him off balance. He began having sexual liaisons in a pretty indiscriminate and careless kind of way during that period. He moved his family to Montgomery, sort of dropped them off at an apartment there, and hit the road, planning for the next election.[19]

---

[16] See "George Wallace Settin' the Woods on Fire."
[17] John Kohn, interview by Dan T. Carter, 1988.
[18] Ibid.
[19] See "George Wallace Settin' the Woods on Fire."

But the substantive change in George Wallace, the politician, was realized in those agonizing yet necessary moments when the defeated candidate grappled with what went wrong. Losing to his opponent, John Patterson, by such a large margin was particularly difficult for Wallace, as he had not yet experienced political defeat. In the aftermath of the election, Wallace and his aides agreed that Patterson's success was due to his stance on segregation, which was stronger than Wallace's had been, and the support he enjoyed from the Klan. At this point Wallace reportedly said, "Well boys, no other son-of-a-bitch is ever going to out-nigger me again."[20]

Over the years there has been some dispute as to whether Wallace actually made this statement, and Wallace maintained that he never said it. Marshall Frady used the quote in his 1968 biography of Wallace; however, Stephen Lesher, who was Wallace's official biographer, sides with Wallace. And Bill Jones, who was with Wallace that night, cannot recall Wallace making the statement. But to borrow a line from the movie *The Man who Shot Liberty Valance*, "When the legend becomes fact, print the legend." Therefore, this unadulterated example of political ambition run amok has become a part of the Wallace lore. Moreover, whether or not Wallace actually said that he would not be "out-niggered again" is secondary. His actions following his 1958 loss strongly suggest that this was his motive, regardless of the accuracy of the quote.

Wallace's use of demagoguery for the purposes of attaining political power and playing on racial fears catapulted him into the national spotlight for more than a decade. After his infamous 1958 vow to be a hardliner on segregation, Wallace spent the next four years developing a gubernatorial campaign centered on segregation. He built alliances with organizations that opposed him in 1958 that were also sympathetic to segregation's cause. In the 1962 election for governor, he won by a landslide.

---

[20] Dan T. Carter, *The Politics of Rage* (Baton Rouge: Louisiana State University Press, 2000), 96.

Wallace's inauguration speech on Monday, January 14, 1963, and his subsequent actions that year had a significant effect, fairly or unfairly, in defining who Wallace was, from his lasting impact on the political discourse of the 1960s up to the present day. In fact, his inaugural address may have set the tone for the year that would be one of hope and hostility.

January 14, 1963, was the coldest day on record in Montgomery in almost eighty years, but that did not deter huge crowds from celebrating the inauguration of the man who had adopted the campaign slogan "Stand Up for Alabama."

The symbolism of the speech could not have been better orchestrated had it been written by a member of the Screen Actors Guild. Thirteen days after the centennial of the Emancipation Proclamation, declaring "that all persons held as slaves" within the rebellious states "are, and henceforward shall be free,"[21] standing where Davis took the oath of office as President of the Confederacy, Wallace was on the brink of becoming the standard bearer for a politics that claimed to be supported by the Constitution but in essence is better defined as the perpetuation of hate.

Before the ceremony, Wallace and his staff hinted to the press that the speech would contain some noteworthy moments. They worked the national press for weeks, suggesting that the three major networks send national correspondents to cover the inauguration.[22] In hindsight, Wallace's appeals to the press were not simply the hyperbole of a zealous politician clamoring for media attention. Wallace also had some understanding of the moment that he was about to experience. While it is doubtful that Wallace understood in totality the impact he would have by igniting this powder keg, there is enough evidence to conclude that his inauguration speech was no mere accident of history.

Wallace brought "tent revival" fervor to his audience. The burden

[21] Featured Documents: Emancipation Proclamation,
http://www.archives.gov/exhibits/featured_documents/emancipation_proclamation/
[22] Carter, *The Politics of Rage*, 9.

14

on Wallace was not to say something new, but to say what the crowd wanted to hear in the way they wanted to hear it. He was not appealing to the better angels of the white citizens of Alabama; he instead was appealing to the same primordial impulses of fear and hatred that got him elected. In this context, Wallace was the preacher charged with giving people hope based on maintaining their notion of the status quo, even if all that meant was clinging to the legalized superiority of the whiteness of their skin. His was an ambition that did not call people to reach higher; rather, it invited them to dig deeper into the abyss of evil. Though initially it would appear that Wallace's congregation was made up of the white people of Alabama, on January 14, 1963, he became the surrogate pastor for the entire southern region sympathetic to the cause of segregation.

Like any good charismatic preacher, Wallace began his address by deliberately using innocuous terms:

I shall fulfill my duty in working hard to bring industry into our state, not only by maintaining an honest, sober, and free-enterprise climate of government in which industry can have confidence but in going out and getting it . . . so that our people can have industrial jobs in Alabama and provide a better life for their children. I shall not forget my duty to our senior citizens . . . so that their lives can be lived in dignity and enrichment of the golden years, nor to our sick, both mental and physical . . . and they will know we have not forsaken them. I want the farmer to feel confident that in this state government he has a partner who will work with him in raising his income and increasing his markets. And I want the laboring man to know he has a friend who is sincerely striving to better his field of endeavor. I want to assure every child that this state government is not afraid to invest

in their future through education, so that they will not be handicapped on every threshold of their lives.[23]

Inaugural Address (1963), The "Segregation Now, Segregation Forever" Speech, Governor George Wallace of Alabama,
http://web.utk.edu/~mfitzge1/docs/374/wallace_seg63.pdf

There was nothing in Wallace's initial remarks that warranted national coverage. The governors of California, Illinois, and New York, or any other state in the Union, could have easily delivered the first 800 words of Wallace's address. But this is where any congruence with his forty-nine other colleagues would end. It did not take long for Wallace to give the people what they wanted. The next 4,100 words of this speech would set Wallace apart, giving those in attendance the red meat they were hoping for. Wallace was about to deliver the line that speechwriter Asa Carter, a former Klan member, had stated was "gonna catch everybody."[24] Wallace continued:

Today I have stood, where once Jefferson Davis stood, and took an oath to my people. It is very appropriate then that from this Cradle of the Confederacy, this very Heart of the Great Anglo-Saxon Southland, that today we sound the drum for freedom as have our generations of forebears before us done, time and time again through history. Let us rise to the call of freedom-loving blood that is in us and send our answer to the tyranny that clanks its chains upon the South. In the name of the greatest people that have ever trod this earth, I draw the line in the dust and toss the gauntlet before the feet of tyranny . . . and I say . . . segregation now . . . segregation tomorrow . . . segregation forever.[25]

By placing white Southerners on the side of the oppressed—invoking God, the spirit of self-determination, and the memory of the Founding Fathers—Wallace delivered one of the most memorable speeches of 1963. With one phrase, Wallace had simultaneously revamped the rebel yell and resurrected Stonewall Jackson.

He rallied Southerners with just enough historical accuracy to mask his gross inaccuracies:

There were no government handouts, no Marshall Plan aid, no coddling to make sure that our people would not suffer; instead the

---

[24] Carter, *The Politics of Rage*, 10.
[25] Inaugural Address.

South was set upon by the vulturous carpetbagger and federal troops, all loyal Southerners were denied the vote at the point of bayonet, so that the infamous, illegal Fourteenth Amendment might be passed. There was no money, no food, and no hope of either. But our grandfathers bent their knees only in church and bowed their head only to God.[26]

Wallace's comments rang true because they were not directed toward the 30 percent of Alabamians who toiled under the oppressive heat of Jim Crow segregation. But a mere six words placed the speech in the pantheon of memorable moments of 1963. Just as Kennedy would electrify the crowd in Berlin on June 26, saying, "Ich bin ein Berliner," as would King when he told those on the Washington Mall on August 28, "I have a dream," on January 14, Wallace became infamous with "segregation now, segregation tomorrow, segregation forever."

In many ways Wallace's 1963 inaugural address was reminiscent of Jefferson Davis's farewell address in the Senate on the morning of January 21, 1861. In announcing Mississippi's decision to secede from the Union, Davis delivered what many consider one of the great speeches in American history:

It has been a conviction of pressing necessity—it has been a belief that we are to be deprived in the Union of the rights which our fathers bequeathed to us—which has brought Mississippi to her present decision. She has heard proclaimed the theory that all men are created free and equal, and this made the basis of an attack upon her social institutions; and the sacred Declaration of Independence has been invoked to maintain the position of the equality of the races. That Declaration is to be construed by the circumstances and purposes for which it was made. The communities were declaring their independence; the people of those communities were asserting that no man was born—to use the language of Mr. Jefferson—booted and spurred, to ride over the rest of mankind; that men were created

---

[26] Inaugural Address.

equal—meaning the men of the political community; that there was no divine right to rule; that no man inherited the right to govern; that there were no classes by which power and place descended to families; but that all stations were equally within the grasp of each member of the body politic. These were the great principles they announced; these were the purposes for which they made their declaration; these were the ends to which their enunciation was directed. They have no reference to the slave; else, how happened it that among the items of arraignment against George III was that he endeavored to do just what the North has been endeavoring of late to do, to stir up insurrection among our slaves? Had the Declaration announced that the Negroes were free and equal, how was the prince to be arraigned for raising up insurrection among them? And how was this to be enumerated among the high crimes, which caused the colonies to sever their connection with the mother country? When our Constitution was formed, the same idea was rendered more palpable; for there we find provision made for that very class of persons as property; they were not put upon the equality of footing with white men—not even upon that of paupers and convicts; but, so far as representation was concerned, were discriminated against as a lower caste, only to be represented in the numerical proportion of three-fifths. So stands the compact which binds us together.[27]

Hindsight allows for easy deconstruction of the arguments put forth by Wallace and Davis. But placed in their context, they were extremely persuasive speeches. Of the two speeches, Davis's is the more intellectually honest. In fact, Davis's argument was supported by the *Dred Scott* decision in 1857 and the Compromise of 1789.

In the *Dred Scott* decision, the Supreme Court ruled that people of African descent imported into the United States and held as slaves, as well as their descendants—whether or not they were slaves—could never be citizens of the United States, and that the United States

---

[27]Jefferson Davis, farewell address, January 21, 1861, in *American Speeches: Political Oratory from the Revolutionary to the Civil War*, ed. Ted Widmer (New York: The Library of America, 2006), 702–703.

Congress had no authority to prohibit slavery in federal territories. The Compromise of 1789, which remains one of the dark moments in U.S. History, was the agreement reached, between the North and the South, that male slaves were counted, for census purposes, as 3/5 of a person. This dreadful compromise at the formation of the Constitution may have been politically necessary in order to head off the secession that was to come seventy-six years later, but it actually served to legitimize in too many hearts that African slaves were not fully human.[28]

Though Wallace may have embraced a loose association with the arguments put forth by Davis, the basis of his contention was not unlike the William F. Buckley/Barry Goldwater conservatism of the 1950s and 60s—these men felt the federal government's intrusion into matters of the state was more egregious than its systematic dehumanization of Negro citizens—and sided with segregationists and against the principles of the Civil Rights Movement.[29]

The genius of Wallace was to adopt the spirit of Davis but to cloak it in the populism of former Louisiana Governor Huey Long. In doing so, his inaugural address delivered to an enthusiastic crowd transformed Alabama into the citadel for segregation. Wallace campaigned in 1962 as a governor who would not bend to the will of the federal government. He made it clear in his address that the action taken by the Kennedy Administration the year before in Oxford, Mississippi, when it sent federal troops to protect James Meredith as he integrated the University of Mississippi, would not be tolerated in his state. He referred to the Kennedy Administration as "pseudo-liberal spokesmen and some Harvard advocates" who had "never examined the logic of its substitution of what it calls 'human rights' for 'individual rights.'"[30] He

---

[28] Seating for the House of Representatives is based on census population. To fully count the slaves would have given the South an advantage, but to not count them at all would have greatly advantaged the North, hence the compromise.

[29] Goldwater, and to a lesser extent Buckley, would reverse their positions.

[30] Inaugural Address.

dismissed their actions in his inaugural address as a "propaganda play on words that has appealed to the unthinking." [31]

The speech was a win-win for Wallace and his white constituency. Wallace gave them what they desired, and in return he received what he wanted—national attention that would feed his unrestrained ambition. He was covered by *Time Magazine*, *Newsweek*, and *The New York Times*, which provided Wallace with the headline: "North Denounced by Gov. Wallace."[32]

Later in the evening on January 14, 1963, Kennedy gave his State of the Union address. While Wallace left no doubt with the faithful segregationists as to where he stood, Kennedy took a more measured approach. In his approximately 5,400-word address, which covered tax cuts, Social Security, mental health, West Berlin, Cuba, and Vietnam, Kennedy dedicated sixty-five words to the topic of race and the anniversary of the Proclamation. Up to this point, Kennedy had deliberately avoided taking a definitive stand on civil rights, and he had no intention of taking the bait offered by the Governor of Alabama, no matter how fiery the rhetoric. In the most benign and perfunctory way possible, short of completely ignoring the topic altogether, Kennedy said:

And the most precious and powerful right in the world, the right to vote in a free American election, must not be denied to any citizen on grounds of his race or color. I wish that all qualified Americans permitted to vote were willing to vote, but surely in this centennial year of Emancipation all those who are willing to vote should always be permitted.[33]

---

[31] Ibid.

[32] Editorial, "North Denounced by Gov. Wallace," *The New York Times*, January 15, 1963, p. 16.

[33] Kennedy's Annual Message to the Congress on the State of the Union was taken from the website The American Presidency Project, http://www.presidency.ucsb.edu, delivered on January 14, 1963

Terry Sanford

The response that many within the Civil Rights Movement hoped Kennedy would give that night came from a rather unlikely source four days later. On January 18, North Carolina Governor, Terry Sanford, delivered his "Emancipation" address before the North Carolina Press Association at the Carolina Inn in Chapel Hill, North Carolina. Not only did he commemorate the centennial of the Emancipation Proclamation, but also he challenged the people of North Carolina to treat its Negro citizens with fairness and dignity.

"Now is the time in this 100th year not merely to look back to freedom, but to look forward to the fulfillment of its meaning," Sanford said.[34]   He called on residents of North Carolina and elsewhere, "to quit unfair discrimination and to give the Negro a full chance to earn a decent living for his family and to contribute to the higher standards for himself and all men."[35]

Sanford's remarks did not receive the public notoriety that Wallace had four days prior. It was nevertheless a powerful counter to Wallace in style and substance. Where Wallace offered a firebrand style, Sanford was more genteel; Wallace appealed to what was, while Sanford focused on what could be. In doing so, Sanford demonstrated the South was not an evil cabal that was in lockstep, firmly committed to an ethos of second-class citizenship for Negroes. In 1963, Wallace and Sanford were two southern governors on opposite ends of the civil rights spectrum. Many hoped that the president would publicly address the importance of the Emancipation Proclamation as well as use the bully pulpit of the Oval Office to support civil rights legislation. But, poignantly, it was another southern governor who sought to fill the shoes of a reluctant president.

---

[34] Southern Sources,
http://www.lib.unc.edu/blogs/shc/index.php/2010/05/02/video-of-governor-terry-sanfords-emancipation-speech-to-the-north-carolina-press-association/
[35] Ibid.

But the president's lukewarm response could not temper the situation. On January 14, the roles of the three men pivotal to civil rights in 1963 were defined. King and Wallace would prod from the left and right respectively, while Kennedy would use all of his political skill to remain in the amorphous middle. Since the 1960 campaign, Kennedy's high expectations, fostered by his "stroke of the pen" promise, had fallen short in the minds of those pushing for a stronger civil rights agenda. King and his followers wanted the morality of the country, woven into the nation from its inception, to change. Wallace was the ravenous beast whose ambition fed on the toxins of hatred. Kennedy was the politician driven by pragmatism and his 1964 reelection bid. The last thing Kennedy wanted was to antagonize the South any more after what had already occurred in Oxford, Mississippi, the year before. In 1963, however, Wallace was prepared to push the envelope well beyond Kennedy's desires to remain in the middle for political reasons.

Wallace Beyond the Year of Hope and Hostility

The political odyssey of Wallace—who went from a young war veteran entering politics advocating progressive policies, only later to descend into the politics of racism following the loss of his lifetime dream of being elected Governor of Alabama in 1958—is a case study in unbridled ambition. Moreover, any attempt to understand Wallace's political motives beyond ambition might prove oxymoronic. There is no doubt that Wallace's ambition served him well in some cases, but it permanently damaged him historically in others.

In 1963, Wallace was gaining national attention by offering segregationists in Alabama and elsewhere momentum to a cause that had been on the defensive for nine years. But in the years to come, his ambition would prove to be his Achilles' heel and make him an unwitting ally to the Civil Rights Movement led by Martin Luther King Jr. After two terms as governor, one third-party presidential campaign, and one run as the Democratic Presidential Candidate,

Wallace would become even more of an enigma. In 1983, Wallace was returned to the governor's mansion with the overwhelming support of the black people of Alabama, whom he once sought to deny equal protection under the law. In 1963, it would have been impossible for the staunchest optimist to see a day when Wallace would be a supporter of civil rights, but it would eventually happen.

However the Wallace legacy is parsed out, it is hard to deny that beginning in 1963, he ushered in a brand of southern populism that made him one of the most influential politicians in the last half of the twentieth century and into the fledgling stages of the twenty-first.

Harvey Gantt

The bold and brash Wallace made it clear he would not acquiesce to any court-ordered desegregation as did his South Carolina counterpart, Governor Ernest (Fritz) Hollings, whom Wallace ridiculed for allowing Clemson University to be integrated without much opposition. [36] Wallace also blatantly objected to the less than confrontational way Harvey Gantt became the first Negro to integrate into South Carolina's Clemson University on January 28, 1963.

The combined character of Clemson University President Robert C. Edwards and Harvey Gantt made the desegregation of Clemson University the antithesis to what would play out in Alabama later that year. What occurred in South Carolina would be called "Integration with Dignity."[37] It was a well-planned effort to avoid the type of violent hostility that the world would witness in Alabama later that year.

Harvey Gantt was born January 14, 1943. Ironically, on the same day Wallace was proclaiming the virtues of segregation in his

[36] Carter, 113.
[37] Harvey Gantt and the Desegregation of Clemson University, http://www.clemson.edu/oirweb1/fb/factbook/Historical%20Enrollment/Integration.htm

inaugural address, Gantt was celebrating his twentieth birthday and preparing to chart a very different course in the Palmetto State. He was one of four children born to Wilhelmina Gordon and Christopher Gantt. As far as Negroes were concerned at that time, the Gantts were a middle-class family in Charleston, South Carolina. Harvey's parents graduated from Burke Industrial School in Charleston, and he also graduated from Burke High School on June 3, 1960. He ranked second in his class of 262 students. When Gantt graduated from Burke High School, he already had set his sites on becoming an architect. He also knew that the color of his skin made his chances of attending the best engineering school in the state fall somewhere between improbable and impossible.

But the single-minded determination that would ultimately lead to Gantt managing a successful architectural practice—Gantt Huberman Architects, in Charlotte, North Carolina—was present early in Gantt's life. In a 1986 interview, Gantt said:

I'm one of those fortunate people who early on recognized that I wanted to be an architect and that was in ninth grade. I consider that to be early, I mean, you toy around with a lot of things and I did probably as most kids do, wanting to be everything from a pharmacist to a doctor to a preacher to a lawyer. But finally it was putting together my aptitude for drawing and my interest in the technical aspects of putting things together that led me to architecture.[38]

Gantt set history in motion by submitting a letter to Clemson's Office of Admissions on July 1959. In the world of segregation, most Negro students of Gantt's academic caliber attended the historically black colleges: Tuskegee Institute in Tuskegee, Alabama; Howard University in Washington, D.C., and North Carolina A&T in Greensboro, North Carolina.

Of those three, Gantt applied only to Howard. But being a National Achievement Scholar out of high school meant that Gantt would receive a full scholarship to any school that accepted him. With

[38]Harvey Gantt, interview by Lynn Haessly, January 6, 1986. Recorded in the Southern Oral History Program Collection, #4007, in Charlotte, North Carolina.

the exception of Clemson, Gantt was accepted to every school that he applied to; he ultimately settled on Iowa State University located in Ames, Iowa. But two things stopped him from staying in the Midwest: Gantt did not like Iowa State, and he had already taken legal action to be admitted into Clemson.

Though Gantt was mature beyond his years, he also benefited from living in a political house. Dinner table conversations would take the form of political activism. On April 1, 1960, while still attending Burke High School, Gantt was arrested on a trespassing charge at S.H. Kress department store in Greensboro for participating in a sit-in that was part of the national civil rights movement to desegregate lunch counters. Martin Luther King Jr., eight years later, in his final speech before his assassination, would note the significance of this movement. In referring to the sit-in movement that night, King said:

I knew that as they were sitting in, they were really standing up for the best in the American dream. And taking the whole nation back to those great wells of democracy, which were dug deep by the Founding Fathers in the Declaration of Independence and the Constitution.[39]

Gantt was hardly an unsuspecting patsy that happened to be at the right place at the right time, accidentally participating in a rendezvous with destiny. But Gantt's primary reason for attending Clemson had more to do with his education goals than proving a political point. Matthew Perry, an attorney who was in Charleston to defend students who were arrested during another lunch-counter sit-in protest and who would later represent Gantt in his quest to desegregate Clemson University, recalled his initial encounter with Gantt. "He approached me with his right hand extended and introduced himself," Perry recollected. "'I'm Harvey Gantt, a senior at Burke High School, and I

---

[39] Martin Luther King Jr., *Testament of Hope: The Essential Writings of Martin Luther King, Jr.*, ed. James Washington (San Francisco: Harper, 1986), p. 286.

want to be an architect. I want to attend Clemson, which has the best engineering program . . . but I think that might be a problem.'"[40]

The next three years took Gantt on a political and legal trek during which any juncture could have ended his historic quest. Meanwhile, Gantt maintained his excellent scholarship while attending Iowa State. On December 7, 1962 *Time* magazine wrote the following optimistic piece about Gantt's upcoming hearing:

Gantt's request for admission to Clemson is before Federal Judge Cecil C. Wyche, 77, a fair-minded South Carolinian who is expected to rule in Gantt's favor if Clemson fails to disprove discrimination.[41]

But on December 21, 1962, Wyche dismissed Gantt's case because "he failed to prove" that Clemson used the issue of race to deny him admission.[42] According to Wyche, "the plaintiff's case [was] based upon circumstantial evidence."[43] Wyche included in his decision that Clemson could admit Gantt "voluntarily" without violating any laws of the State of South Carolina. Perry appealed the decision to the U.S. Court of Appeals for the Fourth Judicial Circuit on January 4, 1963.

The case was argued on January 9, and on January 16, the court reversed Wyche's decision. Two days after the court's decision to admit Gantt, the Clemson Board met to discuss the situation. Realizing they had exhausted their legal options to prohibit Gantt from attending, they made one last appeal directly to U.S. Chief Justice Earl Warren, who promptly denied it. The Board then voted to adopt recommendations to maintain "law, order, peace, and dignity."[44]

---

[40] Dr. H. Lewis Suggs "Harvey Gantt and the Desegregation of Clemson University 1960–1963" essay (Clemson, South Carolina: Clemson University, n.d.), p. 20.

[41] "Education: They Don't Want Riots," *Time Magazine*, December 7, 1962, http://www.time.com/time/magazine/article/0,9171,829634,00.html.

[42] Suggs, 35–36.

[43] Suggs, 36.

[44] Ibid.

When Gantt arrived to the Clemson campus on January 28, nothing happened. The tension that had occurred with James Meredith at the University of Mississippi three months earlier was non-existent. There are several reasons for Gantt's uneventful entrée onto the Clemson campus. First and foremost was Gantt himself: his wisdom, confidence, commitment of purpose, and integrity, along with his impeccable scholarship, made his denial all the more absurd.

Second was the leadership of Clemson President Edwards who understood the winds of change early on and did not want Clemson to be a bastion of violence that was justified by the same erroneous arguments of interposition and nullification embraced by its southern counterparts. He was the architect of the dignified and restrained approach that Clemson would embrace. But it would have been impossible for Edwards to carry this alone.

Speaking at the fortieth anniversary of Gantt's admission to Clemson, Edwards told of the importance of so many other people who worked behind the scenes to prepare for the successful desegregation. "I'll never be able to tell you how much I appreciate the support of the faculty, staff, and students, especially the students," Edwards said.[45]

Credit must also be given to South Carolina Governor Fritz Hollings. While Hollings was not facing reelection, his gubernatorial term was to expire thirteen days before Gantt began taking courses at Clemson, which may have accounted for his measured approach. He did, nevertheless, appeal for dignity and restraint. While Wallace was positioning himself as the primary defender of segregation, Hollings in his farewell address before the state legislature stated forthrightly: "We are running out of courts, we are running out of appeals, and time."[46] That speech set a tone that minimized any Wallace-like

---

[45] Heroes Recall Historic Day,
http://www.thetigernews.com/printStory.php?aid=1879.
[46] Fritz Hollings,
http://digital.tcl.sc.edu/cdm/compoundobject/collection/how/id/291.

theatrics among elected officials. And it helped to make Harvey Gantt's entrance to Clemson an uneventful one indeed.

Harvey Gantt and Michael Jordan

Twenty days after Gantt entered Clemson, basketball star Michael Jordan was born. The importance of this otherwise non sequitur would not be appreciated until 1990, when Harvey Gantt was in a hotly contested race against hardline Republican Jesse Helms for the North Carolina U.S. Senate seat. The race would be marred by the infamous "hands" TV commercial, which depicted the hands of a white man receiving a rejection letter for a job allegedly because of a racial quota. The commercial ran the weekend before the election; Gantt lost the race by less than 100,000 votes.

Michael Jordan, who hails from North Carolina, was at the time the quintessential sport's icon in the country, if not the world. He was the most effectively marketed athlete of his generation. His shoe contract with Nike alone was worth tens of millions of dollars to him and hundreds of millions to the company. It was believed that a public endorsement of Gantt, given Jordan's unmistakable star power, could have made a difference in the race. But when asked to endorse Gantt, Jordan reportedly declined simply by saying, "Republicans buy sneakers, too."

Whatever was to be gained politically by publicly endorsing Gantt was not worth Jordan risking his endorsement with Nike. This is not to suggest that Jordan was the reason for Gantt's 1990 defeat. Nor does it suggest Jordan was wrong for his decision not to endorse. But it does reveal an irony in the year of hope and hostility.

The day Jordan was born, the country had not witnessed the full brunt of the hostility that would define a good portion of the year. In 1963, to be Michael Jordan—a global sports icon whose Madison Avenue endorsement carried so much weight for millions—was inconceivable, especially in a southern state like North Carolina. It was the dignity, courage, and hope offered by Harvey Gantt and others that year that afforded Jordan circa 1990 the luxury to make the type of pragmatic business decisions that he did.[47]

Wallace's inaugural speech was a noteworthy highlight of January 1963, but Gantt's groundbreaking achievements were no less significant in defining the year. They were opposites in demeanor and objective. But there could not have been two better representatives to catapult the year of hope and hostility.

---

[47] Jordan did contribute to Gantt's 1996 campaign against Helms.

Chapter Two:

Fidel Castro, Kennedy's Nagging Thorn

On February 8, 1963, the Kennedy Administration prohibited travel to Cuba and made financial and commercial transactions with Cuba illegal for U.S. citizens. It was the final piece put in place to cement a policy—and, in large part, a mindset—that would continue into the present day. This simple act ensured that the thorn that had been in Kennedy's side since the beginning of his administration—Fidel Castro—would continue to nag him. Cuba was the sight of Kennedy's worst military blunder and greatest diplomatic victory. But history also indicates that had the events of November 22, 1963[48] had not occurred, U.S. policy toward Cuba might look very different today.

United States–Cuba Relations

In late 1958, when it became clear that Castro's revolution would overthrow Fulgencio Batista's regime, the philosophical and political

---

[48] The date of John F. Kennedy's assassination. This event will be discussed in detail in Chapter Eight.

leanings of the movement remained obscured. The burning question for the Eisenhower Administration was, "Is Castro a Communist?"

Castro's rise to power was due in part to his being the only viable leader in what was a broad-based coalition galvanized more by its unwillingness to continue living under Batista's dictatorship than a centralized ideology. It wasn't until December 2, 1961, in a nationally broadcasted speech, that Castro declared that he was a Marxist-Leninist and that Cuba was embracing Communism.

From the U.S. perspective, the initial problem with Castro, like his predecessor Batista, was that upon assuming power on January 1, 1959, he had no plans for resuming free elections. (In 1954, Vice President Richard Nixon visited Havana to congratulate Batista on winning an election in which his name was the only one that appeared on the ballot.) But unlike Batista, Castro showed little interest in bending to the political will of the United States. Kennedy signed the embargo in 1963 not only because of the ongoing Cold War, but also because of the widespread fear known as the domino theory.[49] The Cold War and ostensibly Communism was an area where Kennedy in 1963 could ill-afford to appear weak.

But Cuba under Castro posed new challenges for the United States. More than any other country in the hemisphere, Cuba had been, for centuries, a barometer with which America would judge its level of power in relation to other countries. The thought of having a Soviet satellite state roughly 90 miles from the United States was more than an irritant; it represented the possible growing power of Communism and the potential weakness of America globally.

The main problem was that Cuba was within the U.S. sphere of influence, and the United States wanted to control that domain. Such thoughts have been a part of American foreign policy—at times obsessively—since the ratification of the Constitution. In 1809, President Thomas Jefferson sent General James Wilkinson to Spain in

---

[49] The domino theory speculated that if one country in a region became Communist-controlled, then the surrounding countries would also become Communist-controlled.

an attempt to purchase Cuba. He wrote a letter to his eventual successor James Madison, revealing, "I candidly confess that I have ever looked upon Cuba as the most interesting addition that can be made to our system of States . . . With Cuba and Canada we should have such an empire for liberty as she has never surveyed since the creation."[50]

The Monroe Doctrine (1823) furthered Jefferson's imperialistic desires to make the Caribbean and Latin America vital parts of America's economy and military. In America's quest to be, as Jefferson put it, "masters of the Caribbean" in the twentieth century, the United States occupied or intervened openly in the following Latin American countries: Honduras (1912), Haiti (1915), Guatemala (1954), the Dominican Republic (1916 and 1965), Nicaragua (1927 and 1980s), and Panama (1989). The United States also confirmed the acquisition of Puerto Rico in 1952 and Cuba in 1898 and again in 1961.

The invasion of Cuba in 1961 was the Kennedy Administration's baptism into Cold War politics that led ultimately to the brinksmanship between Cuba, the United States, and the Soviet Union.

Kennedy had inherited an apparent renegade government—renegade in the sense that Cuba under Castro showed little interest in becoming part of America's dominion—less than one hundred miles from U.S. shores. And Kennedy knew that open defiance could propel other Latin American countries to rebel. In the roughly one thousand days of the Kennedy Administration, Castro is prominently featured in both its high and low moments. But the lowest point came a mere three months into the new Kennedy Administration.

Bay of Pigs

In April 1961, Kennedy approved the invasion of Cuba at the Bahía de Cochinos, the Bay of Pigs, and on April 17, some 1,500 armed Cuban

---

[50] Thomas Jefferson to James Madison, 24 October 1823, in *The Jeffersonian Cyclopedia*, edited by John P. Foley (New York: Funk & Wagnalls, Co., 1900), 222.

exiles landed on the south coast of Cuba from their U.S.–funded training camps in Guatemala.

The idea to overthrow Castro was birthed in the Eisenhower Administration in 1960. On March 17, Eisenhower ordered the CIA to "organize the training of Cuban exiles, mainly in Guatemala, against a possible future date when they might return to their homeland."[51] Moreover, the growing number of Cubans sympathetic to Batista, who had made Miami their home in exile, supported momentum for this plan.

On the day of the invasion, the main force of Cuban rebel soldiers—who had been training in Guatemala with the CIA since May 1960 and who were supplied with arms by the U.S. government— advanced across the island to Matanzas and set up a defensive position. The rebels intended to provoke an insurrection in Cuba, overthrowing Castro's Communists. The United Revolutionary Front sent leaders from South Florida and established a provisional government. The success of the plan depended on the Cuban population joining the invaders.[52] But despite the year of preparation and U.S. support, the Cuban army easily defeated the rebels, and by April 20, most were either killed or captured.

The unsuccessful invasion provoked anti–U.S. demonstrations in Latin America and Europe and further embittered U.S.–Cuban relations. After the failure, the invasion was dispraised as poorly planned and executed, which subjected President Kennedy to severe criticism at home. It was an ill-conceived mission that invoked the justifiable ire of the world community, while making Kennedy appear weak as a leader.

The CIA planned this invasion believing its goals for overthrowing Castro could be achieved without U.S. military involvement. The unsuccessful attempt culminated in Castro releasing 1,113 captured rebels in exchange for $53 million in food and

---

[51] Herbert Parmet, *Eisenhower and the American Crusades* (Piscataway, NJ: Transaction Publishers, 1998), 561.

[52] "The Bay of Pigs" John F. Kennedy Presidential Library and Museum, http://www.jfklibrary.org/JFK/JFK-in-History/The-Bay-of-Pigs.aspx

medicine raised by private donations in the United States. It was an embarrassing defeat for the Kennedy Administration.

What remains somewhat unclear is the exact point that Kennedy decided to sponsor a Cuban invasion. By the fall of 1960, thousands of Cubans had already fled to the United States, it was the height of the Cold War, and Castro's Communist leanings were still only speculation. With an ongoing presidential election, Kennedy, out to prove his Cold War toughness, repeatedly stated that the United States should support Cuban exiles.

This prompted Vice President Richard Nixon, Kennedy's Republican rival, to respond during one of their presidential debates:

I don't know what Senator Kennedy suggests when he says we should help those who oppose the Castro regime. But I do know this: that if we were to follow that recommendation that we would lose all of our friends in Latin America, we would probably be condemned in the United Nations, and we would not accomplish our objectives. And I know something else: it would be an open invitation for Mr. Khrushchev to come in.[53]

Nixon's response was hardly the prophetic musing of a potential president, though history would prove him right. Nevertheless, Nixon failed to add in his response that he was already working with the CIA on a Cuba invasion plan.

Nixon would later blame CIA agent Allen Dulles for having briefed Kennedy in advance about the invasion plans during the campaign.[54] Dulles had briefed Kennedy in July 1960, and it remains uncertain if he divulged any specific plans to invade Cuba. But in his haste to dismiss political charges of timidity and to perhaps "out-

---

[53] Richard Nixon, presidential debates, 21 October 1960, from Tom Gjelten, "Ten Presidents, One Dictator: U.S.–Cuba Policy." National Public Radio, August 4, 2006.

[54] Richard Nixon, *RN: The Memoirs of Richard Nixon* (New York: Simon & Schuster, 1990), 22.

Nixon" Nixon, Kennedy's hard-hitting campaign rhetoric may have unwittingly backed him into a corner once he assumed the presidency.

As Nixon was well aware, the Eisenhower Administration had been working on a plan to oust Castro. On December 8, 1960, the CIA presented to Eisenhower a strategy that consisted of sixty to eighty guerrillas, air strikes from Nicaragua, and an amphibious landing consisting of 600 to 750 armed men, with the objective being to secure a limited area of Cuba and hopefully inspire other dissident Cubans to participate.[55]

Reportedly, Eisenhower was supportive of the idea of removing Castro, who had referred to the American embassy as a "nest of spies"[56] in January 1961. This statement prompted the Eisenhower Administration to officially break diplomatic relations, further convincing Eisenhower that military action against Cuba was warranted. On January 19, Eisenhower met with president-elect Kennedy. Eisenhower urged his younger counterpart to continue his efforts to support the anti-Castro forces, which were being trained in Guatemala. When Kennedy assumed the presidency the next day, he inherited a plan that was gaining momentum and developing a life of its own. In his attempt to demonstrate he was as much if not more of a Cold War hawk than Nixon, Kennedy assumed a staunch activist stance toward liberating Cuba from the Castro regime. Kennedy's calls for U.S. support for Cuban exiles against Castro may have confounded Nixon during the campaign, but they also may have placed Kennedy in a political straightjacket that left an ill-advised invasion as the only alternative. Whether Kennedy's unadulterated support for Cuban exiles was a political endeavor remains a topic of speculation—this support may have ruined any potential Eisenhower plans to invade

---

[55]Lawrence Freedman, *Kennedy's Wars* (New York: Oxford University Press, 2000), 126.

[56] George Gedda, "Diplomat Recalls Cuba Break in 1961," http://www2.fiu.edu/~fcf/diplobrk1101.html (January 1, 2001).

Cuba prior to the 1960 election, and had Eisenhower invaded, the close election may have swung to Nixon.

Once Kennedy assumed the presidency, the CIA suggested that the invasion commence sooner rather than later.[57] According to the CIA, the Cuban exiles trained in Guatemala were ready. In addition, the Guatemalan president was under pressure[58] to discontinue the training camps and deport the exiles, which could have landed some in Miami. This would have opened Kennedy up to criticism that he was not as supportive of Cuban exiles as he had originally claimed—a charge that the still-popular Eisenhower was more than able to levy, especially given his backing of the original plan.

Hindsight easily reveals the problems associated with the CIA plan. The first major error occurred on April 15, 1961, when the CIA dispatched eight B-26 bombers from Nicaragua to attack Cuban airfields. Though the bombers were painted to look like Cuban Air Force planes, they were from World War II and were obsolete. The operation failed to destroy the entire arsenal of planes as planned, leaving most of Castro's air force intact. As news broke of the attack and American complicity became apparent after photos of the repainted planes became public, President Kennedy cancelled the second air strike.

On April 17, the Cuban-exile invasion force landed at beaches along the Bay of Pigs and immediately came under heavy fire. The Cuban planes that had gone unharmed in the April 15 air attack strafed the invaders, sank two escort ships, and destroyed half of the exiles' air support. Bad weather hampered the ground force, which had to work with soggy equipment.

Within the next twenty-four hours, Castro had 25,000 troops advancing on the beach, and the Cuban Air Force continued to control the skies. As the situation grew increasingly grim, President Kennedy authorized an "air-umbrella" at dawn on April 19, which called for six

---

[57] Michael Beschloss, *Kennedy Versus Khrushchev* (London: Faber and Faber, 1991), 103–104.

[58] Freedman, 125.

unmarked American fighter planes to help defend the brigade's B-26s flying in from Nicaragua. But the B-26s arrived one hour later than expected and were shot down by the Cubans. The invasion was crushed later that day. Some exiles escaped by sea, while the rest were killed or rounded up and imprisoned by Castro's forces. Almost 1,200 Brigade members had surrendered, and more than 100 had been killed. As former Secretary of State Dean Acheson allegedly quipped to Kennedy, it did not require Price, Waterhouse to conclude that 1,500 Cuban exile guerillas were no match for 250,000 Cuban soldiers.[59]

Mass trials were held for the 1,189 men captured, and each was sentenced to thirty years in prison. After twenty months of negotiation with the United States, most were released in exchange for the $53 million in food and medicine.

Ted Sorensen, former Kennedy speechwriter and Counselor, in writing about the Bay of Pigs in his biography of Kennedy, noted five fundamental problems with the plan based on erroneous assumptions:

Kennedy thought he was approving a quiet, though large-scale infiltration of 1,400 Cuban exiles back into their homeland.

Kennedy thought he was approving a plan whereby exiles, should they fail to hold and expand the beachhead, could take up guerilla warfare with other rebels in the mountains.

Kennedy thought the Cuban exiles, represented by their Revolutionary Council and brigade leaders, could decide whether they wished to risk their own lives and liberty for the liberty of their country without any overt American support.

Kennedy thought he was approving a plan calculated to succeed with the help of the Cuban underground, military desertions, and, in time, an uprising of a rebellious population.

Kennedy thought he was approving a plan rushed into execution on the grounds that Castro would later acquire the military capability to defeat it.[60]

---

[59] Douglas Brinkley *Dean Acheson: The Cold War Years, 1953–71* (New Haven, CT: Yale University Press, 1992), 127.

[60] Theodore Sorensen, *Kennedy* (New York: Harper & Row, 1965), 302–303.

Within the history of U.S. policy, has there been as set of assumptions so crucial to a situation that were so misguided? Kennedy's five assumptions, as articulated by Sorensen, demonstrate a plot overflowing with disaster. Contrary to Kennedy's assumptions, the mission was hardly a secret, the guerillas were given contradictory instructions as to what to do on the beachhead, members of the brigade believed that the United States would back them up with force, Castro already possessed the requisite forces to defeat the guerillas, and the pro-Castro forces were stronger than originally believed.

As a result of the U.S. failure at the Bay of Pigs and the diplomatic embarrassment that followed, Kennedy fired CIA Director Allen W. Dulles and Deputy Director Charles P. Cabell, as well as Deputy Director Richard Bissell, who was principally responsible for the failed operation. Kennedy then publicly assumed full responsibility for the failure, and he ordered a full investigation of the operation. The resulting report, written by CIA Inspector General Lyman Kirkpatrick, concluded that ignorance, incompetence, and arrogance on the part of the CIA were responsible for the fiasco. It criticized nearly every aspect of the CIA's handling of the invasion: misinforming Kennedy Administration officials, planning poorly, using faulty intelligence, and conducting an overt military operation beyond "agency responsibility as well as agency capability." The report also said "the agency reduced the exile leaders to the status of puppets."[61]

The implementation of the Bay of Pigs policy was an obvious disaster, but the ensuing politics remain an example of success and serve as an illustration of the Kennedy mystique. At first, the mishandling of the invasion made Kennedy look weak globally, and it bolstered the pre-election concerns that many had had that the young senator from Massachusetts was not ready to lead the Free World. However, by taking full public responsibility in the weeks following,

---

[61] Craig Nelson, "CIA Takes Blame for Bay of Pigs," 23 February 1998, http://www.cubanet.org/CNews/y98/feb98/23e1.htm.

Kennedy's faux pas lifted him to an 83 percent approval rating according to Gallup.[62]

Though Kennedy was the model of contrition publicly—leading to his zenith approval ratings—the Bay of Pigs disaster would bring to fruition everything Nixon had forewarned during their debate. The fiasco was a public relations bonanza for Castro—he could rightfully claim that his tiny island, assuming the role of David, had defeated the Goliath known as the mighty U.S. Empire, especially because it was such a political embarrassment for the fledgling Kennedy Administration. Unbeknownst to most Americans, Kennedy's public humility hid his private reaction, which some would observe as an obsession with Castro.

The Kennedy Administration's obsession provided the foundation for a covert policy known as Operation Mongoose.

Operation Mongoose

Approved by the president in November 1961, Operation Mongoose was a secret plan with a primary mission to foster rebellion in Cuba that the United States could support. The goal of Mongoose was to disrupt Cuba's economic infrastructure, and the assassination of Castro was considered a viable option to meet that goal.

President Kennedy assigned Brigadier General Edward G. Lansdale, Assistant for Special Operations to the Secretary of Defense, to act as chief of operations. Lansdale coordinated Mongoose activities along with the CIA and the Departments of State and Defense. The CIA units in Washington and Miami were primarily responsible for implementing Mongoose operations, which included military, sabotage, and political propaganda programs.

---

[62] Roper Center, "Job Performance Rating for President Kennedy," March 1961, Public Opinion Archives, http://webapps.ropercenter.uconn.edu/CFIDE/roper/presidential/webroot/presidential_rating_detail.cfm?allRate=True&presidentName=Kennedy#.UMX7_Y6hDFI.

According to the 400 pages of declassified documents relating to Operation Mongoose released in 2001, the Kennedy Administration sought to disable or destroy Cuban power plants in Cuba, lay mines to disrupt shipping, and undermine or destroy Castro's leadership. To achieve these goals, the architects of Mongoose proposed placing American intelligence operatives in Cuba.

A secondary objective for Operation Mongoose was to assassinate Castro. Mongoose offered several possible ways to carry out the mission, including poisoning cigars with botulism toxin and presenting them to Castro as a gift, poisoning a drink for Castro, and even rigging explosives to rare seashells on the sea floor to tempt Castro, who was an avid diver.

Mongoose was also involved in psychological warfare. Lansdale created an anti-Castro radio broadcast that covertly aired in Cuba. Leaflets were distributed depicting Castro as overweight and opulent at the citizens' expense.

Yet the main thrust of Lansdale's plan was a series of large-scale "dirty tricks" meant to evoke a call to arms against Cuba in the international community. One plan called for a space launch at Cape Canaveral to be sabotaged and blamed on Cuban agents. Operation Bingo called for a staged attack on the U.S. Navy base at Guantanamo Bay in hopes of creating conditions that would demand for the U.S. military overthrow of Castro.

When the Church Committee, headed by Idaho Senator Frank Church, investigated the actions of the national intelligence agencies in the wake of the Watergate scandal in 1974, notes on Operation Mongoose surfaced publicly for the first time. The committee commented not only on the assassination plots, but also on the "dirty tricks" proposed by Lansdale.

But Mongoose existed on paper more than in practice. While there were elements of propaganda dissemination, in 1964, President Lyndon Johnson abandoned the program after Kennedy's death. The fatal flaw in Mongoose was that it appeared to be a reactionary attempt to right a wrong by using a methodology similar to the initial Bay of

40

Pigs blunder. However, Kennedy's obsession with Castro lingered. He remained the nagging thorn.

On February 3, 1962, Kennedy issued Presidential Proclamation 3447, initiating the existing U.S. embargo against Cuba, banning nearly all trade between the two countries.[63] He did so, however, only after satisfying his personal self-interest.

Former Kennedy Press Secretary Pierre Salinger, in November 2002, wrote of the somewhat amusing events leading to the Cuban embargo proclamation:

Several months later, the president called me into his office in the early evening.

"Pierre, I need some help," he said solemnly.

"I'll be glad to do anything I can, Mr. President," I replied.

"I need a lot of cigars."

"How many, Mr. President?"

"About 1,000 Petit Upmanns."

I shuddered a bit, although I kept my reaction to myself. "And, when do you need them, Mr. President?"

"Tomorrow morning."

The next morning, I walked into my White House office at about 8 a.m., and the direct line from the president's office was already ringing. He asked me to come in immediately.

"How did you do, Pierre?" he asked, as I walked through the door.

"Very well," I answered. In fact, I'd gotten 1,200 cigars. Kennedy smiled, and opened up his desk. He took out a long paper, which he immediately signed. It was the decree banning all Cuban products from the United States. Cuban cigars were now illegal in our country."[64]

This embargo prohibited importers and tourists from bringing in goods of Cuban origin. It also restricted Cuba's use of American ports,

---

[63] American Presidency Project, www.presidency.ucsb.edu.

[64] Pierre Salinger, "Great Moments: Kennedy, Cuba, and Cigars" http://www.cigaraficionado.com/webfeatures/show/id/Great-Moments-Kennedy-Cuba-and-Cigars_7840.

which hurt the Cuban government economically but failed to remove Castro from office. This became a political opening for Republicans to use against the Kennedy Administration with an impending mid-term election in November. The Republican Senatorial Campaign Committee announced that Cuba would be the dominant political issue of the 1962 elections.[65]

Throughout 1962, two forces drove Cuban policy: Kennedy's obsession and the public's opinion of Kennedy. Mongoose, though hardly a successful policy, bore witness to Kennedy's obsession with Castro and Cuba.

Cuba was the only nation polled that gave the Kennedy Administration negative ratings (62 percent); 70 percent of Cubans wanted the U.S. to take some type of action short of war, including "starving" them out" as one of the possibilities.[66]

Cuba and the Soviet Union

The Kennedy Administration's obsession with Castro and Cuba was not necessarily excessive; concern was due with such a hostile country so close to U.S. shores. Kennedy's Soviet Union counterparts would have behaved similarly, if not even more extremely, in order to demonstrate their regional dominance. When the Soviet Union was confronted with a similar situation in 1956, Khrushchev took decisive action to quell the hostility.

During the Hungarian uprising, from October 23 until November 10, the people of Hungary spontaneously revolted against their government and its Soviet-backed policies. The revolt began with peaceful demonstrations by students in Budapest. They demanded an end to Soviet occupation. Through arrests and tear gas, police tried to disperse the masses, but after students attempted to free those who were arrested, police began to fire on the crowd.

---

[65] Sorensen, 670.
[66] Freedman, 161.

42

In response, the students demolished the statue of former Soviet leader Joseph Stalin; they brought it down to chants of "Russians go home." On November 4, Khrushchev, who had become increasingly concerned about the uprising, sent in the Soviet Red Army, which led to the death of an estimated 3,000 Hungarians. Roughly 450 were arrested and subsequently executed, and over 200,000 immigrated to other countries. In comparison, the Kennedy Administration's obsession with Castro could be considered mild. But events in October 1962 would mark a dramatic change in Kennedy's perception toward the Soviet Union and Castro.

The Cuban Missile Crisis

The Cuban Missile Crisis should be understood as the triangular confrontation between the United States, the Soviet Union, and Cuba during the height of Cold-War tension. After deflecting the Bay of Pigs invasion, Cubans believed there was an ongoing possibility of another U.S. invasion. It was on the heels of the Bay of Pigs that Castro formally declared Cuba a satellite of the Soviet Union, but this formality merely made official what many had believed to be true since the Cuban Revolution in 1959.

The Cuban Missile Crisis was as close as America came to nuclear war. While many continue to debate whether the Kennedy Administration actually prevented this war, there is little doubt that the danger was real.

Former Secretary of Defense Robert McNamara wrote about the severity of the crisis in his book, *Argument Without End*.

According to McNamara, "No one should believe that had United States troops been attacked with tactical nuclear warheads, the United States would have refrained from responding with nuclear warheads. And where would it have ended? In utter disaster."[67]

In 1962, the Soviet Union was behind the United States in the

---

[67] Robert McNamara, James Blight, and Robert Bringham, *Argument Without End* (New York: PublicAffairs, 2000), 10.

arms race. Soviet missiles possessed the capability to be launched only against Europe, while U.S. missiles were capable of striking the entire Soviet Union. In late April 1962, Soviet Premier Nikita Khrushchev conceived the idea of placing intermediate-range missiles in Cuba. A deployment in Cuba would double the Soviet strategic arsenal and provide a real deterrent to a potential U.S. attack against the Soviet Union. And because Castro was already seeking ways to defend Cuba from any repeat performances of the Bay of Pigs, missile installation in Cuba was a fait accompli. In the summer of 1962, the Soviet Union worked quickly and secretly to build its missile installations in Cuba.

In early September 1962, American U-2 spy planes discovered that the Soviet Union was building surface-to-air missile (SAM) launch sites in San Cristobal, Cuba. In addition, they discovered an increase in the number of Soviet ships arriving in Cuba, raising fears that the Soviets were enhancing Cuba with new supplies of weapons. Though SAMs were not considered offensive in nature, the new installations did allow Cuba the capability to shoot down U-2s.

These discoveries put Kennedy in a difficult situation. Moreover, mid-term elections were about to take place for the United States Congress in November. And Cuba remained an issue where Kennedy appeared weak, according to opinion polls. The prospects of losing Democratic seats in a Congress already unable to pass much of Kennedy's key legislation would be exacerbated with this potential fiasco. The prospect of planes being shot down during reconnaissance missions may have contributed to Kennedy's decision to restrict U-2 planes over Cuba. Pilots were allowed to perform flyovers, but they were ordered to avoid flying the entire length of the island.

The crisis officially began on October 15, 1962, when reconnaissance photographs revealed that Soviet missiles with long-range capabilities were under construction in Cuba. On October 16, Kennedy was informed of the missile installations. He immediately organized a group of advisors known as the Executive Committee of the United States National Security Council (ExComm). The team consisted of President Kennedy; Vice President Lyndon Johnson;

44

Attorney General Robert Kennedy; National Security Advisor McGeorge Bundy; Secretary of State Dean Rusk; Secretary of the Treasury C. Douglas Dillon; Secretary of Defense Robert McNamara; Director of Central Intelligence John McCone; U.S. Army Chairman of the Joint Chiefs of Staff General Maxwell D. Taylor; Under Secretary for Economic, Business, and Agricultural Affairs George Ball; Ambassador to the Soviet Union Llewellyn Thompson; Deputy Secretary of Defense Roswell Gilpatric; and Special Counsel to the President Ted Sorensen.

This assembled group met several times, debated different strategies, and finally determined the following possible ways to handle the situation:

Do nothing; ignore the missiles in Cuba. This was reasonable because the United States had military bases in 127 different countries, including Cuba. The United States also had nuclear missiles in several countries close to the Soviet Union (including Turkey) that had nuclear capabilities.

Negotiate and propose the Soviet Union dismantle their missiles in Cuba; in exchange the United States would withdraw its nuclear missiles from Turkey and Italy.

Invade. Send United States troops into Cuba to overthrow Castro's government.

Create a naval blockade. Use the United States Navy to stop military equipment arriving in Cuba from the Soviet Union.

Bomb missile bases. Utilize conventional air strikes against Cuban missile bases and other military targets.

Use nuclear weapons against Cuba and/or the Soviet Union.[68]

After the initial ExComm meetings, the team generally felt that air strikes would be the best option. But this choice was encouraged mostly by the CIA, and given their poor recommendations during the Bay of Pigs, Kennedy chose to embrace a more cautious posture.

---

[68] Theodore Sorensen, *Kennedy* (New York: Harper & Row, 1965), 682.

Kennedy's caution created a more judicious climate within ExComm as they began to ponder the Soviet Union's potential counter moves if the United States went ahead with the proposed air strikes. ExComm continued to meet for an additional two days. The CIA and the military still supported bombing raids and/or an invasion. General Curtis LeMay, Air Force Chief of Staff, argued strongly with the president that a military attack was essential. When Kennedy questioned the possible Soviet response, LeMay assured him they would counter by moving against Berlin, a possibility that was always lurking in the back of Kennedy's mind.[69]

By Wednesday, October 17, McNamara became the naval blockade's strongest supporter. He argued that the blockade was a strong yet not overbearing response that kept the United States in control of the situation. The majority of the committee also moved in favor of a naval blockade of Cuba. Later that day, Kennedy met with Russian representative Andrei Gromyko, though this meeting had been scheduled prior to the discovery of the missiles.

Gromyko informed Kennedy that the United States should cease its threats toward Cuba and that the aid the Soviets were providing was for food and land development. He also told the president the Soviets were sending Cuba a few "defensive"[70] weapons. Kennedy explained to Gromyko that the situation would become dire if offensive weapons were placed in Cuba. Gromyko assured the president that the Soviet Union would never engage in such a scenario and that the defensive weapons that were placed in Cuba would never threaten the United States. But Gromyko said this as photos taken by U-2 flights over Cuba that morning that showed between sixteen and thirty-two nuclear missiles with one-thousand-mile capability were sitting on Kennedy's desk.

By this time, however, Kennedy viewed the naval blockade as the most viable option in a situation that did not offer, in his mind, "any

---

[69] Conversation between John F. Kennedy and Curtis LeMay. White House Tape 31.2. 9:45 AM, October 19, 1962.

[70] 13 Days in October, http://microsites.jfklibrary.org/cmc/oct18.

satisfactory alternatives."[71] Though the blockade was far from perfect, the other options carried extreme downsides. The Air Force, in spite of LeMay's assurances, could not guarantee 100 percent destruction of all the missiles nor predict the potential Soviet response if an invasion were to occur. Moreover, assuming the invasion was successful in destroying all missiles, the attack would have to be followed up by an invasion. The shortcoming of the military plan most likely recalled too much the Bay of Pigs scenario for Kennedy's comfort. So Kennedy instructed Sorensen to write a speech in which he would explain to the nation and the world why the naval blockade was necessary.

Addressing the nation on October 22, the president said, "Within the past week, unmistakable evidence has established the fact that a series of offensive missile sites is now in preparation on that imprisoned island."[72] But Kennedy did not share with the country just how close the administration already was to full-blown war.

Kennedy also placed the Air Force on alert to prepare for an attack on Cuba and the Soviet Union. The army positioned 125,000 men in Florida and was told to wait for orders to invade Cuba. If the Soviet ships carrying weapons for Cuba failed to respect the blockade by refusing to turn back or be searched, war would have been the most likely outcome. Kennedy also promised his military advisers that if any of the U-2 spy planes were fired upon, he would give orders for an attack on the Cuban SAM missile sites.

U.S. allies were notified and military preparations were made for the blockade. Kennedy ordered armed forces to be at DEFCON-2, which increased force readiness to just below the maximum. It is not certain how many times this level of readiness has been reached or if the maximum, DEFCON-1, has ever been ordered.

On Wednesday, October 24, the United States announced the blockade. The blockade line was initially set at 800 miles but was later

---

[71] Ibid.

[72] John F. Kennedy, National Address on the Cuban Missile Crisis, October 22, 1962. Transcript from Fordham University Sourcebook, www.Fordham.edu/halsall/mod/1962Kennedy-cuba.html.

reduced to 500 miles to give the Russians additional time to consider the ramifications. Kennedy ordered the ships in the Caribbean to refrain from interfering with any of the ships that had stopped short of the line; they were to give them every possible opportunity to turn around. By mid-morning, Navy Intelligence reported that two Russian ships were approaching the blockade line, and that a Russian submarine had moved in between the ships. This complicated matters because the original plan was to send a cruiser in to conduct the boarding, but the appearance of the sub created additional danger.

If the submarine refused to surface, the United States would counter, forcing it up by dropping small depth charges. Moreover, orders had been given to shoot the rudders and propellers of any Soviet cargo ship that failed to stop. At approximately 10:25 AM, CIA Director John McCone was informed that the Russian ships had stopped in the water, indicating their compliance with the blockade.

Later that day, the UN suggested that the blockade should be lifted for a few weeks if Russia agreed not to send missiles to Cuba. Khrushchev agreed, but Kennedy declined. While Kennedy stated he would be open to discuss a peaceful solution, he felt because the missile crisis was created under secret and duplicitous methods, it would be counterintuitive to now give the Soviets the benefit of the doubt.

The morning the blockade was initiated, the already daily low flyovers of Cuba were increased to eight planes, twice a day. On October 23, Khrushchev sent a letter to Kennedy that stated, "The actions of the USA with regard to Cuba are outright banditry, or, if you like, the folly of degenerate imperialism."[73]

Khrushchev also stated that Soviet ships would not follow American orders. Kennedy's reply on October 25 was similar to his response to the United Nation's request that the blockade be lifted. He cited the Soviets' deception as the reason for the crisis. The president also ordered the low-level flights to be increased to once every two

---

[73] Nikita Khrushchev to John F. Kennedy, October 23, 1962, http://www.bbc.co.uk/dna/place-lancashire/plain/A563852

hours, and in case invasion by ground became the only option, he ordered that leaflets preparing Cubans for a provisional government be dropped from the planes.

That evening, the most bizarre moment of the crisis unfolded: Khrushchev sent a telegraphed letter to the president, which Robert Kennedy referred to in retrospect as "very long and emotional."

Khrushchev wrote about the atrocities of nuclear war, and how he only wished to "compete peacefully, not by military means."[74] He offered to stop placing missiles in Cuba and to remove or destroy all those that currently existed if the United States would lift the blockade and pledge to not invade Cuba.

Later, another letter to Kennedy arrived from Khrushchev, suggesting that missile installations in Cuba would be dismantled if the United States dismantled its missile installations in Turkey. ExComm met to discuss what the course of action should be. Many supported military action but were willing to give the Russians one last chance. However, Robert Kennedy and Ted Sorensen felt they should respond to Khrushchev's first letter and simply ignore the second, which is exactly what the president decided to do.

Robert Kennedy then met with Ambassador Dobrynin. He informed the ambassador that if the Russians could not come to some type of agreement by the next day, the United States would remove those missile sites for them.

Khrushchev then announced on October 28 that he would dismantle the installations and return them to the Soviet Union, expressing his trust that the United States would not invade Cuba. Further negotiations were held to implement the October 28 agreement, including a United States demand that Soviet light bombers also be removed from Cuba and specifications about the conditions of the United States not invading Cuba.

---

[74] Sergei N. Khrushchev, *Nikita Khrushchev and the Creation of a Superpower* (University Park, PA: Pennsylvania State University Press, 2001), 593.

The Russians agreed to the terms outlined in the United States response to Khrushchev's first letter. The missiles in Cuba were removed along with the blockade, the United States pledged not to invade Cuba, and several months later, the missiles in Turkey and Italy were removed.

The Cuban Missile Crisis was widely viewed as a triumph for the Kennedy Administration. Kennedy looked tough against the Soviet Union, and he had seemingly put Fidel Castro in his place. Given his actions between 1961 through the embargo signed on February 8, 1963, Kennedy had positioned himself as the least likely to passively tolerate the Castro regime.

But the events that would come next shifted Kennedy's position, and had they fully materialized, they may have put the president in an "Only Nixon could go to China"–type of situation, meaning though the public believed he would not conduct a major policy shift, he would have likely made changes nonetheless. These events would provide one of the great "what-ifs" had Kennedy lived. In 1963, Kennedy flirted with a different approach regarding Castro by embracing a more accommodationist stance that included covert dialogue.

The United States' current antipathy toward and public policy surrounding Cuba—a holdover from the Cold War—might look very different had Kennedy lived beyond 1963. Having well-established bona fides in his opposition to the Communist regime less than one hundred miles from America's shores, Kennedy may very well have been the only president who could have co-existed with Castro and not paid a big political price in the process.

A recorded conversation seventeen days before Kennedy's assassination between the president and National Security Advisor McGeorge Bundy reveals a discussion of the possibility of a secret meeting in Havana with Castro. On the recording, Bundy is briefing the president on Castro's invitation to William Attwood, a U.S. official at the United Nations, to come to Havana for a secret discussion on improving relations with Washington. Kennedy approves provided that official U.S. involvement can be denied. This tape, in particular, represents a 180-degree turnaround from Kennedy's bombastic campaign rhetoric and his actions during the Bay of Pigs, Operation Mongoose, the Cuban Missile Crisis, and the economic embargoes. But the shift in policy must be understood in the broader context of Kennedy's natural pragmatism as a politician.

This pragmatism, which may have betrayed Kennedy initially on his stances with civil rights, and that gives pro-Kennedy historians justification to suggest that the outcome in Vietnam would have been different had he lived, had all the makings of being on the money in Cuba. A good portion of Kennedy's political career reads as though he was usually willing to subordinate his personal beliefs in exchange for what was possible politically.

Less than one month after Kennedy signed the Cuban embargo in 1963, and thereby during the aftermath of Kennedy's perceived victory in the Cuban Missile Crisis, the tangible evidence reveals the possibility of Kennedy's shift in policy toward Cuba. The Kennedy Administration saw this path as more politically advantageous than the CIA-led covert actions to overthrow Castro.

Top Secret declassified documents indicate that Castro shared a mutual interest in improving relations between Cuba and the United States. In May 1963, Castro told correspondent Lisa Howard that a rapprochement with Washington was indeed a possibility.

Lisa Howard began her career as an off-Broadway theater and TV soap opera actress, appearing in the CBS soap opera *The Edge of Night* in the 1950s. When her acting career began to fade, Howard made the switch to journalism. It was while working for the Mutual Radio Network that Howard became the first American reporter to interview Khrushchev. In 1961, she was hired by ABC and became the host of *The News Hour with Lisa Howard.*

In April 1963, Howard went to Cuba to make a documentary. Castro agreed to private as well as on-camera interviews, where he made it clear to Howard that he was amenable to opening relations with Washington. Howard returned to the United States and reported this revelation directly to Kennedy.

This was a rather serendipitous disclosure because on March 4, 1963, less than one month after Kennedy signed the final embargo against Cuba, White House aide Gordon Chase wrote an internal memo at the behest of National Security Advisor Bundy titled "Mr. Donavan's trip to Cuba." In that memo, Chase wrote, "The president does not agree that we should make the breaking of Sino/Soviet ties a non-negotiable point. We don't want to present Castro with a condition that he obviously cannot fulfill. We should start thinking about more flexible lines." He concluded writing this important addendum: "The above must be kept close to the vest. The president, himself, is very interested in this one."[75]

Chase's final point strongly suggested the president's political pragmatism was on high alert. Kennedy was willing to give up some of his high approval ratings as a result of the Cuban Missile Crisis if the exchange could improve the United States' existing relationship with Cuba. He would have to face criticism from Republicans and a public who knew Cuba as the only area where Kennedy polled below 50 percent.

A White House memorandum written by Chase to Bundy, dated April 11, 1963, further amplified the Kennedy Administration's change of course. It read:

1. We are concerned about solving our Cuba problem, but so far, we have been looking at only one side of the coin—ways to hurt Castro by varying degrees of overt and covert nastiness. We have not looked seriously at the other side of the coin—quietly enticing Castro over to us.

2. If this sweet approach turned out to be feasible and, in turn, successful, the benefits would be substantial. In the short run, we would probably be able to neutralize at least two of our main worries about Castro—the reintroduction of offensive missiles and Cuban

[75] National Security Archive,
http://www.gwu.edu/~nsarchiv/NSAEBB/NSAEBB103/630304.pdf.

subversion. In the long run, we would be able to work on eliminating Castro at our leisure from a good vantage point.[76]

Point Two in Chase's memo clearly indicates that the potential policy was driven in some measure by not wanting to repeat anything reminiscent of the Cuban Missile Crisis, and the obsession to remove Castro from power remained part of the policy. Chase does not, however, declare by what means they would "eliminate" Castro— perhaps through diplomatic or economic channels, or as noted in the first point, some form of "covert nastiness."

But the United States was also aware of the chaos that would ensue if Castro were assassinated. In a May 1 CIA memo that recounted Lisa Howard's extensive interview with Castro, the Kennedy Administration stated that "neither [Che] Guevara nor Raul Castro [Fidel's brother] would be able to rule Cuba"[77] if Fidel was indeed eliminated. The memo also noted that Howard stated that Castro was open to possible rapprochement with Kennedy.

There was a constant stream of memos throughout the summer emanating from White House representatives, all with what appears as tacit support from the president, clearly indicating that the administration was moving to change its existing relationship with Cuba. On September 20, 1963, Kennedy authorized Attwood to engage in direct dialogue with Ambassador Lechuga. Bundy suggested that Lisa Howard have a small reception at her house in order to give the meeting a casual appearance. Howard and Lechuga met at Howard's Park Avenue apartment on the evening of September 23. Bundy recorded on November 5 that "the President was more in favor of pushing towards an opening toward Cuba than was the State Department, the idea being—well, getting them out of the Soviet fold

[76] National Security Archive,
http://www.gwu.edu/~nsarchiv/NSAEBB/NSAEBB103/630411.pdf.
[77] National Security Archive,
http://www.gwu.edu/~nsarchiv/NSAEBB/NSAEBB103/630501.pdf.

and perhaps wiping out the Bay of Pigs and maybe getting back into normal."[78]

On November 17, five days before his assassination, Kennedy met with French journalist Jean Daniel, who he asked to relay to Castro that he was ready to negotiate normal relations and drop the embargo. Kennedy sent a coded message to Castro in a speech delivered on November 19. The speech included the following passage: "Cuba had become a weapon in an effort dictated by external powers to subvert the other American republics. This and this alone divides us. As long as this is true, nothing is possible. Without it, everything is possible."[79] The same day that Kennedy delivered the speech, an optimistic Chase wrote to Bundy, "The ball is now in Castro's court. As soon as Lechuga calls Bill [Atwood] to set up a discussion for an appointment to set up an agenda, Bill will get in touch with us."[80] The "agenda" was in regard to a November 8 memo from Chase to Attwood about a direct meeting with Castro.

But fate would obviously deal a major blow to the prospects of normalized relations between Cuba and America. In a bitter irony, White House representatives were planning for the potential negotiations as Kennedy was gunned down in Dallas.

Three days after the assassination, Chase submitted a follow-up memo to Bundy accessing the potential of Lyndon Johnson picking up where Kennedy left off in Cuba, specifically the continuation of Attwood's activities. He wrote:

My own thinking on this, vis-à-vis the events of November 22, is still very fluid. Basically, the events of November 22 would appear to make accommodation with Castro an even more doubtful issue than it was. While I think that President Kennedy could have accommodated and gotten away with it with a minimum of domestic heat, I'm not sure

---

[78] National Security Archive,
http://www.gwu.edu/~nsarchiv/NSAEBB/NSAEBB103/clip.mp3,
[79] Carlos Lechuga, http://www.spartacus.schoolnet.co.uk/JFKlechuga.htm,
[80] National Security Archive,
http://www.gwu.edu/~nsarchiv/NSAEBB/NSAEBB103/631119.pdf.

of President Johnson. For one thing a new President who has no background of being successfully nasty to Castro (e.g. President Kennedy in October, 1962) would probably run a greater risk of being accused, by the American people, of "going soft."[81]

Chase also noted that accused Kennedy assassin, Lee Harvey Oswald, possessed pro-Castro ties that would make any normalization with Cuba increasingly difficult. Though Chase did not rule out rapprochement with Cuba entirely, as his November 25 memo goes to great lengths to outline possible strategy, the door to the idea remained cracked. At least in theory, Attwood's work was effectively finished.

If the February 12, 1964, memo, however, were any indicator, it would appear that Castro had not concluded that proposed normalization between Cuba and the United States was terminated. Using Lisa Howard as an interpreter, Castro sent a memo to Johnson, stating, "Please tell President Johnson that I earnestly desire his election to the Presidency in November."[82]

Castro even resorted to lighthearted banter with the president. "If there is anything I can do to add to his majority (aside from retiring from politics), I shall be happy to cooperate," he said.[83] He added, "Seriously, I observe how the Republicans use Cuba as a weapon against Democrats. So tell President Johnson to let me know what I can do if anything. Naturally, I know my offer of assistance would be of immense value to the Republicans—so this would remain our secret."[84] Castro praised Kennedy for his political courage and assured Johnson that "if he decided to continue the Kennedy approach,"[85] he would guarantee absolute secrecy.[86]

[81] National Security Archive, http://www.gwu.edu/~nsarchiv/NSAEBB/NSAEBB103/631125.pdf.
[82] National Security Archive, http://www.gwu.edu/~nsarchiv/NSAEBB/NSAEBB103/640212.pdf.
[83] Ibid.
[84] Ibid.
[85] Ibid.
[86] Ibid.

But as Chase had forewarned, the momentum in 1964, with the country reeling over an assassinated president and an election on the horizon, had all but dissipated.

Though a smattering of discussions of potential reform continued, most much less extreme than what Kennedy had considered, by July Chase had sent a memo to Bundy with concerns about Lisa Howard's role because she was now in contact with UN Ambassador Adlai Stevenson. Chase recommended they consider removing Howard from direct participation in lieu of Lechuga.

The fleeting momentum that might have altered the course of history has yet to be recaptured. In the five decades of Cuban policy since Kennedy's assassination, every president has maintained a stay-the-course policy. It has indeed created one of the great "what-ifs" in American political history. Kennedy supporters like Pierre Salinger believe that Kennedy would have dramatically changed the course of Cuba–U.S. relations. "If Kennedy had lived," Salinger said, "I am confident that he would have negotiated that agreement and dropped the embargo because he was upset with the way the Soviet Union was playing a strong role in Cuba and Latin America. Cuba would be a different country now and Castro would not be in power any more."[87]

Declassified documents support Salinger's assertion. But advocates of the Salinger perspective cannot ignore that Operation Mongoose was still in effect as were discussions of eliminating Castro in 1963.

But Kennedy speechwriter Ted Sorensen positions Kennedy's overtures to Castro as the forward thinking of a president with high approval ratings, who had successfully stood up to the Communist during the Cuban Missile Crisis. "Let's not overstate the situation," Sorensen said. "Kennedy felt things were going his way and that Castro had been disillusioned by Khrushchev being the statesman by taking his missiles out of Cuba. Kennedy thought if Castro was angry

[87] *Cuba: A Country Study*, ed. Rex Hudson (Department of the Army, 2002), 1.

at Khrushchev maybe there was a chance of turning Castro into another Josip Tito."[88]

Tito had been a longtime Communist, but he eventually broke with the Soviet Union because of his belief in independence and self-determination. According to Sorensen, though Kennedy did not place as much emphasis on turning Castro as the dry documents might indicate, it does show Kennedy as a leader unwilling to rest on his popularity. He was willing to examine the possibility of normalizing relations with Castro while paradoxically keeping Operation Mongoose in effect.

But in 1963, Castro was indeed the nagging thorn in America's side, and he ruled Cuba for forty-nine years through the administrations of ten U.S. presidents. What failed to happen in 1963 is but another example of how the issues from this monumental year continue to influence America into the present day.

---

[88] Ted Sorensen interview with author, June 24, 2009.

Chapter Three:

In Birmingham Because Injustice Is Here

In the spring of 1963, activists in Birmingham, Alabama, led by Martin Luther King, launched one of the most influential and improbable campaigns of the Civil Rights Movement.

This two-month campaign that used peaceful demonstrations as its hallmark would be met with violent attacks using high-pressure fire hoses and police dogs on men, women and children, producing some of the most iconic images of the year. It changed the nation, providing a stepping-stone that by August would make King America's unquestioned moral voice, and it also began the process that moved President John F. Kennedy from lukewarm support to putting the power and prestige of the presidency behind those in the Movement.

But it was improbable for two reasons: Birmingham lay at the core of a state that had made itself the stronghold for segregation; and the perception of weakness within the Movement on the heels of the campaign in Albany, Georgia, in 1962.

58

The Albany Campaign

Between 1961 and 1962, civil rights protestors spent over a year in Albany, Georgia, attempting to integrate the city's public facilities. By the end of 1962, however, it was a widely held belief that the movement suffered a defeat. The *New York Herald Tribune* called it "one of the most stunning defeats of King's career."[89] In a 1965 *Playboy Magazine* interview, King acknowledged that if he had to do it over, he would conduct a different campaign in Albany.[90]

The Albany Movement was a desegregation effort that began in November 1961. Dr. William G. Anderson, a local black physician, initiated the movement along with local activists from the Student Nonviolent Coordinating Committee (SNCC) and the National Association for the Advancement of Colored People (NAACP). According to Anderson:

The Albany Movement was sort of a spontaneous thing. The name itself speaks eloquently to that spontaneity. What else is going to be called a movement? What happened was the result of this catalyst, and the catalyst was of course the SNCC students coming in, as a result of that catalytic reaction in the city of Albany, a number of the civic and social organizations sort of got together and—and decided all in one night—the people in the community apparently are ready for whatever is happening . . . And so after, a good deal of conversation about what shall we call ourselves? And naturally we tossed around all sorts of names, but when the words "Albany Movement" were spoken it sort of took hold at that time. And we never looked at any other names.[91]

---

[89] Lynne Olson, *Freedom's Daughters: The Unsung Heroines of the Civil Rights Movement* (New York: Simon & Schuster, 2002), 237.

[90] Martin Luther King Jr., "50 Years of the Playboy Interview," *Playboy Magazine*, January 1965,
   http://www.playboy.com/playground/view/50-years-of-the-playboy-interview-martin-luther-king.

[91] William G. Anderson interview by James Divinney, "Eyes on the Prize," Atlanta, GA, 7 November 1985,
   http://digital.wustl.edu/e/eop/eopweb/and0015.1042.003drwilliamganderson.html

The "spontaneous thing" that Anderson referred to at the inception of the Albany Movement may have contributed to the overall perception that the campaign was not a success.

Anderson had relocated to Albany in 1957 after completing his residency in Flint, Michigan, and began his medical practice. But the harsh segregationist policies and racist attitudes made it difficult for Anderson to treat patients. Anderson decided to respond to this unjust resistance by spearheading the Albany Movement. He called on Martin Luther King Jr., who was a family friend and childhood neighbor, to support him in his efforts to strike down segregation.

The movement quickly became a broad attack on every aspect of segregation within Albany. SNCC was already involved in a voter-registration center in town, and this provided a base of operations for various sit-ins and protests. King's involvement began in December 15, 1961, and his presence, though not universally embraced, immediately transformed the Albany Movement into a King-led effort that brought national media attention to the semi-rural town, which had a population of approximately 50,000.

The day after King's arrival, Reverend Ralph Abernathy led a march of 250 protestors to City Hall, where all 250 were arrested. Albany Police Chief Laurie Pritchett trained his officers to apply passive law enforcement to handle the protesters, which would be a hallmark of his strategy. Pritchett insisted that prisoners were treated very courteously, diffusing the power of nonviolent protests.

Pritchett had carefully studied the movement's prior strategies, developing his own strategy designed to subvert the movement's efforts. He used mass arrests, avoiding any type of dramatic, violent acts that could attract national publicity. Pritchett also arranged to disperse the prisoners to county jails all over southwest Georgia to prevent his jail from filling up. The absence of physical conflict meant there would be no media bonanza and no national outrage. Without the benefit of national press coverage, Albany became a series of negotiations and mass arrests, which offered the public the perception that King's efforts were unsuccessful. While the press waited for an explosive confrontation that never occurred, behind-the-scenes Albany officials promised to desegregate bus and rail terminals but later reneged on such promises. This was the consistent pattern throughout the movement.

King and Abernathy were sentenced to jail terms in July 1962, and they hoped this would revive the interests of the media. They refused to pay the $178 fine that would have exempted them from serving time, but to avoid publicity, local authorities paid the fine for them, effectively kicking them out of jail and deflating the possibility of a sensational news story.

Another problem for King while he was in Albany was that violence did break out, but from the wrong side. Roughly two thousand protestors became frustrated and impatient with the nonviolent methods and the city's obvious disingenuousness to comply with previous desegregation agreements. They threw rocks and bottles at the police that had been operating nonviolently in their duties and maintaining law and order. King held a prayer vigil to quell the violence, but he had lost the perception of the moral high ground. He was arrested for holding the vigil, and the city of Albany also managed to obtain a federal injunction that banned King and his followers from further public protests. Police hostility would have given the Albany Movement national attention, but it was the protestors, not Chief Pritchett, who were perceived as the instigators of violence. The shrewd methods employed by the City of Albany officials to dishonor any agreements made with the protesters in combination with the lack of sensationalism that the press was seeking gave the Albany Movement the appearance of failure.

At face value, Albany seemed to be a disjointed effort where Chief Pritchett had out-strategized King. With the police chief's "gentle" methods, Albany's refusal to allow King to languish in jail, and the pressure the movement received from Attorney General Robert Kennedy to abide by federal laws, there was little hope for victory in Albany in a literal sense. But others would contend the lessons of Albany were hardly the defeat that conventional wisdom might offer.

As historian Howard Zinn, who participated in the Albany Movement, would opine:

That [Albany defeat] always seemed to me a superficial assessment, a mistake often made in evaluating protest movements. Social movements may have many "defeats"—failing to achieve objectives in the short run—but in the course of the struggle the strength of the old order begins to erode, the minds of people begin to change; the protesters are momentarily defeated but not crushed, and have been lifted, heartened, by their ability to fight back.[92]

There is no question strategic mistakes were made. Unlike previous civil rights efforts, the Albany Movement did not attack segregation with any particular demand. Instead it was a movement that wanted all forms of segregation eliminated, rejecting gradualism, but opening the door to the type of insincere negotiations that ultimately led to frustration. The Albany Movement's demands may have been too general—protesting against segregation as whole, rather than specific issues. The failure to address specifics left many protestors frustrated and unable to maintain the discipline required to engage in nonviolent action.

But the one specific that did come out of Albany, according to former Southern Christian Leadership Conference (SCLC) Director of Voter Registration Jack O'Dell, was the realization that gradualism was no longer a viable option for the movement.[93] King and the SCLC had been stung by the empty promises of gradualism along with the unhurried pace it represented. Gradualism was not something they wished to replicate going forward.

From the movement's perspective, gradualism was simultaneously the disingenuous tool of those who wished to maintain the inhumane status quo and the comfortable pragmatic political option for the Kennedy Administration, which sought to balance the

---

[92] Howard Zinn, *You Can't Be Neutral on a Moving Train* (Boston: Beacon Press, 2002), 54.

[93] Jack O'Dell, interview with author, May 29, 2009.

needs of civil rights protestors along with those of southern states that were key to its reelection hopes in 1964. By 1963, gradualism had become unacceptable to those who bore the burden of the sweltering heat of unequal protection under the law.

As a stand-alone effort, Pritchett's efforts in Albany were successful, but within the gamut of a systematic strategy that would lead into Birmingham and the March on Washington in 1963, the Albany Movement takes on a different look. This linkage was beautifully articulated by King in his last speech on April 3, 1968, when he said that the defeat of the Albany Movement was the moment that Negroes "decided to straighten their backs up."[94] He added, "Whenever men and women straighten their backs up they're going somewhere because a man can't ride your back unless it is bent!"[95]

By 1968, King had embraced a viewpoint of Albany in line with that of Howard Zinn's. Whatever failure the Albany Movement experienced in its inability to foster substantive change was unimportant; the movement instigated a transformative change that was stronger than the segregation laws. As an isolated event, it might appear to have been a defeat, yet as part of a systematic strategy, it was integral. But despite this broader viewpoint of Albany, in 1962, King knew that another defeat in the upcoming movement in Birmingham would permanently label him a failure for the movement's cause.

On to Birmingham

Late in 1962, when the Southern Christian Leadership Conference (SCLC) began planning for the Birmingham campaign, they based their preparations on the lessons learned from Albany. With the benefit of hindsight, the tactics that were subsequently applied in Birmingham were not only more effective but they also demonstrated that Albany was hardly a failure.

---

[94] Martin Luther King Jr., speech delivered at Mason Temple, Memphis, Tennessee, on April 3, 1968.

[95] Ibid.

As the winds of change headed steadfast toward Birmingham in 1963, the purveyors of segregation, the architects of the movement, and the Kennedy Administration would each engage in a rendezvous with destiny, each riding the crest of three different and competing agendas: maintaining the status quo in Birmingham, encouraging social and legal transformation, and handling politics with an eye toward reelection, respectively.

The SCLC's relationship with the Kennedy Administration was complicated. The goal of the SCLC, post Albany, was to end segregation in the South. They had lost all appetite for gradualism. But the politics of the issue made gradualism the preferred choice of the Kennedy Administration.

In 1960, John F. Kennedy won a close election against Richard Nixon with help from many of the southern states that imposed segregation laws. But overtly being portrayed as supporting the SCLC's cause would have been the Kennedy Administration's preferred choice, as evidenced by the October 1962 confrontation between President Kennedy and Mississippi Governor Ross Barnett over admitting James Meredith, the first black student, to the University of Mississippi. Unfortunately, Kennedy's firm support of integration in this instance had created lingering feelings of disapproval throughout the South. And furthermore, the pace of social tension within the South was moving faster than the Kennedy Administration was comfortable with. The issue of civil rights was an intra-party battle that threatened to pit Kennedy against Democratic leadership in the South.

The tenuous nature of the relationship between southern Democrats and the rest of the party began in earnest in 1948 when South Carolina Governor Strom Thurmond led a third-party presidential run after Harry Truman desegregated the U.S. Army, proposed the creation of a permanent Fair Employment Practices Commission, and openly supported the elimination of Poll Taxes and expressed his desire to draft federal anti-lynching laws. Thurmond still holds the record for the longest filibuster in Senate history—twenty-four hours and eighteen minutes—to block the Civil Rights Act of 1957. At the beginning of 1963, the Kennedy Administration saw any potential civil rights bill as dead on arrival because many key committee chairmanships in the Senate were held by southern senators sympathetic to segregation. And their proven ability and historical commitment to filibuster civil rights legislation meant certain defeat from the Kennedy Administration's perspective. Moreover, it would be a crushing political blow for an administration to send legislation to Congress that could not make it out of committee. For the Kennedy Administration, in early 1963, it simply wasn't worth the political risk to send a civil rights bill to Congress—lots of downside potential with very little upside.

The Kennedy Administration's political pragmatism created growing frustration within the civil rights community, who saw them as failing to make good on their 1960 civil rights campaign promises. Kennedy felt he could be more effective using executive orders, bypassing Congress. But this was viewed, from the SCLC perspective, as a tepid response to an issue they felt required Lincolnesque boldness and determination. With January 1, 1963, marking the centennial anniversary of the Emancipation Proclamation, King had made multiple appeals to Kennedy to issue a second proclamation that would outlaw segregation.[96]

Further complicating the relationship between the Kennedy Administration and the SCLC was the separate agenda pursued by FBI Director J. Edgar Hoover, who was particularly hostile toward King. By 1963, the FBI had assigned to King full enemy status. Moreover, by 1963, the FBI no longer notified King when their surveillance

---

[96] On December 13, 1961, King sent a telegram to the president urging a second Emancipation Proclamation. He followed up with a sixty-four page appeal requesting a "national rededication to the principles of the Emancipation Proclamation and for a executive order prohibiting segregation" on May 17, 1962, http://www.nytimes.com/2012/05/17/opinion/kings-forgotten-manifesto.html?_r=0

revealed a possible assassination attempt.[97] Hindsight may indeed be the enemy of dispassionate historical examination, but Hoover's overt hostility toward King and the movement remain a grim chapter in U.S. history. This tragedy is magnified not only by the movement's commitment to nonviolent civil disobedience, but also by its deeply rooted belief in the Declaration of Independence and the Constitution. The movement transformed itself into the unintended consequence of the Founding Fathers' revolutionary efforts. Beyond any proposed legislation or speech to the nation, there was little the Kennedy Administration could do to directly to aid the Birmingham campaign.

If the Albany Movement represented a defeat for King, taking on Birmingham would appear nothing short of ludicrous, if not masochistic. But with Albany having proved the futility of gradualism to King and the movement, Birmingham was the obvious next step. In fact, Birmingham would become a hard-fought victory, making a persuasive case that Albany was not a defeat in a linear sense, but rather a learning experience that would ultimately bear the fruit of success for the movement's cause. The Birmingham campaign would also demonstrate that some of King's harshest criticisms would not be directed toward staunch segregationists but to moderate clergy who advocated for the virtues of gradualism rather than the confrontational style that the movement would embrace.

There were several tangible and intangible differences between Albany and Birmingham that made the latter city the movement's obvious next adversary. The major difference may have been that Birmingham was an intentional target of the SCLC. Unlike Albany, where a movement had already existed before King's involvement, the Birmingham campaign was the brainchild of the SCLC. Albany was a King-led movement largely because of his presence and national notoriety. But it is a different undertaking when one is attempting to place his or her efforts on top of what has already been created rather than being part of a plan at its inception. Neither the SNCC nor the

---

[97] Taylor Branch, *Parting the Waters: America in the King Years 1954–1963* (New York: Simon & Schuster, 1988), 692.

NAACP was active in Birmingham the way they were in Albany, reducing the possibility of turf rivalries. In fact, the NAACP was outlawed in Alabama when the SCLC began its campaign. The only real presence that the SCLC had to contend with was the Alabama Christian Movement for Human Rights, headed by Reverend Fred Shuttlesworth. And it was Shuttlesworth who invited King to come to Birmingham.

Shuttlesworth is an icon in the movement's lore. His participation goes back as far as the movement's official beginnings in 1955. He participated in sit-in protests at lunch counters as well as the Freedom Rides in 1961. On Christmas Day, 1956, he survived a bomb blast that destroyed his home. And he would be hospitalized as a result of the injuries sustained by high-powered fire hoses during the Birmingham campaign. As long as King and Shuttlesworth could co-exist, it would give the Birmingham effort an advantage over Albany. Shuttlesworth had demonstrated a willingness to put his life on the line for freedom's cause that would gain King's admiration.

Another difference between Albany and Birmingham was location. While Albany, located in southwest Georgia, was largely rural, Birmingham was a city of 340,000 that had a significant industrial base. It possessed the highest per-capita income for blacks of any city in the South. Steel, iron ore, and mining were among the industries that hired black workers. Birmingham was the second property of U.S. Steel; the first was Pittsburgh, Pennsylvania. But in 1964, King summed up the best reason for targeting Birmingham:

If you visited Birmingham before the third of April in the hundredth anniversary year of the Negro's emancipation, you might come to a startling conclusion. You might conclude here is a city which has been trapped for decades in a Rip Van Winkle slumber; a city whose fathers have apparently never heard of Abraham Lincoln, Thomas Jefferson, the Bill of Rights, the Preamble to the Constitution, the Thirteenth, Fourteenth, and Fifteenth Amendments, or the 1954 decision of the United States Supreme Court outlawing segregation in public schools.[98]

The planning sessions about going into Birmingham bore a distinct difference from those held before Albany. In addition to being a movement orchestrated by the SCLC, it was very strategic in who would be involved in those meetings. A good portion of the SCLC was omitted. King also limited the number of non-SCLC clergy that would be involved.[99] The SCLC members active in the planning with King were Abernathy, Reverend Wyatt Tee Walker, Reverend Andrew Young, Reverend James Lawson, Stanley Levison, Clarence Jones, and Jack O'Dell.[100]

It was Walker, the SCLC's executive director, who presented the detailed strategy to the group called Project C (for confrontation), calling for a combination of targeted sit-ins at the lunch counters of department stores, economic boycotts of the downtown business section with larger protests, and massive demonstrations designed to give attention to the boycotts as well as fill the jails. Finally, the plan would call on those outside of Birmingham to descend upon the city, increasing the attention on the boycotts and overcrowding the jails. The movement was designed to gradually build, culminating with a crescendo of national attention.

There was little dissent concerning Walker's plan—much of the discussion centered on other matters. King needed assurances from Jack O'Dell that there was a plan in place to ensure the necessary resources were available to carry out the strategy. The movement could not afford to fill Birmingham's jail and be unable to make bail. King was also concerned about press perceptions of the potential monetary issue: "If we run dry again in the next few months, the press

---

[98] Martin Luther King Jr., *Why We Can't Wait* (New York: New American Library, 1964), 47.
[99] Branch, 688.
[100] Jack O'Dell, interviewed by author, May 29, 2009.

will say we went into Birmingham just to get out of debt," he said.[101] King was the movement's best fundraiser nationally, but he was also needed on the ground in Birmingham. The plan would require a well-thought-out use of King's time. Could King conduct fundraising tours across the country while he was simultaneously needed in Birmingham?

After O'Dell assured King the resources and the accompanying plan were in place, they were ready to move into action. Once the decision to go to Birmingham was finalized, King concluded with a brutally grave possibility: "There are eleven people here assessing the type of enemy we're going to face," he said. "I have to tell you in my judgment, some of the people sitting here today will not come back alive from this campaign. And I want you to think about it."[102]

King was offering a realistic understanding of the task ahead. Alabama, under the leadership of Governor George Wallace, had become the citadel of segregation, and Birmingham was its shining example. In the words of Jack O'Dell, Birmingham was the "Johannesburg of the South."[103] Long before Wallace's "Segregation today, segregation tomorrow, segregation forever" inaugural address, Birmingham already possessed the nickname "Bombingham" because of eighteen unsolved bombings over a six-year period, which all occurred in black neighborhoods. In 1962, instead of adhering to a Supreme Court ruling to integrate public facilities, Birmingham chose to close thirty-eight public playgrounds, eight swimming pools, and four golf courses. It was this legacy that, according to O'Dell, led King to call Birmingham "the most thoroughly segregated city in the United States."[104] And no one personified the spirit of this legacy more than Theophilus Eugene "Bull" Connor.

---

[101] Branch, 691.
[102] Branch, 691–692.
[103] O'Dell interview.
[104] Ibid.

Bull Connor

On July 11, 1897, in Selma, Alabama, Theophilus Connor was born the son of a train dispatcher and telegraph operator, whose work required frequent travel. During Connor's childhood, his family lived in several states. His mother died of pneumonia when he was eight years old, and his father continued to travel for work, so Connor spent much of his childhood and early teenage years living with relatives. He attended high school but did not graduate.

In 1922, Connor became a popular sports-radio announcer for the local minor league baseball team, the Birmingham Barons. Connor gained local notoriety by using a megaphone to forward telegraph reports of baseball games to Birmingham pool halls. It was also during this time he acquired his nickname, "Bull"; it was based on a local newspaper cartoon character, Dr. B. U. L. Conner.

In 1934, Connor ran for a seat in the Alabama House of Representatives as a Democrat. He won, due largely to his name recognition as a radio personality. In 1937, Connor was elected Birmingham's Commissioner of Public Safety, a position that gave him administrative authority over the police and fire departments, schools, the public health service, and libraries. Connor portrayed himself as a defender of working-class white people, tough on crime, and an uncompromising proponent of racial segregation—gradualism was not in Connor's vocabulary.

As Public Safety Commissioner of Alabama, Connor was lord and Birmingham was his fiefdom. In 1948, Connor's officers arrested Idaho Senator Glen Taylor, the running mate of the Progressive Party candidate and former Vice President Henry Wallace. Taylor's crime was his attempt to speak to the Southern Negro Youth Congress, which violated Birmingham's segregation laws. And Connor paid no price for his mistreatment of a sitting United States Senator. With the bulk of Birmingham's key services under his jurisdiction, Connor in essence ran the city.

Efforts by future Birmingham Mayor David Vann, who helped organize a referendum that changed Birmingham's form of government, would prove pivotal in the movement's success and Connor's ultimate downfall. In November 1962, the voters of Birmingham changed their form of government, calling for the mayor to work with the nine-member city council rather than the three county commissioners, thereby eliminating Connor's position as Commissioner of Public Safety. It was the first clear sign that the city wanted to move away from the negative perceptions that led to the nickname "Bombingham." This move necessitated that Connor run for mayor if he wanted to maintain a role in public life.

For decades, Connor and his tactics may have represented the soul of a majority, but in the beginning of 1963, it remained unclear if the white people of Birmingham wanted him as the face of their city.

The Birmingham mayoral race was scheduled for March 5, 1963, with Connor and State Senator Albert Boutwell as the leading candidates. In comparison to Connor, Boutwell was a moderate on segregation. While Boutwell's moderation may have been more appealing to the black voters of Birmingham—he was the lesser of two evils—he still represented the continuation of Jim Crow segregation, albeit in a potentially less violent form, which made him appealing in the eyes of much of Birmingham's white population. Though in many respects, Boutwell represented the gradualism of the Albany Movement, which the SCLC did not wish to repeat.

Project C Versus Bull Connor

In January and February, King maintained a hectic schedule speaking across the country, raising money for the Birmingham effort, which was scheduled to commence in March. But the March 5 mayoral election caused King to move back the official start of Project C. This was a disappointment because the strategy outlined by Wyatt Walker was set to begin in the first week of March and peak through Easter, which was the second largest shopping season of the year. There was a feeling within the movement that a public demonstration in the midst of a mayoral election might unintentionally aid the cause of Connor. King agreed to postpone the demonstrations until two weeks after the election, but in what might be viewed later as a serendipitous event for the SCLC, the March 5 results did not produce a clear winner. Boutwell and Connor were scheduled for an April 3 runoff that would further set back Walker's timeline.

Even though Governor Wallace endorsed Connor, Boutwell easily defeated him in the runoff. The city was bustling with a sense of renewal, unaware of the confrontation that was about to take place. The next day, the headline of the local paper read, "New Day Dawns for Birmingham."[105] The white voters of Birmingham had seemingly turned a page; they wanted Boutwell's moderation over Connor's excess. But here is where Connor first became the "gift" that kept on giving to the SCLC's cause.

Racial moderates along with business and civic leaders hoped that Boutwell's victory would open the door to peaceful compromises with civil rights leaders. They hoped that incidents like the tragedy of the Freedom Riders in Birmingham on Mother's Day, 1961, would never be replicated.

On that 1961 Sunday, two Freedom Riders' busses were brought to a halt by a mob from Birmingham. The first bus, a Greyhound, was firebombed outside of Birmingham, and the iconic photos showing the bus engulfed in flames made global headlines. The mob met the second bus in Birmingham, where they severely beat the passengers. Connor claimed he posted no officers at the bus depot to protect the Freedom Riders because of the Mother's Day holiday. It was later revealed that the FBI knew of the planned attack and knew that Birmingham police would not be available. Moreover, Reverend John Rutland, Connor's pastor, reportedly pleaded with him that morning to protect the Freedom Riders, but to no avail.[106] As much as moderates

---

[105] Stephen B. Oates, *Let the Trumpet Sound: A Life of Martin Luther King, Jr.* (San Francisco: HarperCollins, 1993), 216.

[106] Branch, 420.

may have wished to put this type of public mayhem behind them, Connor had other plans.

As an elected official, Connor argued against the recent election results—as far as he was concerned, he still had two years remaining on his term and had no intention of leaving. Connor, along with two other commissioners, took legal action, prohibiting Boutwell from taking office. Until it was decided in the courts, the city of Birmingham would be bogged down in the internal strife of having two competing forms of government—the one they wanted in Boutwell and the one they had in Connor—making Birmingham vulnerable to the goals of Project C, and Bull Connor accountable to no one.

The headwind of gradualism was blowing briskly in the face of the SCLC's movement. If the Birmingham mayoral election results were any accurate indicator, the voters wanted some form of change from the way their city was perceived publicly. Gradualism was certainly the preference of the Kennedy Administration that at best was functioning as a quasi-supporter of the SCLC.

But the SCLC wanted confrontation—they needed it, and they had a willing accomplice in Connor. In retrospect, Bull Connor, desperate to prove his relevance to a city that clearly did not want him as mayor, was tailor-made for SCLC's campaign.

April 3, 1963, became what the SCLC called B-Day (for Birmingham). Wyatt Walker comprised a jail list of protestors willing to go to jail, which was between 250 and 350 individuals.[107] But only sixty-five volunteers showed up in the basement of First Baptist Church of Ensley, where King's younger brother, Rev. A.D. King, was the pastor. After a brief soliloquy on nonviolence by Martin Luther King and Rev. James Lawson, the protestors went to the Sixteenth Street Baptist Church to meet Rev. Shuttlesworth and begin the demonstrations. Shuttlesworth had begun handing out the group's "Birmingham Manifesto" to the press, which stated that the

---

[107] Walker touted 350, but King later stated it was 250.

Birmingham campaign was based on the "moral witness to give our community a chance to survive."[108]

The sixty-five volunteers were divided into five groups, and each group headed toward specifically targeted lunch counters for a confrontation that would lead to arrest. Four of the five lunch counters had prepared themselves by adopting methods they'd learned from Albany Police Chief Pritchett, to avoid confrontation. When the protestors sat down, the lunch counters simply cut off the lights and closed for the day. But one lunch counter, Britt's, called the police, and twenty-one demonstrators were taken to jail.[109]

Ironically, the first-day results were met with disappointment from both King and Connor. For King, the first day was reminiscent of the Albany Movement: very little fanfare, few arrests, and not much for the press to report. It certainly raised the question of whether or not Boutwell's defeat of Connor was enough to assuage the fire for nonviolent civil disobedience. For Connor, attempting to show his importance to a city that no longer wanted his leadership, it was a missed opportunity to fulfill his pledge to cram the jails with protestors. If Birmingham was unwilling to cooperate with his plan to meet the movement's confrontation with his brand of retaliation, how could he remain in office after April 15, the date he was originally scheduled to leave office after the mayoral election? However, though it was unlikely they knew it at the time, King and Connor would become the improbable duo that would alter the movement's fortunes.

The initial stages of Project C were hardly a success; storeowners frustrated the movement's efforts by failing to engage in the confrontation that was initially hoped for. The media had been promised these types of conflicts as well, but at this point they remained few in number. The Kennedy Administration made no public statements regarding the Birmingham campaign. The only direct contact that the SCLC received from the administration was from

---

[108] Birmingham Manifesto, http://www.crmvet.org/docs/bhammanf.htm.
[109] Branch, 709.

Burke Marshall, on behalf of Attorney General Robert Kennedy, urging the movement to delay its efforts.

In April 1963, anything except violent confrontation was simply not a front-page news item. The systematic denial of constitutional rights to some of America's citizens alone was not a high priority for a nation in the throes of the Cold War and coming off of the tension and success of the Cuban Missile Crisis. It naturally furthered a climate for gradualism because it represented change without anyone enduring the prerequisite for change, which is discomfort. A strong argument could be made that America in 1963, let alone Birmingham in 1963, was hardly in a mood for the type of discomfort that the SCLC and Bull Connor would demonstrate.

As with the Albany Movement, the initial stages of the Birmingham campaign were making King appear increasingly like yesterday's news. But unlike Albany, Birmingham was much more King's doing. He planned it, made public statements in advance, and put his reputation as a national figure on the line. It appeared that Project C had the makings in the beginning of "Project N"—that is, Project Nonstarter.

On Wednesday, April 10, 1963, the city of Birmingham filed a complaint and requested an injunction in state circuit court. They charged those involved in Project C—139 individuals in two organizations—guilty of committing and/or encouraging participation in certain movements such as sit-in demonstrations, mass street parades, trespasses on private property after being warned to leave the premises by the owners, mob congregations upon public streets and other public places, unlawful picketing in private places of business in the City of Birmingham, and being in violation of numerous other ordinances and statutes of the City of Birmingham and State of Alabama.

The complaint stated that these infractions of the law were expected to continue and would "lead to further imminent danger to the lives, safety, peace, tranquility, and general welfare of the people of the City of Birmingham," and that "remedy by law [was] inadequate."[110]

The circuit judge granted a temporary injunction, making illegal the very methods outlined in Project C. The ramifications of the SCLC's next move would raise a plethora of philosophical, theological, and ethical debates that would ultimately invoke thinkers and writers such as Augustine, Thomas Jefferson, John Bunyan, and Jesus of Nazareth before a suitable answer could be sorted out. Could the SCLC's movement be just, as they claimed, while knowingly breaking the law?

At the time of the injunction, few beyond those intimately involved were following to movement, and Birmingham had yet to reach the nation's radar screen. There was no twenty-four-hour news cycle in those days. In fact, the nightly news broadcast was still fifteen minutes in length. CBS Evening News with Walter Cronkite became the first to expand to thirty minutes on September 2, 1963. A nation still focused primarily on a Communist threat might view the violation of the injunction as simply a matter of breaking the law rather than analyze the situation through an Augustinian prism and question whether or not Birmingham's injunction represented a just law. Moreover, there was not wide print media coverage from either the mainstream or Negro newspapers in the early stages of the protest effort. In terms of public perception, in April 1963, it would be highly unlikely a majority of Americans would view Negro leadership leading a protest that violates the law as being consistent with the democratic values of the nation, especially without the proper context. This was the challenge confronting King and the movement.

The turning point came as King was vacillating between engaging in one of the civil disobedience acts defined as illegal by the injunction, which would result in his being arrested, or addressing the SCLC's need to raise additional money. King was also running into opposition from Birmingham's Negro business community, who were

---

[110] Injunction requested by the City of Birmingham against Protesters http://www.crmvet.org/docs/bhammanf.htm.

far more amenable to the idea of giving Boutwell a chance to make progress on segregation once he took office than having protestors armed with nothing more than a belief in equality going up against Bull Connor's police force. Adopting the language of Jim Crow proponents, the Negro business community saw King and the SCLC as outside agitators and viewed their actions as more harmful than beneficial to any desegregation efforts.

Moreover, though the numbers tend to fluctuate a bit, it is fair to conclude that of the several hundred black churches in Birmingham and the surrounding areas, less than 10 percent directly participated in some manner with Project C. The folklore, which tends to exaggerate over time, conjures the vision of black churches in mass solidarity, nonviolently marching, praying, and singing their way to victory over the oppressive hand of Jim Crow. This was not the case.

As Project C commenced, the SCLC was told by an anxious Kennedy Administration to wait until Birmingham's election status was cleared up, and that same message was given to them by a number of black business leaders. Likewise, a majority of Birmingham's black churches sent a similar message.

Six days into Project C, the SCLC was running low on resources and the funding to bail out the few protestors who actually participated; the black business community continued to oppose them, and they still received little support from black churches. The percentage of jail-commitment cards that translated into actual participation rivaled the percentage of black churches that contributed to the movement's efforts. The only thing that may have prevented the movement's beginnings from appearing to be a complete failure was the fact that the press included the onlookers as part of the participants, which exaggerated the overall numbers.[111] But promises to the press of a major confrontation seemed to lack credibility. It was shaping up disastrously as an "Albany Redux."

Because of Birmingham's mayoral election, the movement could not take full advantage of the Easter time frame offered in Walker's

---

[111] Branch, 730.

initial plan. Though Walker's plan had called for a gradual increase in pressure, the early stages of Project C languished well below expectations. There was not an overwhelming outcry of support from the Negro business community, the Negro church, or the Negro community at-large. But Good Friday, 1963, serendipitously served as the turning point for Project C and for King as a national leader.

Incarceration

Good Friday, in the Christian tradition, was the necessary evil precursor to the resurrection, and in Birmingham on this day in 1963, a number of symbolic events were on display as the story was simultaneously being preached in pulpits across the world. Good Friday, 1963, was the day that Pope John XXIII, in one of his last public appearances due to his terminal cancer, interrupted services at St. Peter's Basilica to call for the reference to "perfidious Jews" to be removed from the liturgy. The Pontiff's display of ecumenical goodwill did not change the fact that Martin Luther King Jr. had reached a decision on his moral divide of whether to go to jail or to travel the country to replenish the SCLC's coffers on a fundraising campaign. On Good Friday, 1963, he would go to jail.

Was King going to jail for the Negroes of Birmingham or for himself? Was he, as part of both the Negro and white communities of Birmingham suggested, "an outside agitator" All tangible evidence up to this point seemed to indicate that the results in Birmingham were to be a duplication of Albany, which would diminish King's stature in the cause for civil rights. The decision to go to jail was certainly not based on the desires of the Negro business community, nor was it based on the active participation of Negro churches and the larger Negro community of Birmingham. Nonetheless, King's Good Friday actions must be placed in comparison to the story of Jesus at Gethsemane.

Gethsemane is the garden at the foot of the Mount of Olives in Jerusalem where Jesus and his disciples prayed before Jesus' arrest and crucifixion. The gospel according to Luke portrays Jesus as anguished about the Good Friday decision. King must have felt a similar torment in his soul. On the evening he decided to violate the injunction that would result in his arrest, at the Gaston Motel, in Room 30, King did not make his decision with his trusted inner circle; rather, he removed himself from the debate. After spending time alone in his bedroom, he returned to the larger group wearing uncustomary "work clothes." "I don't know what will happen," he said. "I don't know where the money will come from, but I have to make a faith act."[112]

As King and Abernathy left the Sixteenth Street Baptist Church along with roughly fifty protestors, the cheering onlookers who lined the sidewalk again erroneously gave the impression of much more participation by Birmingham Negroes. Not long after King and Abernathy began marching, they, along with the fifty protestors, were arrested.

Connor was well aware of the Albany playbook orchestrated by Chief Pritchett, but following Albany's lead would undermine Connor's reason to remain in office. He wanted to make an example of King that would send a message to the Negro community as well as the white business community, which had long grown tired of Connor's methods for enforcing segregation, if not segregation itself. Isolated from other inmates, King was placed in solitary confinement, he was denied any communication with his attorney, and he could not make any phone calls, including to his wife Coretta who had given birth to their fourth child, Bernice, on March 28. In addition, King was deprived of a mattress or linen.

Four days after his arrest, King finally saw his attorney Clarence Benjamin Jones. Jones informed King that SCLC Director Wyatt Tee Walker and entertainer Harry Belafonte were working to alert the Kennedy Administration of King's conditions. But the mood in the White House was not overtly sympathetic, in large part because they were initially opposed to the Birmingham campaign. Moreover, King remained in jail by choice, his incarceration not the product of unfortunate happenstance.

---

[112] Branch, 729.

But the Kennedy Administration was not the only group at odds with the movement's methods. Though the motivations varied, there was a unique coalition of dissenters comprised of white business leaders, Alabama's white politicians, Negro business leaders, and even a large percentage of Negro churches. They had all reached similar conclusions that the SCLC, as an outside agitator, was making things more difficult for the Negroes of Birmingham. Though none of the criticism garnered King's attention, it did attract the notice of several white clergymen, who were predisposed to support the civil rights efforts.

Letter from Birmingham Jail

A statement published on April 12, 1963, in the local Birmingham newspaper was titled "A Call for Unity," and it was reprinted by the American Friends Service Committee, the Quaker-led organization long known for its commitment to social justice. The statement read:

We the undersigned clergymen are among those who, in January, issued "an appeal for law and order and common sense," in dealing with racial problems in Alabama. We expressed understanding that honest convictions in racial matters could properly be pursued in the courts, but urged that decisions of those courts should in the meantime be peacefully obeyed.[113]

The statement's third paragraph was particularly stinging, for it could have easily been written by any number of white business leaders in opposition to Project C, by referring to the seemingly universal view that saw King as an outside agitator:

However, we are now confronted by a series of demonstrations by some of our Negro citizens, directed and led in part by outsiders. We recognize the natural impatience of people who feel that their

---

[113] Alabama clergyman, public statement. Birmingham, Alabama, 12 April 1963, http://www.stanford.edu/group/King//frequentdocs/clergy.pdf.

hopes are slow in being realized. But we are convinced that these demonstrations are unwise and untimely.[114]

The clergy specifically noted in their statement that they supported the efforts of "certain local Negro leadership, which has called for honest and open negotiation of racial issues in our area."[115] A number of Negro clergy, jealous of King, would have most likely supported this suggestion, as it would have placed them in a role of local prominence.

Alluding to the promise offered with Boutwell's victory over Connor in the Birmingham mayoral race, a view shared by the Kennedy Administration, they added:

Just as we formerly pointed out that "hatred and violence have no sanction in our religious and political traditions," we also point out that such actions as incite to hatred and violence, however technically peaceful those actions may be, have not contributed to the resolution of our local problems. We do not believe that these days of new hope are days when extreme measures are justified in Birmingham.[116]

The eight clergymen closed with a direct appeal to Birmingham's Negro community to reject King's methods on nonviolent civil disobedience:

We further strongly urge our own Negro community to withdraw support from these demonstrations, and to unite locally in working peacefully for a better Birmingham. When rights are consistently denied, a cause should be pressed in the courts and in negotiations among local leaders, and not in the streets. We appeal to both our white and Negro citizenry to observe the principles of law and order and common sense.[117]

---

[114] Ibid.

[115] Ibid.

[116] Ibid.

[117] Ibid.

Though the full statement was a mere 428 words, it was the most powerful statement against King and the SCLC's efforts in Birmingham. Among King's detractors, this was no doubt the most stinging blow. Not once did the clergy address King by name, but their references did not conceal that he was the target of their disagreement.

The Negro clergy, who did not directly participate in the movement, could be dismissed due to their jealousy of King and fear of possible reprisal had they actively participated, as could the Kennedy Administration, which viewed the problem through a myopic political lens. But these eight white clergymen were not apologists for Jim Crow. They had engaged in public displays of defiance against the tradition of segregation. They had been critical of Alabama Governor George Wallace's inaugural address in January. Several of these clergymen had taken personal stands not only in support of civil rights, but also against issues such as the death penalty, and later some would speak out against the Vietnam conflict. Their theological perspective was rooted in a place where King believed he could find solidarity. This reality no doubt fueled King's dismay as Jones slipped him the newspaper that contained the clergymen's statement as he passed by the guards on duty. But Jones was doing more than covertly keeping King abreast of what was happening on Birmingham's streets while he was incarcerated.

On Jones's next visit, he was greeted with a letter that King said he was writing in response. By Jones's own admission he did not take the writing seriously at first; he was busy holding up the legal end of the situation and working with Belafonte, who was in contact the Kennedy Administration, and Walker, who coordinated events on the ground in Birmingham, especially with King incarcerated. Moreover, King's response was written on the sides of newspaper or whatever he could get his hands on. With each subsequent visit, Jones found it challenging to keep King focused on the business at hand, as King seemed preoccupied with working on his response. But Jones decided to pacify King; he realized writing might be the only thing that stood between hope and hopelessness as King languished in Bull Connor's jail.

82

What Jones did not know at the time was that the newspaper he had slipped to King—outlining the clergy's strong disagreement of his methods—would unleash a political, theological, historical, and moral epistle that had been dormant in King's soul. The final product, King's "Letter from Birmingham Jail," is an unparalleled document in American history. It is a 6,800-word retort that is masterfully organized around what Aristotle considered the three primary forms of persuasion: ethos, pathos, and logic. It remains, in the opinion of many, not only King's best work of 1963, but also the pinnacle of his writing throughout his illustrious career.

It is unlikely any other group of dissenters could have unearthed the prophetic impulses that King demonstrated in his Letter. Yet King's response was as if he had made the clergymen stand proxy for those opposed to Project C as he deftly moved from humble pastor to prophetic theologian to American historian deeply committed to the country's democratic values. While the clergy limited their critique to the events of Birmingham, King not only responded to their local charges, but he also widened the response by taking the clergymen on a whirlwind historical journey as he reviewed the ongoing epic battle between justice and injustice. King drew on the Judeo-Christian traditions of the Old Testament prophets. He linked the movement to the Exodus narrative, so critical to the liberation efforts of African slaves and their theology in America. He called on the thinking of the Roman Catholic theologian St. Thomas Aquinas, American Protestant theologian Paul Tillich, Jewish philosopher Martin Buber, and poet T. S. Eliot, among others. But King's Letter was not merely a lofty piece of prose formulated into a concise document.

King attacked the provincial notion that not being from Birmingham made him an outside agitator, reminding the clergy, "injustice anywhere is a threat to justice everywhere."[118] And King wrote from the perspective of the suffering Negro:

---

[118] Martin Luther King Jr., "Letter from Birmingham Jail," 16 April 1963, http://www.africa.upenn.edu/Articles_Gen/Letter_Birmingham.html.

Perhaps it is easy for those who have never felt the stinging darts of segregation to say, "Wait." But when you have seen vicious mobs lynch your mothers and fathers at will and drown your sisters and brothers at whim; when you have seen hate-filled policemen curse, kick, and even kill your black brothers and sisters; when you see the vast majority of your twenty million Negro brothers smothering in an airtight cage of poverty in the midst of an affluent society; when you suddenly find your tongue twisted and your speech stammering as you seek to explain to your six-year-old daughter why she can't go to the public amusement park that has just been advertised on television, and see tears welling up in her eyes when she is told that Funtown is closed to colored children, and see ominous clouds of inferiority beginning to form in her little mental sky, and see her beginning to distort her personality by developing an unconscious bitterness toward white people; when you have to concoct an answer for a five-year-old son who is asking, "Daddy, why do white people treat colored people so mean?"; when you take a cross-country drive and find it necessary to sleep night after night in the uncomfortable corners of your automobile because no motel will accept you; when you are humiliated day in and day out by nagging signs reading "white" and "colored"; when your first name becomes "Nigger," your middle name becomes "Boy" (however old you are), and your last name becomes "John," and your wife and mother are never given the respected title "Mrs."; when you are harried by day and haunted by night by the fact that you are a Negro, living constantly at tiptoe stance, never quite knowing what to expect next, and are plagued with inner fears and outer resentments; when you are forever fighting a degenerating sense of "nobodiness," then you will understand why we find it difficult to wait.[119]

King used history to indicate that the clergymen's observations of the SCLC's tactics of breaking the law were overly simplistic:

We should never forget that everything Adolf Hitler did in Germany was "legal" and everything the Hungarian freedom fighters

---

[119] Ibid.

did in Hungary was "illegal." It was "illegal" to aid and comfort a Jew in Hitler's Germany. Even so, I am sure that, had I lived in Germany at the time, I would have aided and comforted my Jewish brothers. If today I lived in a Communist country where certain principles dear to the Christian faith are suppressed, I would openly advocate disobeying that country's anti-religious laws.[120]

King directly addressed the clergymen's point that the demonstrations were untimely given that Boutwell had defeated Connor:

One of the basic points in your statement is that the action that I and my associates have taken in Birmingham is untimely. Some have asked: "Why didn't you give the new city administration time to act?" The only answer that I can give to this query is that the new Birmingham administration must be prodded about as much as the outgoing one, before it will act. We are sadly mistaken if we feel that the election of Albert Boutwell as mayor will bring the millennium to Birmingham. While Mr. Boutwell is a much more gentle person that Mr. Connor, they are both segregationists, dedicated to maintenance of the status quo. I have hoped that Mr. Boutwell will be reasonable enough to see the futility of massive resistance to desegregation. But he will not see this without pressure from devotees of civil rights. My friends, I must say to you that we have not made a single gain in civil rights without determined legal and nonviolent pressure. Lamentably, it is an historical fact that privileged groups seldom give up their privileges voluntarily. Individuals may see the moral light and voluntarily give up their unjust posture; but as Reinhold Niebuhr has reminded us, groups tend to be more immoral that individuals.[121]

On being called an extremist, King did not shy away from the characterization. He responded directly to the charge using pathos,

---

[120] Ibid.
[121] Ibid.

ethos, and logic to turn the definition of *extremist* on its head using an inverted order of history to make his point. He wrote:

But though I was initially disappointed at being categorized as an extremist, as I continued to think about the matter I gradually gained a measure of satisfaction from the label. Was not Jesus an extremist for love: "Love your enemies, bless them that curse you, do good to them that hate you, and pray for them which despitefully use you, and persecute you." Was not Amos an extremist for justice: "Let justice roll down like waters and righteousness like an ever-flowing stream." Was not Paul an extremist for the Christian gospel: "I bear in my body the marks of the Lord Jesus." Was not Martin Luther an extremist: "Here I stand; I cannot do otherwise, so help me God." And John Bunyan: "I will stay in jail to the end of my days before I make a butchery of my conscience." And Abraham Lincoln: "This nation cannot survive half slave and half free." And Thomas Jefferson: "We hold these truths to be self-evident, that all men are created equal . . ." So the question is not whether we will be extremists, but what kind of extremists we will be. Will we be extremists for hate or for love? Will we be extremists for the preservation of injustice or for the extension of justice? In that dramatic scene on Calvary's hill three men were crucified. We must never forget that all three were crucified for the same crime—the crime of extremism. Two were extremists for immorality, and thus fell below their environment. The other, Jesus Christ, was an extremist for love, truth and goodness, and thereby rose above his environment. Perhaps the South, the nation and the world are in dire need of creative extremists.[122]

King had transformed the local criticism of eight clergymen into a national response for the movement. His "Letter from Birmingham Jail" is probably the most important document written during the Civil Rights Movement. Not even the depravity of being confined to Bull Connor's jail cell could derail this work—though it did not hurt that King's isolation allowed him to center his thoughts. Like the Apostle

---

[122] Ibid.

Paul, King had produced this stellar document while incarcerated. He was inspired by the 428 words emanating from those whom King may have wrongly assumed understood the movement's plight. And if these eight clergy could not understand, it could stand to reason that America did not understand. The "Letter from Birmingham Jail" responds to its collective critics, and it inspires its supporters in philosophical, theological, political, and moral tones that the gradualism previously experienced in Albany, Georgia, what many moderate-liberal forces were now advocating in Birmingham, was simply unacceptable.

Jones may not have initially understood the impact of King's Letter; his primary focus, as an attorney, lay elsewhere. But Walker fully understood the magnitude. Walker reportedly stayed up nights dictating and deciphering King's penmanship from the scraps of paper and newspapers that King used to write on as he formulated his thoughts.

The impact of King's letter initially was felt far more internally than externally. The Birmingham effort was not riding on an apex of momentum at the time King wrote the letter. Walker's enthusiastic embrace of the letter was not shared as he attempted to place it in various publications. It was far too long for most mainstream publications, the Negro press did not publicize it, and only a few theological journals showed any interest. But King's time in jail had not been in vain. Nine days after his arrest, he was released on bail. The enthusiasm King created by writing his letter had not reached masses, as Birmingham had not changed much in the nine days he sat behind bars. But the enthusiasm the letter sparked internally would soon be experienced externally by a most unlikely source.

The Children's Crusade

SCLC staff member James Luther Bevel, who had been working in Mississippi, radically proposed that the SCLC use local students for the demonstrations. Bevel's rationale was simple: adults fearing reprisal, such as the loss of their jobs, were reluctant to participate, but children were not held to similar restrictions, increasing the likelihood of their participation. Bevel was probably the most unlikely person to advocate this proposal.

Most accounts of Bevel describe him as charismatic and eloquent. Bevel was known as a man of passion and peculiarity. He often wore a yarmulke in honor of Old Testament prophets. Bevel possessed an unorthodox persona that caused discomfort in several SCLC members, but not King—at least not in the manner that would prohibit him from hearing the value of Bevel's words and ideas.

Bevel was the Director of Direct Action of Nonviolent Education of the Southern Christian Leadership Conference. He is associated with three of the movement's most widely known successes: the 1965 Selma Voting Rights Movement, the 1966 Chicago Open Housing Movement, and the 1963 Children's Crusade campaign.

Bevel, one of seventeen children, was born on October 19, 1936, in Itta Bena, Mississippi, and divided his childhood between there and Cleveland, where he worked in the steel mills as a teenager.

In later life, Bevel's career would take a somewhat eccentric if not bizarre turn, as he would move to the right politically by supporting Ronald Reagan's presidency, and, in 1992, by becoming running mate for Lyndon LaRouche Jr., the fringe candidate for president.

Bevel's unpredictable biography corresponds with the feelings he engendered among several of his contemporaries in 1963. For King to see the wisdom of Bevel's strategy above the cacophony of dissent is a testament to his leadership qualities. Jack O'Dell stated that King's listening skills were one of the underrated aspects of his leadership. O'Dell spoke of King's desire to hear the perspective from all those at the table on an issue before making a decision.[123] For the sake of the movement, King heard Bevel, though not initially. King had his own reservations but did not dismiss Bevel's suggestion outright. After hearing from all sides, he agreed to the Children's Crusade, hoping

---

[123] O'Dell interview.

that the action would "subpoena the conscience of the nation to the judgment seat of morality."[124]

Whether the movement was about to command the nation's collective conscience was not the immediate concern. King and the movement had agreed upon a strategy that would send children into Bull Connor's jail—a far cry from Chief Laurie Pritchett in Albany. Needless to say, the Negro residents of Birmingham did not universally embrace this latest tactic, the most controversial to date.

The SCLC and the Alabama Christian Movement for Human Rights' members began canvassing colleges and high schools for volunteers to be trained in the tactics of nonviolent direct action. May 2, 1963, would be the seminal moment for the movement, for it would deliver what had been promised since Project C began, providing the results that King had hoped for.

On Thursday, May 2, more than a thousand Negro students skipped their classes, opting instead to congregate at the Sixteenth Street Baptist Church to commence on a march that would take them downtown. As they approached police barricades, they were immediately arrested and carried off in paddy wagons and school buses. They were packed in like sardines, but it was not a deterrent. The following day, hundreds of young people gathered for their opportunity to see the inside of Bull Connor's jail. At the same time, something was unleashed in Connor that cemented the city of Birmingham as the stronghold of racial bigotry.

As Birmingham's Commissioner of Public Safety, Connor directed the local police and fire departments to apply an increased use of force to halt the demonstrations. What the nation and the world saw were horrifying images of children being blasted by high-pressure fire hoses, clubbed by police officers, and attacked by aggressive police dogs. As the dogs were unleashed, a smug Connor reportedly said,

---

[124] "Children's Crusade," Martin Luther King Jr. and the Global Freedom Struggle. Stanford University, Petaluma, CA,
  http://mlk-
kpp01.stanford.edu/index.php/encyclopedia/encyclopedia/enc_childrens_crusade/.

"Look at those niggers run!"[125] Connor's feeling of superiority blinded him to the fact that everyone did see, including the Associated Press.[126]

On Saturday, May 4, the front pages of newspapers around the country displayed the gruesome brutality of police dogs attacking unarmed, nonviolent students and children. The *New York Times* printed the photo with the accompanying headline: "Violence Explodes at Racial Protests in Alabama."[127] Television brought the undeniable brutality into living rooms across the nation and finally showed how the South was severely running against the values found in the Declaration of Independence and the Constitution.

That evening, at the Sixteenth Street Baptist Church, King sought to reassure parents of the student protesters. He said, "Don't worry about your children; they are going to be alright. Don't hold them back if they want to go to jail, for they are not only doing a job for themselves, but for all of America and for all of mankind."[128] This was quintessential King, tying the movement to a greater significance beyond the immediate pain of Jim Crow and making it a cause to improve the nation. He sensed those in the North, immune from the impact of segregation, had now been given a visual wake-up call through newspaper photos and the advancing impact of television.

Reaction from the White House

Attorney General Robert Kennedy, who did not share King's patriotic observation, issued a statement criticizing King and Connor.

It read: "These demonstrations are the understandable expressions of resentment and hurt." The attorney general was still

---

[125] Stephen Oates, *Let the Trumpet Sound: A Life of Martin Luther King, Jr.* (San Francisco: HarperCollins, 1994), 234.

[126] Nick Bryant, *The Bystander: John F. Kennedy and the Struggle for Black Equality* (New York: Basic Books, 2006), 387.

[127] Ibid.

[128] "Children's Crusade."

holding on to the belief that confrontation could have been avoided if the gradualism that Boutwell represented would have been given the opportunity to take place. He then added a direct attack on King, stating, "Schoolchildren participating in street demonstrations is dangerous business. An injured, maimed, or dead child is a price none of us can afford to pay."[129]

Robert Kennedy's statement demonstrated the bifurcated existence he held in the White House. As the president's thirty-five-year-old brother who had very scant legal background, he was hardly qualified to serve as attorney general, in comparison to many who had served before him. This may have caused Robert Kennedy to feel that the demonstrations and violence reflected on the Justice Department and him specifically. He was also the president's campaign manager/caretaker, regardless of any official title, and Bull Connor's police dogs and fire hoses made the Kennedy Administration look bad on the domestic and international fronts. By any standard, the photos taken in Birmingham juxtaposed with the United States' rhetoric as the paragon of democracy; it came off as thinly veiled hypocrisy at the height of the Cold War. Whatever was achieved globally during the Cuban Missile Crisis could be torn down domestically in less than a year.

But the attorney general's statement also missed the impact the photos from Birmingham would have on the nation. Before Connor unleashed his fire hoses and police dogs, 4 percent of Americans felt civil rights were the nation's most pressing issue, but after viewing the photos, 52 percent felt it was the most pressing issue. There was a shift in the nation. As King hoped, the nation was indeed forced into "the judgment seat of morality."[130]

Many historians have previously observed this fact, but it bears repeating. Connor may have done more for civil rights in a single episode than King had accomplished in eight years of putting his life on the line. The still footage and videos of the high-powered fire hoses

---

[129] Bryant, 387.
[130] Ibid.

and police doges attacking students engaged in nonviolent civil disobedience was indelibly etched in America's psyche that day. Connor was also responsible for the nation's worst publicity since the Bay of Pigs in 1961. President Kennedy would observe in the aftermath of the confrontation in Birmingham, "the civil rights movement should thank God for Bull Connor. He's helped it as much as Abraham Lincoln."[131]

Connor had not grasped the enormity in which he had damaged his own cause. As the confrontation continued on May 7, the Reverend Fred Shuttlesworth, one of the movement's masterminds, was caught under the full power of the fire hoses while leading a group of schoolchildren from the Sixteenth Street Baptist Church. A delighted Bull Connor told reporters, "I wish they had carried him away in a hearse."[132]

On May 8, the negative national publicity that Birmingham garnered, largely through the efforts of Connor, caused Birmingham's white business community to agree to most of the protestor's demands. Their approval, tacit or otherwise, of Bull Connor's methods left an indelible stain on the city. Two days later, the political community also acquiesced. The City of Birmingham agreed to desegregate lunch counters, restrooms, drinking fountains, and fitting rooms within ninety days, and they agreed to hire blacks in stores as salesmen and clerks. Those in jail would be released on bond or their own recognizance. But on May 11, Birmingham once again reprised the role that gave rise to its colloquial identification "Bombingham," as a bomb destroyed the Gaston Motel where King was staying. King had left only a few hours before the bomb went off.

Aftermath of Project C

Project C was a success. The SCLC and local officials reached an agreement to end the Project C demonstrations if downtown stores

---

[131] William A. Nunnelley, *Bull Connor* (Tuscaloosa, AL: University of Alabama Press, 1991), 164.

[132] Bryant, 390.

were desegregated and all protestors were released from jail. Project C's achievement was partially due to the unfulfilled aspirations of Albany, as this time, the movement kept the effort securely away from the domain of gradualism. But the success of Project C must be viewed well beyond any tangible achievements agreed upon in May 1963. In fact, if one simply judged its success on the outcomes of Birmingham, its victory was minor—nothing more than the gradualism the movement vowed to eschew after Albany. The hatred that existed before the campaign began would still exist.

But Project C transformed the nation as to how it viewed civil rights—going from an issue that was primarily a Negro problem to one that carried national implications. It managed to create a measure of discomfort—the prerequisite for change—throughout the nation. It was an amazing achievement for a group of citizens armed with only a deeply held belief in America's core values, who had pledged themselves to a set of ten commandments, which read as follows:

I hereby pledge myself—my person and body—to the nonviolent movement. Therefore I will keep the following ten commandments:

1. Meditate daily on the teachings and life of Jesus.

2. Remember always that the non-violent movement seeks justice and reconciliation—not victory.

3. Walk and talk in the manner of love, for God is love.

4. Pray daily to be used by God in order that all men might be free.

5. Sacrifice personal wishes in order that all men might be free.

6. Observe with both friend and foe the ordinary rules of courtesy.

7. Seek to perform regular service for others and for the world.

8. Refrain from the violence of fist, tongue, or heart.

9. Strive to be in good spiritual and bodily health.

10. Follow the directions of the movement and of the captain on a demonstration.

I sign this pledge, having seriously considered what I do and with the determination and will to persevere.[133]

Moreover, the events in Birmingham provided the first glimpse of the impact television would have on the nation's conscience. Project C was a moral tug-of-war, pitting the "never" of hostility exemplified by Bull Connor's fire hoses and police dogs against the "now" of hope that rested on a foundation of nonviolent civil disobedience and an unwavering belief in the values of America. It set the stage for the upcoming March on Washington. And it was also an integral part of the momentum for the Civil Rights Act of 1964 and the Voting Rights Act of 1965.

---

[133] King, 63–64.

Chapter Four:

All Free People Are Citizens of Berlin

Two speeches in June 1963 serve as bookends and display how much President Kennedy matured in his approach toward the Soviet Union that year; Kennedy ultimately banned nuclear weapons tests in the atmosphere, outer space, and underwater.

Rarely do historical events occur in isolation. To appreciate what culminated with the signing of the Limited Nuclear Test Ban Treaty in October 1963, the Cold War had to come as close as possible to a nuclear confrontation, that being the Cuban Missile Crisis one year earlier. But while Cuba may have been disconcerting from the United States' perspective—to have a satellite of the Soviet Union so close to America's shores seemed dangerous, to say the least—from the perspective of Soviet Premier Nikita Khrushchev, all Cold War roads led to Berlin.

The Cold War and Berlin

The city of Berlin was the epicenter of the Cold War struggle. By 1948, Berlin was divided into four occupied sections—U.S., Soviet

Union, British, and French. The divide ran simultaneously on parallel tracks, functioning as the tangible evidence of divisions within a city hardened by the tension between East and West. Ironically, the Cold War began its slow and consistent simmer about the same time John F. Kennedy became a freshman member in the House of Representatives in 1947.

By November 1958, Khrushchev issued an ultimatum to the West to withdraw from Berlin within six months, making it a free, demilitarized city. If the West complied, the Soviet Union would grant East Germany complete control of West Berlin. The West would have access to West Berlin by permission of the East German government. Through his ultimatum, Khrushchev was in effect nullifying the 1948 agreement in order to place Berlin under the sole jurisdiction of East Germany, with the caveat that if the West refused, there would be war.

In May 1959, Khrushchev withdrew the ultimatum, opting instead to meet with those occupying West Berlin. He visited President Eisenhower in September 1959 at Camp David. Eisenhower reportedly told Khrushchev, "There was nothing more inadvisable in this situation than to talk about ultimatums, since both sides knew very well what would happen if an ultimatum were to be implemented."[134] Khrushchev reportedly responded that he found it incomprehensible that a peace treaty could be regarded as a threat to peace.[135] But underneath Khrushchev's external displays of bluster and recklessness was his vulnerability concerning Berlin.

Though the Soviet sector was roughly half the city, with the remaining portion divided equally among the United States, French, and British, the main division was between two central ideologies. Post–WWII Berlin represented the visible aftermath of an alliance based on defeating the Nazis, but it was unable to forge any lasting sustainability. Nowhere else were the two competing ideologies so close geographically and on global display. What Khrushchev

---

[134] Department of State: Office of the Historian, http://history.state.gov/historicaldocuments/frus1958-60v10p1/d130.
[135] Ibid.

understood was that those who inhabited East Germany were consistently voting with their feet as to which system they preferred.

By the time Kennedy assumed the presidency in 1961, more than two million East Berliners had made an exodus since the German Democratic Republic took control of East Berlin in 1949. Food shortages in 1960 enhanced desires to leave. In February 1961, 13,576 people left East Germany, 40 percent more than the number that left in February 1960.[136] By March that number increased to 16,098.[137] By the time Kennedy had his June 1961 summit with Khrushchev in Vienna, both men were weakened, though Khrushchev not as obviously as Kennedy. The Soviet premier used the bluster of appearing out of control to camouflage the reality of a failing system. For Kennedy, 1961 was the single worst year in foreign affairs that he would have to deal with; it may have been the worst any U.S. president had seen yet or has seen since.

JFK's Foreign Policy, 1961

Kennedy, already weakened in the eyes of Khrushchev by the Bay of Pigs fiasco, inadvertently provided Khrushchev additional fodder to demonstrate his superiority over the younger, less experienced politician. The aftermath of the Bay of Pigs gave Khrushchev the impression that Kennedy was not only erratic but also timid, as he was unable to complete the mission, which may explain the bombastic behavior Khrushchev would exhibit at their summit in Vienna and during the Berlin crisis that was to follow.

On the issue of nuclear testing while in Vienna, Khrushchev told Kennedy that he saw no need for a nuclear test ban. His resistance to discontinue testing was due to his belief that it was the only way for the Soviet Union to reach a level playing field with the United States. A call for a nuclear test ban was hardly a novel concept; it had publicly

---

[136] Lawrence Freedman, *Kennedy's Wars* (New York: Oxford Press, 2000), 59–60.
[137] Ibid, 60.

been a global concern since 1955,[138] as it was known that aboveground nuclear testing created atmospheric radioactive fallout. The initial negotiations between the United States and the Soviet Union stalled under the weight of proposals and counter proposals. In 1958 both sides suspended testing, but two years of increasing Cold War tension would eventually bring an end to any apparent goodwill.[139]

As historian Robert Dallek offered in his biography on Kennedy, Khrushchev's primary goal at Vienna was to demonstrate his superiority and undermine U.S. standing.[140] It was also to mask his vulnerability in Berlin. Of the myriad topics discussed in Vienna, Berlin was the one that proved to be an immediate crisis—it was Khrushchev's greatest concern. He reminded Kennedy that the Soviet Union had lost more than twenty million people during WWII, and the enhanced military strength of Germany could lead to a larger, more devastating third world war.[141] His solution was simple: the Soviet Union intended to sign a peace treaty with both Germanys—at the very least with East Germany—invalidating all post-1945 agreements. If Kennedy agreed, Berlin would remain a "free city"; if not, the West would lose all rights to Berlin.[142] Khrushchev presented Kennedy with a similar ultimatum to the one he proposed in 1958—a treaty on Khrushchev's terms or war. Though it was hardly a rational proposal, it did coincide with the aura of irrationality that Khrushchev had established. Khrushchev's performance left the impression that he indeed had dominated his American adversary.

---

[138] In May 1955, the United Nations Disarmament Commission brought together the United States, the United Kingdom, Canada, France, and the Soviet Union to begin negotiations on ending nuclear weapons testing.

[139] "Nuclear Test Ban Treaty," John F. Kennedy Presidential Library and Museum,

  http://www.jfklibrary.org/JFK/JFK-in-History/Nuclear-Test-Ban-Treaty.aspx.

[140] Robert Dallek, *An Unfinished Life: John F. Kennedy 1917–1963* (New York: Little Brown, 2003) 407.

[141] Ibid., 411.

[142] Ibid.

For Kennedy, it marked the second time in less than five months that he appeared to have lost his footing on the world stage. Kennedy was wrong about the Bay of Pigs in April, and he now appeared to be weakened further by Khrushchev's irresponsible threats. Though Kennedy made clear to Khrushchev that the United States would not be bullied by his threats on Berlin, the agenda and tone of the meetings in Vienna were set by the Soviet premiere. The Bay of Pigs fiasco gave Khrushchev little reason to appreciate Kennedy's judgment. Why shouldn't Khrushchev see how far he could push his young, less-experienced adversary?

Kennedy may have prepared for a summit, but Khrushchev had prepared for a competitive sport that dangled the prospects of a nuclear confrontation. This left Kennedy confused and frustrated. In the aftermath of Vienna, Kennedy famously told *New York Times* reporter James Reston, "Now we have a problem in making our power credible and Vietnam is the place."[143] It was a comment that might explain the formative stages of the Vietnam conflict before it became a decades-long quagmire, but it would prove inaccurate, for it was not how Kennedy would establish his power credibility with Khrushchev. The key international issue facing Kennedy in 1961 was Berlin, and the pressure placed on Kennedy was not coming exclusively from the Kremlin, but also from the American people. In July 1961, polls indicated that nearly 85 percent supported "standing firm" on Berlin, with a mere 3.5 percent advocating some type of concessions.[144] And 54 percent were prepared to go to war over Berlin.[145]

At the Vienna meeting, Khrushchev gave Kennedy an aide-mémoire that demanded a settlement on the Berlin issue in "no more

---

[143] James Carroll, "Credible Presidential Power," *Boston Globe*, http://www.bostonglobe.com/opinion/2012/10/14/new-presidents-set-dangerous-precedents/3BkelmrNmJruLMDYzFTauJ/story.html (October 15, 2012).

[144] Freedman, 68.

[145] Ibid.

than six months."[146] Kennedy needed to respond to Khrushchev's saber rattling. If he took a hard line, it would only escalate the existing crisis. If, however, he chose restraint, he risked appearing weak, reminiscent of former British Prime Minister Neville Chamberlain, whose 1938 Munich Agreement with Adolph Hitler conceded the Sudetenland region of Czechoslovakia to the Nazis and opened the door to further German aggression. Kennedy had realized meteoric approval ratings in the aftermath of the Bay of Pigs by taking public responsibility for the failed mission.[147] But after being weakened by his lackluster performance when he met Khrushchev face-to-face in Vienna, would the American people be so forgiving for the third time, in the first six months of his administration, if he appeared not to be up to the Communist challenge? The press began to coalesce around the notion that Kennedy needed to make a statement on Berlin. His former presidential rival Richard Nixon said at the time, "Never in American history has a man talked so big and acted so little."[148]

In a span of roughly two weeks, Khrushchev appeared emboldened by the Vienna summit and kept the pressure on Kennedy. He told the Russian people in a televised address that Western attempts to force passage to West Berlin could result in a thermonuclear war. He also made his aide-mémoire to Kennedy public, and through the use of delegates, he made it known that he had no interest in pursuing any further test ban negotiations.

Kennedy commissioned former Secretary of State Dean Acheson to write a report on Berlin. When Acheson delivered his report on June

---

[146] Nikita Khrushchev to John F. Kennedy, aide-mémoire, Vienna, 4 June 1963,

http://www.cvce.eu/viewer/-/content/930c38eb-5011-494b-ad72-f8ea5cb1fe30/en.

[147] According to a May 1961 Gallup Poll, conducted after the unsuccessful Bay of Pigs invasion, 83 percent of the American public approved of Kennedy's job performance.

[148] Richard Nixon, News Conference 13, June 28, 1961,

http://www.jfklibrary.org/Researchold/Copy-of-Ready-Reference/Press-Conferences/News-Conference-13.aspx.

28, 1961, it focused on three American objectives: (1) the freedom of the people of West Berlin to choose their own system; (2) the presence of Western troops so long as West Berliners required and desired them; (3) unimpeded access from the West to the city across the East German Autobahn, canals, and air lanes.[149]

Commissioning Acheson was more than petitioning the counsel of an elder statesman who had been battle tested in the developmental phase of the Cold War; there were also political considerations involved. Acheson was far more hawkish against the Soviet Union than many of Kennedy's key advisors. During the 1960 campaign, Kennedy had presented himself as more aggressive against the Soviets than his opponent, Vice President Richard Nixon. Given the level of Khrushchev's bluster, Kennedy was forced to demonstrate that his campaign promise was not merely the musings of an ambitious candidate.

Should Khrushchev interrupt access to West Berlin, was the West prepared to counter in an effective manner? Acheson was of the opinion that the United States must be willing to use nuclear weapons before acquiescing to Khrushchev's bellicose demands. Because Khrushchev was under internal pressure to act, he was a more dangerous threat to Kennedy and the world.

In contrast, Kennedy said little about Berlin publicly, but it was a source of preoccupation for him. When he did speak about Berlin, his comments were measured. The ultimatum deadline was set for December 31. Kennedy made his definitive response on July 25, seven weeks after the two leaders met in Vienna. Kennedy masterfully found the balance between the stark military options championed by Acheson and the diplomatic possibilities offered by key aides such as Arthur Schlesinger and Ted Sorensen. He delivered a thirty-minute address from the Oval Office that placed the blame of the crisis squarely on the shoulders of the Soviet Union. He painted a grave picture of the conflict, making clear the possibility of using nuclear weapons. Linking Cuba and Southeast Asia to Berlin, Kennedy made

---

[149] Sorensen, 564.

the case that the problem must be met head-on, and he explained that America was up to the challenge of protecting its post–WWII interest in Berlin. Demonstrating that the United States would not be boxed in solely to a nuclear option or bullied by Khrushchev's unrealistic demands, Kennedy told the American people his intention to ask Congress for a $3.25 billion appropriation for defense to increase the army from 875,000 to one million soldiers.[150]

Kennedy provided a variation on his words from his inaugural address when he said, "Let us never negotiate out of fear, but let us never fear to negotiate."[151] He succinctly summed up the problems in Berlin, and then he took a jab at Khrushchev, stating, "We cannot negotiate with those who say, 'What's mine is mine and what's yours is negotiable.'"[152]

Kennedy had struck a balance by articulating the problem while demonstrating American resolve and explaining the measured military and diplomatic options, and his speech appealed largely to the nearly 85 percent that supported "standing firm"[153] and the 54 percent prepared to go to war over Berlin. With Kennedy having made his position clear in this Cold War chess match, Khrushchev had the next move.

In response to Kennedy's address, Khrushchev combined harsh retorts with a desire to negotiate. Since Vienna, Khrushchev had been on the rhetorical offensive, but Kennedy's stand had uncovered the weakness of his position. Though it was not viewed as such at the time, Khrushchev was the first to blink. For all of his aggressive posturing, Khrushchev had proposed an unrealistic ultimatum while

[150] John F. Kennedy, radio and television report to the American people on the Berlin Crisis, 26 July 1961, http://www.jfklibrary.org/Research/Ready-Reference/JFK-Speeches/Radio-and-Television-Report-to-the-American-People-on-the-Berlin-Crisis-July-25-1961.aspx.

[151] The Inauguration of John F. Kennedy, 35th President of the United States, 20 January 1961. http://www.jfklibrary.org/Asset-Viewer/Archives/USG-1-12A-r1.aspx.

[152] Ibid.

[153] Freedman, 68.

conveying an aura of recklessness, and he was the one playing a weak hand. He was losing a large number of Germans from the Communist-controlled East to the West. Since he could not bluff Kennedy into accepting his conditions in order to avoid war over Berlin, Khrushchev was left with one option—a rash, face-saving maneuver.

On August 13, the German Democratic Republic began construction on a wall that separated West Berlin from East Germany. At a time when the pace of war between East and West was gaining momentum at a discomforting speed, the wall put an effective end to fearful worries by separating families, keeping the West out and the East imprisoned. Complete with guard towers and anti-vehicle trenches, the Berlin Wall transformed the city of Berlin from a metaphorical symbol of Cold War differences between East and West into a tangible monument to the incongruent philosophies that the two nations embraced.

Kennedy's initial remarks about the wall construction were predictably restrained—a demeanor honed during the failures of the Bay of Pigs that would be present throughout his presidency. Part of his restraint came from his understanding of Khrushchev's problem and his knowing that there was not much that could be done to stop the wall's construction. Prior to the wall's construction, Kennedy told Walt Rostow, Deputy National Security Advisor, that "East Germany is hemorrhaging to death. The entire Eastern bloc is in danger. [Khrushchev] has to do something to stop this—perhaps a wall. And there's not a damn thing we can do about it."[154]

Though the discussions in the immediate aftermath of the Berlin Wall construction were about the implications of the wall and Khrushchev's response to the ongoing saga, the Soviet leader ultimately had to confess that he had no way to stop emigrants beyond the use of force. The Berlin Wall also put an end to any further discussions about an ultimatum. Ironically, the possibility of going to war over Berlin was put to rest, at least temporarily, by the same man

---

[154] Dallek, 425.

that many feared was rash enough to initiate conflict in the atomic age. Khrushchev's retreat bore witness to the effectiveness of Kennedy's measured but firm response. The public perception of Kennedy now was the antithesis of what it was immediately following the Bay of Pigs fiasco and after his less-than-stellar performance at the Vienna summit. After the Bay of Pigs, Kennedy had sought a balance by making his position firm while leaving a path for negotiations. He did this even more so during the Cuban Missile Crisis, and he did it again during the Berlin Crisis.

The construction of the Berlin Wall marked Kennedy's first Cold War victory. It was not a perfect solution, especially for those trapped behind the Wall, but there was no denying that Kennedy's approach effectively called Khrushchev's bluff, forcing the Soviet premiere into retreat. It was a hollow victory, the importance of which could be seen clearer with time. In the moment of 1961, the wall was further evidence of Kennedy's dismal year on the international front. The failure at the Bay of Pigs, Khrushchev's dominance at Vienna, and now the construction of the Berlin Wall fueled the perception that Kennedy was weak. Some historians have persuasively drawn the conclusion that the construction of the Berlin Wall was linked to Kennedy's Bay of Pigs failure. Moreover, Kennedy's failures in 1961 would embolden Khrushchev's actions in 1962. But circumstances such as they were resulted in a paradoxical climate in which the leaders of the two superpowers were in effect leading through their weakness—Kennedy because of his 1961 foreign policy record, and Khrushchev for the vulnerability over Berlin and his internal strife.

The 1961 conflict over Berlin was also the beginning of Kennedy finding his foreign policy voice as president. But the wall created more concern from U.S. allies. For those living in West Berlin, the thirteen-foot-high guarded tower made the twelve-foot-high wall a demoralizing impediment, a constant reminder of Cold War tension. The world watched as Khrushchev constructed what many believed would symbolically transform Berlin into Tombstone, Arizona. Many, like West Berlin Mayor Willy Brandt, wanted Kennedy to take action, but what could he do? Though not an ideal solution, Kennedy saw the wall in a somewhat different light.

Speaking with aide Kenny O'Donnell, Kennedy asked, "Why would Khrushchev put up a wall if he really intended to seize West Berlin?"[155] Kennedy's ability to see events in the larger context was on display. Viewing the construction of the wall as a response to Khrushchev's émigré problem more than any Cold War effort, he rationally added, "There wouldn't be any need for a wall if he occupied the whole city. This is his way out of his predicament. It's not a very nice solution, but a wall is a hell of a lot better than a war."[156]

Though Kennedy was correct in his short-term analysis of the wall, his 1961 actions did raise long-term concerns about the wall's construction. Could the wall have been avoided? The answer to that depends greatly on one's perspective. If one places their emphasis on Kennedy's first-year foreign-policy record, it would be easy to answer in the affirmative. His initial appearance as a rash, undisciplined leader who was not ready for the world stage certainly bolstered Khrushchev's actions. But this perspective undermines Khrushchev's main challenge. He had lost over two million émigrés from East Berlin—a city he would be willing to defend by way of war. From this vantage point, the wall was, as Kennedy observed, Khrushchev's way out.

Kennedy obliged the allies with a symbolic gesture by sending Vice President Johnson to West Berlin. He also sent a letter to Brandt, outlining troop reinforcement and America's commitment to support West Berlin.

In spite of the ongoing tension between East and West, Kennedy was clearly on the offensive. His foreign policy leadership had received a much-needed buoyancy, and he was prepared to build on his newly discovered resilience. But what appeared to be a Soviet retreat in Berlin was quickly offset when Kennedy was given the news that the Soviets had restarted their nuclear testing.

---

[155]Kenneth P. O'Donnell and David F. Powers, *Johnny, We Hardly Knew Ye* (New York: Little Brown, 1972), 350.

[156] Ibid.

For Khrushchev, resuming nuclear testing was a demonstration of Soviet strength, a way to get the United States' attention, and a reminder of the reckless persona he had masterfully crafted. For Kennedy, it was time for him to prove that he had indeed found his voice on matters of foreign affairs, as his response to the Berlin Crisis suggested.

On September 25, Kennedy addressed the United Nations, and his effectiveness as a communicator was on display. It is possible that one can be a great public speaker and not a great communicator. Kennedy was gifted with both qualities.

Kennedy laid out the existing Cold War threat, stating, "Today, every inhabitant of this planet must contemplate the day when this planet may no longer be habitable. Every man, woman, and child lives under a nuclear sword of Damocles, hanging by the slenderest of threads, capable of being cut at any moment by accident, or miscalculation, or by madness. The weapons of war must be abolished before they abolish us."[157] He added, "It is therefore our intention to challenge the Soviet Union, not to an arms race, but to a peace race— to advance together, step by step, stage by stage, until general and complete disarmament has been achieved. We invite them now to go beyond agreement in principle to reach agreement on actual plans."[158]

Kennedy Begins To Find His Foreign Policy Voice

If 1961 began with Khrushchev making unrealistic demands about the future of West Berlin, the momentum shifted in the direction of Kennedy's vision after his July address to the nation. Whatever frustration Kennedy may have felt when learning that Moscow had reconstituted its nuclear testing, it was not evident when he addressed the United Nations General Assembly.

---

[157] John F. Kennedy, address before the general assembly of the United Nations, 25 September 1961.
http://www.jfklibrary.org/Asset-Viewer/DOPIN64xJUGRKgdHJ9NfgQ.aspx
[158] Ibid.

He told those gathered, "I therefore propose, on the basis of this plan, that disarmament negotiations resume promptly and continue without interruption until an entire program for general and complete disarmament has not only been agreed upon, but has been actually achieved."[159]

After defining the issue, Kennedy offered the following solution:

"The logical place to begin is a treaty assuring the end of nuclear tests of all kinds, in every environment, under workable controls. The United States and the United Kingdom have proposed such a treaty that is both reasonable, effective, and ready for signature. We are still prepared to sign that treaty today."[160]

Kennedy's restraint, his ability to frame the issue, and his willingness to provide his adversary an "out" was now driving the discourse between the two nuclear superpowers. In retrospect, Kennedy's inability to charm Khrushchev at Vienna contributed greatly to the crystallization of his foreign policy against his Cold War nemesis. Kennedy used this moment not only to renew calls for a nuclear test ban, but also to position the United States clearly on the side of desiring peace:

But to halt the spread of these terrible weapons, to halt the contamination of the air, to halt the spiraling nuclear arms race, we remain ready to seek new avenues of agreement. Our new disarmament program thus includes the following proposals:

- First, signing the test ban treaty by all nations. This can be done now. Test ban negotiations need not, and should not await general disarmament.

- Second, stopping the production of fissionable materials for use in weapons, and preventing their transfer to any nation now lacking in nuclear weapons.

- Third, prohibiting the transfer of control over nuclear weapons to states that do not own them.

---

[159] Ibid.
[160] Ibid.

- Fourth, keeping nuclear weapons from seeding new battlegrounds in outer space.

- Fifth, gradually destroying existing nuclear weapons and converting their materials to peaceful use.

- And finally, halting the unlimited testing and production of strategic nuclear delivery vehicles, and gradually destroying them as well.[161]

This was not the address of someone who was naive and inexperienced, as many felt Kennedy was when he assumed the presidency. Nor was it a reactionary response to the volatile and unpredictable imagery provided by Khrushchev. It was a rational address that clearly understood the gravity of the problems, offering a sensible solution in the midst of escalating Cold War fears.

But Kennedy also understood that public perception did not align with how he saw events shaping. In a conversation with Adlai Stevenson, Ambassador to the United Nations, about whether to restart nuclear testing, Kennedy said, "What choice did we have? They have spit in our eye three times. We couldn't possibly sit back and do nothing."[162]

Specific to the Cold War public perceptions during the first year of his presidency, Kennedy said, "All this makes Khrushchev look pretty tough. He has had a succession of apparent victories—space, Cuba, the Wall. He wants to give out the feeling that he has us on the run."[163]

Kennedy's policy position against Khrushchev in Berlin in 1961 and his renewed calls for a nuclear test ban did not extinguish the smoldering embers of Cold War tension. It would require another

---

[161] Ibid.

[162] Jeffrey Sachs, To Move the World: JFK's Quest for Peace (New York: Random House, 2013), 27-28.

[163] Glenn T. Seaborg, Kennedy, Khrushchev and the Test Ban (Berkeley, CA: University of California Press, 1983) 88.

crisis in Cuba the following year before any thawing of deeply held differences would be evident.

Cuba, the Cold War Irritant

If Khrushchev was guilty of fanning the flames of nuclear war in 1961, he brought the world even closer to it in 1962. The Cuban Missile Crisis was the closest the world ever came to nuclear war; never before had the United States' armed forces' state of readiness been placed so high. Moreover, the Soviets had alerted their field commanders in Cuba to be prepared to use battlefield nuclear weapons.

The Cuban Missile Crisis found its genesis in the Soviets' inability to match the United States' nuclear arsenal. According to the premier's memoirs, Khrushchev contemplated the idea of nuclear war in May 1962. He knew the United States had the capability of striking the Soviet Union from U.S. territory, but the Soviets had no such response available. Furthermore, Fidel Castro desired to ward off any repeats of the Bay of Pigs attack, and he believed a second attack on Cuba by the United States was high, so he was agreeable to Khrushchev's plans.

On October 27, the Cuban leader sent an "Armageddon Letter" to Khrushchev, advocating that nuclear weapons should be fired if American forces invaded Cuba.[164] What Castro did not understand was that Khrushchev did not share his view. Moreover, Khrushchev was not about to fire the initial salvo that would have undoubtedly launched World War III.

On October 30, two days after the official conclusion of the crisis, Khrushchev offered his feelings about Castro's letter. In a recently published document by the Cold War International History Project, part of Khrushchev's response was reprinted:

In a letter Fidel Castro proposed that we ourselves should be the first to start an atomic war. Do you know what that would mean? That

---

[164] "The Anniversary of the Cuban Missile Crisis," C-SPAN, October 14, 2012.

probably cannot even be expressed at all, we were completely aghast. Castro clearly has no idea about what thermonuclear war is. After all, if a war started it would primarily be Cuba that would vanish from the face of the Earth.[165]

Khrushchev goes on to say, "Only a person who has no idea what nuclear war means or who has been so blinded, for instance, like Castro, by revolutionary passion could talk like that. We did not of course take up that proposal, especially because we had a chance to avert war."[166]

Like the Berlin Crisis in 1956, when President Eisenhower opted for propaganda rather than sending troops to Hungary, the same might have held true in Cuba for Khrushchev. If the United States invaded Cuba a second time, there would be propaganda advantage for Khrushchev, but he was not prepared for war. Cuba was not Berlin.

Kennedy's apparent victory in Cuba also increased the tension between the Soviet Union and the People's Republic of China. Mao Zedong, PRC Chairman, was critical of Khrushchev for his failure to fight the United States: "Khrushchev has moved from adventurism to capitulationism," Mao said.

This tension was reflective of an ongoing feud that led to the Sino–Soviet split. Since Stalin's death in 1953, there had been a growing intellectual divergence between the two largest Communist nations. Both were committed to the overarching ideals of Marxist-Leninist orthodoxy, but Khrushchev and Mao had very different ideas about the future of Communism and its role in the world, especially as it related to capitalism. From 1953 to 1964, any moves Khrushchev made toward thawing Cold War tension were met with heightened conflict with China.

While Khrushchev was beset with problems from China, Kennedy was also plagued with internal problems. He was facing a Congress that was not sold on the prospects of a nuclear test ban

[165] Ibid.
[166] Ibid.

treaty. There was a feeling on Capitol Hill that the Soviets could not be trusted and that entering into a test ban would endanger the security of the United States.

In the West, the perception was that the Cuban crisis was a clear victory for Kennedy. He had stared down Khrushchev, called his bluff, and forced him to retreat. He used his experiences during the Bay of Pigs, the Vienna summit, and Berlin to look past Khrushchev's threats of war and nuclear annihilation and to make clear his own line in the sand, though he always left room for his adversary to pursue a peaceful path out. Later that year, Adlai Stevenson introduced him at a gala in the following manner: "Ladies and gentleman, the author, the producer, the director, and the star of Mr. Khrushchev's new play in Moscow: A funny thing happened to me on my way to Cuba—the president of the United States!"[167]

The "Peace Speech"

The fanfare for Kennedy's foreign success often omitted that it might not have been possible without his failures. In the period spanning from January 1961 to December 1962, it could be argued that Kennedy's on-the-job training and his ability to handle crisis was the most intense of any U.S. president since Franklin Roosevelt, if not since Abraham Lincoln. The lessons he learned during the first two years of his administration would be evident in 1963.

But success in Cuba meant possible defeat as far as a nuclear test ban was concerned. Beginning in 1963, the prospects for a test ban treaty did not look promising; the Soviets had withdrawn any offers to move forward.

Norman Cousins, the editor of the *Saturday Review*, had met with Khrushchev in December 1962 to discuss the potential release of Catholic Bishops and other clergy in an attempt to improve religious relations inside the Soviet Union. According to Cousins, Soviet

---

[167] President Kennedy at the awards dinner of the Joseph P. Kennedy Jr. Foundation, 6 December 1962, http://www.youtube.com/watch?v=WmYqSci3Y6o.

leadership did not trust Kennedy on the issue of nuclear inspections. After another meeting with Khrushchev in April, Cousins returned to suggest to Kennedy that the Soviet premiere was receiving internal pressure to take a harder tack against the United States, not unlike the pressure Kennedy faced from members of Congress. In order to address this dilemma that both leaders shared, Cousins suggested that Kennedy take a "breathtaking new approach toward the Russian people, calling for an end to the Cold War, and a fresh start in American-Russian relations."[168]

Cousins's correspondence to Kennedy, along with his meetings with Khrushchev, put in motion a "peace speech" that offered an olive branch to the Soviet people and its leadership.

But Kennedy had more political reasons to oppose the notion of a speech focused on peace than to support it. As he told Cousins, those who even bothered to write the White House about nuclear testing were running roughly fifteen to one against the ban. In spite of this reality, Kennedy decided in May to use the commencement address at American University on June 10 as the opportunity for his "peace speech."

In a May 22 press conference, Kennedy did not sound as if the two sides were moving toward meaningful negotiations. Nor did he signal that he was on the cusp of giving a major speech that would change the course of U.S.–Soviet relations:

QUESTION: I have a question about the nuclear test ban proposal. Mr. Harold Brown has said before a Senate committee that we could accept as few as six on-site inspections. Do you think that there is further ground for us to move now to approach the Soviet Union in the test ban situation?

JFK: Well, that is the position we have taken more publicly. There have been seven. There has been discussion of six. Mr. Brown, whose judgment I value highly, has not set the official Government position. He was giving his judgment as a scientist. There are a good

---

[168] Freedman, 266.

many other questions to be settled. We have suggested to the Soviet Union that we would consider the make-up of the inspection team, the rules under which the inspection team would operate, the area where there could be drilling, all of these questions, and then if we can get those settled, we could then come finally to the question of the number of tests. The Soviet Union has refused, however, to consider these other matters until we agree with their position of three. That has not been an acceptable negotiating position. We feel that we ought to try to wind up all the other questions which divide us, and then we could finally come and decide what would be, given the arrangements we have made for these other matters, what would be a responsible number of tests. But we are back and forth to the Soviet Union and we are still hoping that we can find a perhaps easing of their position.

QUESTION: Where is the genie, sir? Is it out of the bottle or in the bottle?

JFK: Well, it is neither in nor out right now. But I would say that we will know by the end of the summer whether it is finally out. I said from the beginning that it seemed to me that the pace of events was such in the world that unless we would get an agreement now, I would think the chance of getting it would be comparatively slight. We are, therefore, going to continue to push very hard in May and June and July in every forum to see if we can get an agreement which I regard, but I will say as of now, since December there has been no change in the Soviet position on the number of tests nor willingness to discuss in any way any of these other questions until we accept their position of December, which is not a satisfactory position for us.[169]

Though Kennedy made it through this press conference without mentioning the upcoming commencement speech, Carl Kaysen,

---

[169] Transcript from President Kennedy's press conference, 22 May 1963, http://www.jfklibrary.org/Asset-Viewer/Archives/JFKPOF-060-001.aspx.

Deputy Assistant for National Security Affairs, revealed in a 1966 oral interview that he did in fact have plans for it at the time:

[Ted] Sorensen sent around a memorandum to the usual people saying, "The President wants to make a speech on peace. Do you have any ideas?" And a variety of ideas poured in. Now, a week and a little bit before that speech was due to be made, we had a drafting meeting. This again proceeded in the usual way. Sorensen did a very rough first draft. This was a closely held speech, by the way. And a committee consisting, as I remember, of the Secretary of State and [Adrian] Fisher, probably Adam Yarmolinsky from the Pentagon, Arthur Schlesinger, Mac Bundy, and myself from the White House. [170]

As Kaysen recalls, the president was away making a speech in Los Angeles, and then he went onto Honolulu before returning to Washington to deliver the commencement address at American University. Kennedy and the speech writing team decided that he would include the offer of the moratorium on atmospheric tests.

About the same time, the temperature was thawing in Moscow; Khrushchev made a speech in Berlin, indicating Soviet interest in resuming test ban negotiations. Just before Kennedy returned to deliver the commencement address at American University, Khrushchev sent a message to the White House formally declaring a desire to resume the negotiations in Moscow. Khrushchev's memorandum increased the importance of Kennedy's forthcoming remarks at American University. More than a speech on peace, it was also an opportunity to publicly respond to Khrushchev's invitation to resume talks on a limited nuclear test ban treaty.

What Kennedy delivered was one of the great presidential speeches of the twentieth century. It would prove to be a speech that would ultimately require a retrospective in order to be fully appreciated. Not only did Kennedy publicly answer Khrushchev's desire to resume talks on a limited test ban treaty, he also described the

---

[170] Karl Kaysen, Oral History Interview, JFK #2, 15 July 1966, http://www.jfklibrary.org/Asset-Viewer/Archives/JFKOH-CK-02.aspx.

Soviet people in a three-dimensional way that lifted them from the fly paper of all things Americans held as evil.

Kennedy wasted no time informing those in attendance the purpose of his speech: "I have, therefore, chosen this time and this place to discuss a topic on which ignorance too often abounds and the truth is too rarely perceived—yet it is the most important topic on earth: world peace," he said.[171]

Kennedy went on to declare that his definition of peace was not limited to an American perspective (Pax Americana) but rather "a genuine peace, the kind of peace that makes life on earth worth living, the kind that enables men and nations to grow and to hope and to build a better life for their children—not merely peace for Americans but peace for all men and women—not merely peace in our time but peace for all time."[172]

Seizing on the advice he obtained from Cousins, Kennedy spoke about the internal struggles that he and Khrushchev shared: "Some say that it is useless to speak of world peace or world law or world disarmament—and that it will be useless until the leaders of the Soviet Union adopt a more enlightened attitude. I hope they do. I believe we can help them do it. But I also believe that we must reexamine our own attitude—as individuals and as a nation—for our attitude is as essential as theirs."[173]

Kennedy went on to make unprecedented statements about the Soviet people, somewhat negating the reality that, less than one year prior, the tension between the two nations had reached the level of DEFCON-2. In calling for a collective reexamination of American attitudes toward the Soviet Union, Kennedy declared, "No government or social system is so evil that its people must be considered as lacking in virtue."[174]

---

[171] Commencement Address at American University, 10 June 1963, http://www.jfklibrary.org/Asset-Viewer/BWC7I4C9QUmLG9J6I8oy8w.aspx.

[172] Ibid.

[173] Ibid.

[174] Ibid.

After citing the obvious philosophical differences between the Soviet Union and the United States, Kennedy added, "But we can still hail the Russian people for their many achievements—in science and space, in economic and industrial growth, in culture and in acts of courage."[175] But nothing Kennedy said was more succinct in calling for the elimination of preconceived notions in order to realize a lasting peace than when he told those assembled at the commencement, "For, in the final analysis, our most basic common link is that we all inhabit this small planet. We all breathe the same air. We all cherish our children's future. And we are all mortal."[176]

Prior to Kennedy's American University address, no American president had spoken about the Soviet Union in this manner. Kennedy could do it without fear of internal reprisal, having stood up to Khrushchev during the missile crisis.

The president went on to announce that the Soviet Union, Great Britain, and the United States had agreed "that high-level discussions will shortly begin in Moscow looking toward early agreement on a comprehensive test ban treaty."[177]

As Kennedy predicted, response to the speech was rather lukewarm. The response was not necessarily negative, but judging by the letters the White House received in the aftermath of the speech, there were clearly issues that held more interest for the American people. His "peace speech," like Lincoln's Gettysburg Address almost one hundred years earlier, would require the acute vision of hindsight before its historical value would be truly appreciated.

It did not take Cousins long, however, to appreciate the importance of Kennedy's speech. He sent Kennedy a note the next day complimenting his courage and vision. He lauded the speech for the hope and possibility globally that it offered.

But the lack of appreciation Kennedy received domestically was made up for with the enthusiasm of international responses. A

---

[175] Ibid.
[176] Ibid.
[177] Ibid.

telegram from Copenhagen to the State Department noted the Danish Press "commented extensively and favorably on the president's test ban speech." Other telegrams also indicated that Kennedy's American University address was the main news story in most European papers. The international impression that mattered most was Khrushchev's. If the goal of the speech was peace and to offer a response to Khrushchev's overture, Kennedy accomplished both goals. Khrushchev reportedly said it was the best speech ever given by an American president since Roosevelt.

At the end of June 1963, immediately following negotiations with civil rights leaders for the upcoming March on Washington, Kennedy visited Europe. While in West Berlin, he would give a speech that could have been construed as the rhetorical antithesis of his "peace speech."

"Ich Bin Ein Berliner"

Kennedy's visit to West Berlin was as symbolic as Johnson's visit in 1961 when the Berlin Wall was constructed in that it offered little in the way of palpable change yet sent an unequivocal message of support. Roughly 60 percent of West Berliners turned out to hear the president.

Before Kennedy actually made it to the podium to speak on June 26, 1963, pandemonium had already reached a feverish pitch during the motorcade. Because the shadow of the Nazi regime was still covering Germany, Kennedy's reception and the raucous chants of "Kennedy, Kennedy, Kennedy," also caused some measure of discomfort. German Chancellor Konrad Adenauer said to Secretary of State Dean Rusk, "Does this mean Germany can one day have another Hitler?"[178]

---

[178] Robert Dallek and Terry Golway, *Let Every Nation Know: John F. Kennedy in His Own Words* (Naperville, IL: Sourcebooks, 2006), 192.

The roughly nine-minute address was a far cry from Kennedy's speech at American University, but though he did not draw upon the differences between Communism and democracy, he praised the Russians for their many achievements, calling for peace.

With his words, Kennedy passionately served the red meat that Berliners were hoping for as he drew clear distinctions between the two superpowers. Standing proxy for the hopes of West Berliners, Kennedy said to the ecstatic crowd:

There are many people in the world who really don't understand, or say they don't, what is the great issue between the free world and the Communist world. Let them come to Berlin. There are some who say that Communism is the wave of the future. Let them come to Berlin. And there are some who say in Europe and elsewhere we can work with the Communists. Let them come to Berlin. And there are even a few who say that it is true that Communism is an evil system, but it permits us to make economic progress. *Lass' sie nach Berlin kommen.* Let them come to Berlin.[179]

Kennedy then took a direct swipe at Khrushchev, reminding all that the Wall was a reflection of his inability to address his emigrant problem and the inherent weakness of the Soviet system: "Freedom has many difficulties and democracy is not perfect, but we have never had to put a wall up to keep our people in, to prevent them from leaving us," Kennedy said.[180]

He concluded his remarks in the same manner that he opened. Kennedy began his address by saying, "Two thousand years ago the proudest boast was 'civis Romanus sum,' the Latin phrase that translates, 'I am a Roman citizen,' implying all the rights and privileges associated with the status of Roman citizenship. Today, in

[179] John F. Kennedy, Berlin Speech, 26 June 1963, John F. Kennedy Library and Museum, http://www.jfklibrary.org/Asset-Viewer/Archives/JFKWHA-201-001.aspx.

[180] Ibid.

118

the world of freedom, the proudest boast is 'Ich bin ein Berliner.'"[181] He closed by saying, "All free men, wherever they may live, are citizens of Berlin, and, therefore, as a free man, I take pride in the words 'Ich bin ein Berliner.'"[182]

It has been well documented that the rough translation of Kennedy's words was "I am a jelly doughnut." Kennedy should have said, "Ich bin Berliner," which translates, "I am a Berliner." But anyone viewing a tape of the speech would clearly see, based on the reaction of the German people, that they understood his intent. They heard Kennedy's words with their hearts and desires. For that brief moment, Kennedy's mangled German was perfectly clear.

Limited Nuclear Test Ban Treaty

The speech in Berlin completed an amazing month of oratory for Kennedy. In Volume Two of *American Speeches: Political Oratory from Abraham Lincoln to Bill Clinton*, of the five speeches attributed to Kennedy, three were given in June 1963. In addition to the "peace speech" at American University and the Berlin speech, Kennedy's address to the nation on June 11, 1963, is widely considered the most important speech on civil rights by a president since Abraham Lincoln.

But Kennedy's Berlin speech also provided Khrushchev with a choice similar to the one Kennedy had to confront during the Cuban Missile Crisis. Which speech should Khrushchev focus on in order to move forward on the test ban negotiations: American University or Berlin? Kennedy's fervent emotional appeal to Berliners at the line demarcating East from West could not be an easy pill for Khrushchev to swallow. In Kennedy's own way, was he not retaliating to Khrushchev's bombastic style that was the hallmark of their 1961 meeting in Vienna? But the Soviet premier had already stated that he found Kennedy's speech at the American University to be the best given by an American president since FDR. Khrushchev had to decide

---

[181] Ibid.
[182] Ibid.

whether to focus on the Kennedy who appealed to his audience at American University "to reexamine our attitudes toward the Soviet Union," and who would go on to say that in spite of the philosophical differences that stand between the superpowers, "We can still hail the Russian people for their many achievements," or to focus on the Kennedy who took a direct swipe at the Soviet premier by saying, "We have never had to put a wall up to keep our people in, to prevent them from leaving us."

But the momentum for negotiations was greater than the propaganda spurred by Cold War differences. And after years of on-again, off-again negotiations, it required only ten days to reach an agreement in Moscow. One month after his Berlin speech, Kennedy spoke to the American people about the treaty. On July 26, the president said:

I speak to you tonight in a spirit of hope. Eighteen years ago the advent of nuclear weapons changed the course of the world as well as the war. Since that time, all mankind has been struggling to escape from the darkening prospect of mass destruction on earth. In an age when both sides have come to possess enough nuclear power to destroy the human race several times over, the world of Communism and the world of free choice have been caught up in a vicious circle of conflicting ideology and interest. Each increase of tension has produced an increase of arms; each increase of arms has produced an increase of tension.[183]

The president continued by uttering words that marked not only a highlight of his administration, but also a great source of personal pride:

Yesterday a shaft of light cut into the darkness. Negotiations were concluded in Moscow on a treaty to ban all nuclear tests in the

[183] John F. Kennedy, public address on the Nuclear Test Ban Treaty, 26 July 1963,
http://www.jfklibrary.org/JFK/JFK-in-History/Nuclear-Test-Ban-Treaty.aspx?p=3.

120

atmosphere, in outer space, and under water. For the first time, an agreement has been reached on bringing the forces of nuclear destruction under international control—a goal first sought in 1946 when Bernard Baruch presented a comprehensive control plan to the United Nations.[184]

The Soviet Union and the United Kingdom signed the treaty on August 5; Rusk, along with a bipartisan group of senators representing the United States, was also in attendance. Though the treaty named the United States, the Soviet Union, and the United Kingdom as "original parties," it was opened for signature by additional countries.

Cold War fears, distrust of Khrushchev, and the Cuban Missile Crisis combined to make Senate ratification an uncertain proposition. Would sixty-six senators (as mandated by the Constitution) vote to ratify the treaty? After gaining assurances that underground testing or nuclear use would be affected, Republican Minority Leader Everett Dirksen gave his support.[185] On September 24, the Senate ratified the treaty by a margin of eighty to nineteen.[186] Thirteen days later, the president signed the treaty—seven days before the anniversary of the date when a U-2 plane flying over western Cuba discovered missile sites, officially beginning the Cuban Missile Crisis.

When Kennedy signed the Limited Nuclear Test Ban Treaty, the failure at the Bay of Pigs and the disappointments sustained at Vienna were distant memories now muffled by the courage and vision he displayed at American University, the stature he obtained in Berlin as a world leader, and his conviction to seek peace when events on the ground seemed to point to something other than peace. Kennedy proved up to the challenge of brandishing a steep learning curve in the midst of a rapidly changing thermonuclear world beholden to Cold War differences, where hope and hostility were intertwined with success and failure.

---

[184] Ibid.
[185] Dallek, 629.
[186] Ibid.

While the Bay of Pigs, Vienna summit, and construction of the Berlin Wall are not part of the highlight reel when one remembers the Kennedy Administration, without those failures there is no guarantee that subsequent foreign policy victories would have turned out in the manner they did. For those failures taught Kennedy invaluable lessons of leadership that he probably could not have obtained in any other manner.

Moreover, Kennedy's "peace speech" at American University and his speech in Berlin illustrate the evolution of his leadership. It would have been impossible to imagine Kennedy giving either speech in 1961, but this was 1963. And not only were both speeches possible, they were necessary.

Chapter Five:

"We Are Confronted Primarily with a Moral Issue"

If the events of 1963 are indeed among the most significant our country has seen since that time, then the twenty-four hours spanning between June 11 and June 12, 1963, may have been the most significant, except for, of course, the Kennedy assassination.

Interposition and Nullification

One of the events in those important twenty-four-hours began to unfold on March 11, 1962. George Wallace, who had lost in his initial gubernatorial bid in 1958 and subsequently vowed to never be "out-niggered again," launched his kick-off to become the Yellowhammer State's forty-fifth governor. Sounding the drumbeat for segregation's cause, Wallace vowed to maintain second-class status for Alabama's Negro citizens under his leadership. He made clear, where other southern states had bowed at least to some form of token integration, that Alabama would keep its Jim Crow laws intact. Relying on the mantra of states' rights as guaranteed by the Tenth Amendment, Wallace told those in attendance that the federal government would not send a governor of a sovereign state to prison for standing up for rights rooted in the U.S. Constitution. And if the federal government sought to force any type of school integration, Wallace stated, "I shall refuse to abide by any such illegal federal court order even to the point of standing at the schoolhouse door."[187]

Like his predecessors, Wallace based the legitimacy of his segregationist argument on interposition and nullification. *Interposition* refers to the right of the states to protect their interests from federal violation deemed by those states to be dangerous or unconstitutional. *Nullification* is the theory that states can invalidate any federal law they consider unconstitutional. The Tenth Amendment states, "The powers not delegated to the United States by the Constitution, nor prohibited by it to the States, are reserved to the States respectively, or to the people."[188] When the Tenth Amendment was originally proposed, the Bill of Rights did not apply to the states; it applied only to federal law. States had their own constitutions and their own bills of rights. Some states also had slavery, which was protected under the Tenth Amendment. After the Civil War, the Fourteenth Amendment extended the Bill of Rights and made it applicable to both state and federal law, diminishing much of the Tenth Amendment's power. But this constitutional snag did not discourage Wallace from his bombastic advocacy for the Southern status quo.

Wallace's vow of defiance would prove to be a dangerous, hyperbolic game. In the moment, his declaration that he was willing to face the federal government by placing his body physically in front of progress became one of his most enthusiastic applause lines in his stump speeches. In connecting with the white voters of Alabama, Wallace developed a faithful group of supporters, giving momentum to his unbridled ambition.

---

[187] Dan T. Carter, *The Politics of Rage* (Baton Rouge, LA: Louisiana State University Press, 2000), 105.

[188] 10th Amendment, http://constitution.laws.com/10th-amendment.

Taking a political shot at a photo depicting former governor Big Jim Folsom, who was running again in 1962, drinking scotch with Harlem's flamboyant Negro Congressman Adam Clayton Powell in the Governor's mansion, Wallace declared, "I promise you, I won't serve one drop of alcohol in the Governor's mansion."[189] White voters of Alabama understood that this was not simply the musing of a teetotalist lamenting the days of Prohibition, but rather the thinly veiled politics of race and rage that Wallace came to embody in 1963.

On November 29, 1962, University of Alabama President Frank Rose called Burke Marshall, the Kennedy Administration's assistant attorney general for civil rights, with a proactive concern.[190] Rose worried that a federal court order desegregating the university was forthcoming and that Governor-elect Wallace had already vowed to stand in front of the school door—thereby bringing his dangerous hyperbolic game into fruition. Rose's concern was shared by the Kennedy Administration; they knew this would not be a repeat of James Meredith integrating into the University of Mississippi two months prior.

James Meredith and the University of Mississippi

Mississippi Governor Ross Barnett was no George Wallace in terms of hyperbole, but his staunch segregationist views created a violent climate nevertheless. If there was enough in Wallace's background to conclude he was driven primarily by ambition, one could certainly define Barnett as a true believer for segregation's cause.

"God was the original segregationist," Barnett once said. "He made the white man white and the black man black, and he did not intend for them to mix."[191] He added, "There is no case in history

---

[189] Carter, 107.

[190] Carter, 110.

[191] "Ross Barnett, Segregationist, Dies; Governor of Mississippi in 1960s," *New York Times*, November 7, 1987.

where the Caucasian race has survived social integration; we will not drink from the cup of genocide."[192]

Regardless of their original intent, the outcome for the Negro residents of Alabama and Mississippi was the same: second-class citizenship enforced by the suffocating brutality of Jim Crow.

The tension and perceived victory of the Cuban Missile Crisis in October 1962 were not only successful in keeping James Meredith desegregating the University of Mississippi off of the front pages, but they also caused the press to minimize the mistakes made by the Kennedy Administration and the level of violence that ensued in the desegregation process as well.

Though ultimately successful in desegregating the University of Mississippi, Meredith's admission certainly did not come without violence and bloodshed. Barnett could not be counted on to protect Meredith. And though Meredith had the backing of a federal court order, the Kennedy Administration was forced to assume the reluctant role of Meredith's bodyguard. It wasn't that they were ambivalent towards Meredith's welfare, but rather that they were concerned for the political ramifications of the federal government taking action in an issue defined, at least regionally, as one of interposition and nullification. Kennedy barely defeated Nixon in 1960, and this would prove to be a lingering shadow that would hang over Kennedy throughout his presidency. With an eye already on reelection in 1964, Kennedy did not want to risk alienating Mississippi's eight electoral votes that he had won in 1960, if at all possible. But Barnett would not cooperate.

Moreover, there was an internal divide within the Kennedy Administration, not just with Mississippi but on most matters of civil rights for Negroes, between Lee C. White and historian Arthur Schlesinger, who vigorously fought for civil rights, and Kenny O'Donnell and Larry O'Brien, who were more concerned with politics and did not view civil rights as serving the president's political interest. Though O'Donnell and O'Brien may have been right, based

---

[192] Ibid.

on their short-term political considerations, it was the long-term interest of the nation and the way it would handle civil rights that would ultimately drag the president into the fight—reluctant or otherwise. Oxford, Mississippi, in September 1962 was just the beginning.

Flying debris, bullets, and two deaths—a bystander and a foreign newsperson—marred Meredith's admission and pulled the reluctant Kennedy Administration closer to the center of the controversy. It required more than six thousand federal troops and two hundred arrests for Meredith to enroll at the Oxford, Mississippi campus. Bob Dylan's "Oxford Town" accurately captures the climate and events:

> *Oxford Town, Oxford Town*
> *Ev'rybody's got their heads bowed down*
> *The sun don't shine above the ground*
> *Ain't a-goin' down to Oxford Town*

> *He went down to Oxford Town*
> *Guns and clubs followed him down*
> *All because his face was brown*
> *Better get away from Oxford Town*

> *Oxford Town around the bend*
> *He come in to the door, he couldn't get in*
> *All because of the color of his skin*
> *What do you think about that, my frien'?*

> *Me and my gal, my gal's son*
> *We got met with a tear gas bomb*
> *I don't even know why we come*
> *Goin' back where we come from*[193]

---

[193] Bob Dylan, "Oxford Town," Columbia Records, released December 6, 1962.

Even as Meredith's admission to the University of Mississippi as the first Negro in the university's 118-year history became inevitable, Barnett, who had vigorously fought the court order that went all the way to the U.S. Supreme Court, framed it as Mississippi being "overpowered by the federal government."[194]

It was Justice Hugo Black, a native of Alabama, who issued the Supreme Court ruling that Meredith be admitted in the fall semester of 1962, a move supported by the Justice Department as a "Friend of the Court."

One of the unfortunate political fallouts of Meredith entering the University of Mississippi had to do with the United States Court of Appeals for the Fifth Circuit, which cited Barnett for contempt for his role in denying a federal court. He was assessed a penalty of $10,000 for contempt and was sentenced to jail. But Barnett never served prison time or paid the fine, and the charges were dropped in 1965. The ruling placed the Kennedy Administration in the awkward position of prosecuting a sitting governor in a state that would be in play politically in 1964.

As the violence commenced, Kennedy in a public statement said, "Americans are free to disagree with the law, but not to disobey it. For any government of laws and not of men, no man however prominent or powerful, and no mob however unruly or boisterous is entitled to defy a court of law."[195]

But Kennedy's rational civics lesson, appealing for calm, was countered by Barnett's emotional appeal to the Southern underdog that had proven effective since the days prior to the Civil War. Each offered different arguments and was directed toward dissimilar sensibilities.

---

[194] Al Kuettner, *March to a Promised Land: The Civil Rights Files of a White Reporter, 1952–1968* (Washington, D.C.: Capital Books, 1990), 40.

[195] John F. Kennedy, radio and television report to the nation on the University of Mississippi Station, 30 September 1962,
   http://www.jfklibrary.org/Research/Ready-Reference/JFK-Speeches/Radio-and-Television-Report-to-the-Nation-on-the-Situation-at-the-University-of-Mississippi.aspx.

128

Time did not help Barnett to soften his views. "Generally speaking," he once said years after leaving office, "I'd do the same things again."[196] But the Supreme Court ruling that opened the door in Oxford, Mississippi for Meredith in 1962 would soon make its way across the border to neighboring Tuscaloosa, Alabama.

Wallace and the University of Alabama

In comparison to the Wallace persona, Barnett appeared to be the voice of reason. The concern that Frank Rose expressed to Burke Marshall in November 1962 was well founded. Wallace, upon assuming the office of Governor of Alabama in early 1963, met with the state's educational leader and issued the following warning: "If you agree to integrate your schools, there won't be enough state troopers to protect you."[197] If the threat of violence could be used against university presidents, what lay in store for any Negro who had the audacity to challenge the state's existing codes? Though not exactly the best way to build esprit de corps among the educational group, Wallace viewed the issue of integration and civil rights though a different lens.

Wallace's supporters would view anything short of the governor-elect standing physically in opposition to federal court-ordered integration as an abject violation of a campaign promise. Alabama, in the Wallace political rhetoric, would succeed where other states in the southern region had failed, giving way to the forces of integration and the so-called tyranny of the federal government.

The grainy black-and-white footage from this period can easily leave the impression that white Alabama was in lockstep with the reputation of violence and hatred perpetuated by the public airwaves.

---

[196] "Ross Barnett, Segregationist Dies; Governor of Mississippi in 1960's."New York Times, November 7, 1987,
http://www.nytimes.com/1987/11/07/obituaries/ross-barnett-segregationist-dies-governor-of-mississippi-in-1960-s.html
[197] Carter, 112.

There were those, however, who did not like the way Alabama was publicly portrayed and who did not support Wallace's stance and tactics on civil rights; George LeMaistre was one of those individuals.

LeMaistre, a bank president and former law school professor in Tuscaloosa at the University of Alabama, had trepidation about Wallace's potential response to what he saw was the inevitable. Speaking before the Tuscaloosa Civitan Club, in November 1962, sharing his concerns about the realities of the changing times, he said, "For too long rabble rousing hate groups and loud mouth politicians have undertaken to state the Southern viewpoint on matters which effect our lives."[198]

Citing the Supreme Court as the "final interpreter of the Constitution," LeMaistre stated that no state official "has the right to put himself above the law . . . And that includes a governor or a governor-elect."[199] LeMaistre could not have been more succinct, and his audience's standing ovation could not have been a clearer sign of approval, but the members of the Civitan Club did not represent George Wallace's constituency.

Wallace's infamous "out-nigger me" statement after his gubernatorial defeat in 1958 proved to be more than the frustrations of a losing candidate; it became the personal political theme that drove his quest for national recognition. He unabashedly appealed to southern white populist sentiments with thinly coded language that touted his support for second-class citizenship for Negroes. LeMaistre's concern, based on his understanding of the Constitution, would be Wallace's right to deliver a campaign promise based on his understanding of politics.

Autherine Lucy

When Rose received the applications of Vivian Malone and James Hood, two Negro students who qualified for admittance, he forwarded

---

[198] Carter, 130.
[199] Carter, 130–131.

them to the governor's office. Wallace sent instructions to his staff, stating, "Do what y'all did to Autherine Lucy."[200]

Lucy, a footnote in history, was the first Negro to attend the University of Alabama, in 1956. On the third day of classes, a hostile mob assembled to prevent Lucy from attending class. The police were called to secure her entry to her classrooms, but that evening, the University suspended Lucy on the grounds that it could not provide a safe environment. University officials also claimed that Lucy slandered the university, which gave them grounds for permanent expulsion. It was not until 1980 that the university overturned their horrendous ruling, and Lucy returned to the Tuscaloosa campus in 1982, receiving the master's degree in Elementary Education that had been her original intention in 1956.

But one of the tragic outcomes from the Lucy affair was that the university developed a systematic approach of discouraging Negro applicants. It included hiring private investigators to conduct an extensive background check that would indicate anything that might place the applicant in an unfavorable light.

Willie Painter and Ben Allen were private investigators assigned to conduct background checks on Malone and Hood. Painter and Allen were described has having a long background in investigating Negro applicants, yet their efforts to come up with anything that could be used against Malone and Hood were futile. Al Lingo, who had been appointed by Wallace to head Alabama Highway patrol, was assigned to investigate the Negro students. Though he had limited law enforcement experience, he did come with a reputation of being "hell on niggers."[201]

Malone's reason for applying to the University of Alabama is particularly noteworthy. Unlike James Meredith, she was not interested in proving any political point by challenging the status quo. She had enrolled at Alabama A&M, a historically black university in Huntsville. But Alabama A&M did not offer an accredited accounting

---

[200] Carter, 131.

[201] Carter, 125.

program, and the University of Alabama did. She had the grades to transfer. Were it not for the political and social whirlwinds surrounding her, Malone's decision to transfer would have been the type of pragmatic decision any student in her situation would have been expected to make.

Painter and Allen's failure to dig up any dirt on Malone and Hood called for Wallace to demand a more expansive investigation, but that effort also proved unsuccessful. Other than skin color, the university's tradition, and Wallace's racist populism, there was simply no reason to refuse Malone and Hood from entrance into the University of Alabama. After the second investigation, Allen said as much: "I had a gut feeling Vivian Malone was going to break the color barrier."[202]

Moving Toward a Showdown

Events were quickly moving toward a showdown between Wallace and the Kennedy Administration. The administration did not want to have another confrontation with a Southern Democratic governor over a Negro student being enrolled at its largest state university in less than a year. But Wallace had made such desires impossible. He had placed the Kennedy Administration in an unenviable political corner by giving them the choice either to defend the Constitution but risk losing Southern support for reelection, or to allow Wallace and his interposition argument to rule the day. If there were a way to save face politically by not appearing to be the federal bully that Wallace had warned Alabamans about, the Kennedy Administration would certainly have chosen that option.

But Wallace was playing a different game, one that ultimately directed the chain of events that culminated at the University of Alabama on June 11, 1963. Wallace understood, better than the Kennedy Administration, that if the federal government was perceived as his archenemy, Wallace would win, regardless of the specific

---

[202] Carter, 132.

outcomes. Wallace's ambition and political shrewdness placed him head and shoulders above Governor Barnett. And the handling of James Meredith's enrollment at the University of Mississippi was not exactly something the Kennedy Administration was eager to put on a reelection highlight reel in 1964, especially in the South.

On June 2, 1963, Wallace appeared on NBC's *Meet the Press*. Lawrence Spivak, the show's moderator, pointedly asked Wallace what were his intentions for June 11, 1963, when Malone and Hood were scheduled to enroll. "I shall stand at the door as I stated in my campaign for Governor," Wallace replied. He then added, "The confrontation would be handled peacefully and without violence."[203]

In this latter statement, Wallace was embracing the language of the Civil Rights Movement, drawing a distinction between himself and what the nation witnessed several weeks earlier, as Bull Connor's police dogs and high-powered fire hoses were used against children in the streets of Birmingham, portraying Alabama as the antithesis of peaceful and nonviolent. Wallace would go on to state that he would challenge the Justice Department to "raise constitutional questions that can be adjudicated in the courts."[204] Wallace wasn't taking a stand against integration. Drawing perhaps on images of Sherman taking Atlanta, Wallace instead was opposing the "march of centralized government that is going to destroy the rights and freedoms of the people of this country."[205] In that moment, Wallace was not portraying himself merely as the Governor of Alabama who had already drawn a line in the sand to uphold segregation, but as a defender of constructional rights everywhere.

Wallace was attempting to define Alabama's fight as America's fight. If the Kennedy Administration could run roughshod over his state, as they seemingly did in Mississippi, what would prohibit similar treatment elsewhere? He was effectively using the medium of

---

[203] George Wallace, "Meet the Press with Guest the Honorable George C. Wallace, Governor of Alabama," NBC, Sunday, June 2, 1963.

[204] Ibid.

[205] Ibid.

television. It did not matter that the Supreme Court had struck the basis of his constitutional argument in 1954, and as Barnett was already aware when he led an injunction to block Meredith's admission, the court had also ruled specifically on the matter of desegregation of public universities in 1962.

Moreover, there is simply no way to understate the vortex of change that was occurring in 1963. In 1961, the Berlin Wall was erected, depicting a tangible demarcation separating East and West, and fourteen months later, the Soviet Union and the United States would sit on the brink of nuclear war, and it wasn't until the Associated Press caught Bull Connor's police dogs on film and published photos on the front pages of most of the country's newspapers that civil rights gained national attention. But because the civil rights struggle was symbolized by the Negroes quest for equality, one never knew if or when onlooker fatigue would set in.

Wallace was presenting himself to the nation as a governor whose argument in opposition to Malone and Hood enrolling was not based on the hatred exhibited by Bull Connor but rather on constitutional underpinnings. But two days after appearing on *Meet the Press*, Federal Judge Seybourn Lynne ruled in favor of the Justice Department's request for an injunction against Wallace. The governor was not prohibited from the university on June 11, but any interference with Malone and Hood enrolling would result in his being held in contempt, which would result in fines and jail time. Judge Lynne, who was a graduate of the university and its law school, wrote his ruling in the first-person, stating, "I love the people of Alabama." But he insisted that the law of the land came first. "I know many of both races are troubled and like Jonah of old, are 'angry even unto death.' My prayer is that all of our people, in keeping with our finest tradition, will join in the resolution that law and order will be maintained."[206]

For Lynne, "The concept of the law, the very essence of a republican form of government, rested upon the notion that, once the judicial process had reached a final judgment, all persons thereby are

---

[206] Carter, 139.

134

obliged to obey it."[207] Lynne went on to say, "The Supreme Court of the United States had rejected the doctrine of interposition."[208]

But Lynne was hardly a progressive on integration. In 1956, he was the dissenter in a three-judge panel's decision to integrate city buses in Montgomery, and later that year, he declined a Justice Department recommendation to convene a grand jury to investigate charges that the civil rights of three black ministers had been violated. The next year he had no opinion on a similar panel's warning against setting up a private all-white bus line to circumvent the integration ruling. Over the years, many surmised that Lynn's ruling against Wallace in 1963 was the reiteration of his 1956 court order that allowed Lucy to become the first Negro to attend a public university in Alabama, whom the board of trustees managed to quickly expel.

Regardless of the reason, Lynne's decision was a key moment in civil rights history; he made it clear that Wallace no longer had a legal leg to stand on. Moreover, the Kennedy Administration demonstrated an ability to be quick learners on the job who learned from their previous mistakes. The fiasco of the Bay of Pigs became the triumph of the Cuban Missile Crisis. Likewise, any mishandling in Mississippi would not be repeated in Alabama. The Kennedy Administration was evolving with the changing political climate; it was growing in stature and confidence.

During the 1960 presidential campaign, Kennedy argued that executive and legislative leadership could combat the country's racial discrimination. After he was elected, he soon realized there was no legislative leadership on Capitol Hill to pass civil rights legislation, and Kenny O'Donnell and Lawrence O'Brien argued that such efforts were a no-win politically. They urged the president to wait for a more opportune time.

On June 10, one day before Wallace's much-anticipated standoff, the president gave the commencement address at American University. The speech focused on peace and directed much of its attention toward

[207] Ibid.
[208] Ibid.

the Soviet Union. But while the Kennedy Administration's preference may have been to focus on foreign affairs, America was in the midst of a reexamination of its attitude on civil rights and its importance as an issue. And Wallace was readying America to once again return to the arena of civil rights and race, an area where the administration was less comfortable.

After several weeks of public jousting between Wallace and the Kennedy Administration, June 11 finally arrived. Ultimately, what happened was something that could have very easily been labeled much ado about nothing had it not been for the media coverage. The administration wanted the two Negro students enrolled without violence; Wallace wanted to save face. There must have been a meeting of the minds; if not overtly, there was certainly an implied concurrence.

Assistant Attorney General Nicholas Katzenbach met Wallace alone. It was predetermined that Malone and Hood would stay in the car during this initial confrontation to avoid any possible humiliation by Wallace, to decrease the likelihood of any potential of violence, and to make the standoff about Wallace and the Kennedy Administration and not about the Negro students. With Malone and Hood absent, the Kennedy Administration was also able to avoid charging Wallace with contempt.[209]

As Wallace stood near the podium underneath the designated air-conditioned entrance, Katzenbach stood a few feet away, absorbing the brunt of Tuscaloosa's 95-degree heat. The moment that kept Katzenbach awake all night had finally arrived. The violence in Oxford, Mississippi, and Wallace's seemingly unpredictable nature were on the forefront of his thoughts. The Kennedy Administration felt that Wallace did not want violence to break out, but the question remained whether or not anyone could prevent it. Conversely, Wallace's stern demeanor hid any self-doubt he possessed as to whether he had overplayed his hand.

---

[209] Carter, 147.

136

That morning, after picking up Malone and Hood in Birmingham and prior to his confrontation with Wallace, Katzenbach spoke with Attorney General Robert Kennedy. Katzenbach later reflected on that call, remembering, "Bobby called, [and] he said, 'What are you going to say to Gov. Wallace?' I said, 'I don't really know.' He said, 'Well the president wants you to make him look foolish.' I said, 'Fine, you got any ideas as to how to do that?' He said, 'Oh, don't worry Nick, you'll do fine!'"[210]

Accompanied by the U.S. Attorney and Marshal of Birmingham, Katzenbach approached Wallace; he stopped at the line marking his spot, painted in advance of this event, placing him within approximately twenty feet of the governor's podium. With Katzenbach still in the heat and Wallace still in the shade, Katzenbach moved within four feet of the podium and stated, "I have here President Kennedy's proclamation."[211]

Frustrated and perspiring profusely from the heat, Katzenbach said to an unyielding but cool Wallace, "I have come to ask for your unequivocal assurance that you or anyone under your control will not bar these students."

He then repeated the last statement with a slight variance: "I have come to ask for you unequivocally that you will permit these students who, after all, merely want an education in the great University—"[212]

But Wallace interrupted before Katzenbach could finish, saying, "Now you make your statement, but we don't need a speech."[213]

Agitated by the heat and possibly fortified by the president's urging to make Wallace look foolish, Katzenbach responded, "I'm making my statement, Governor," and he repeated his request that the governor not interfere with the admittance of Malone and Hood, though he did not call them specifically by name.

---

[210] Nicholas Katzenbach, interview on Big Think October 29, 2009. http://bigthink.com/users/nicholaskatzenbach#!video_idea_id=5615
[211] Ibid.
[212] Carter, 149.
[213] Ibid.

Wallace responded with a four-page statement that addressed the state's "sovereignty" and the federal government's "illegal usurpation of power."[214]

Wallace did everything within his power to avoid the issue of race, but it was clear that this in fact had everything to do with race. Wallace had people on his staff—from speechwriters such as Asa Carter to Al Lingo, who headed the Highway Patrol—who were a single phone call away from connecting to the highest echelons of leadership within the Ku Klux Klan. Even Bull Connor was at Wallace's disposal to carry messages to white supremacist organizations, as he did leading up to the June 11 showdown, relaying Wallace's message to stay away from the campus that day.

The fact that the situation was clearly about race and injustice, along with the heat, made Katzenbach even less tolerant of Wallace's political posturing.

As Katzenbach recalled the events, "I said, 'I don't know what the purpose of this big show is. It's just two students, qualified students, trying to get into the university in which they're entitled to be admitted, and I don't see any reason for this show,' and he didn't like that."[215]

But "show," though not initially the goal, became the operative word. As Katzenbach and Wallace faced off for round one, Katzenbach had prearranged with Frank Rose to have Malone and Hood taken directly to the dormitory rooms; they had already been registered, so there was no need to engage the governor.

Round two began as Katzenbach relayed to the president that it was time to bring in the National Guard under the command of Brigadier General Henry V. Graham. About an hour later, a message was sent to Katzenbach that Wallace wanted to be confronted by the military command (Wallace knew General Graham personally); he wanted to make a brief speech and then take his leave. In addition,

---

[214] George C. Wallace, School House Door Speech, 11 June 1963, http://www.archives.state.al.us/govs_list/schooldoor.html.
[215] Katzenbach.

138

Wallace would leave instructions with law enforcement to keep order, and the Kennedy Administration agreed to those plans.

General Graham said that it was his "sad duty'" to order the Governor to step aside.[216] Wallace proceeded to read the second of two statements challenging the constitutionality of court-ordered desegregation, and once he was through, he left. As the *New York Times* reported, "This sequence of events, which took place in a circus atmosphere, appeared to have given the Governor the face-saving exit he apparently wanted."[217]

The most significant indication of change was not caught on camera, nor did it have anything to do with Wallace or Katzenbach. It had to do with Vivian Malone sitting down for the first time in the university cafeteria. She sat by herself at a table, and soon after, two white female students came over and sat down with her. This simple act was perhaps the most transformative of anything that had taken place that day.

The final outcome was a win for both sides. The Kennedy Administration protected the civil rights of Malone and Hood without violence; they avoided holding a second Southern governor in contempt in less than a year. Wallace showed himself as having more stature than Barnett and more courage than Governor Hollings in South Carolina, who virtually put up no resistance when Harvey Gantt became the first Negro to integrate into Clemson University. Wallace had transformed into a national political figure.

Though the Kennedy Administration was right to intervene in Oxford, they had learned a valuable lesson from their mistakes, and that had carried into the University of Alabama confrontation. At the University of Mississippi, people were hurt, a few were killed, there was rioting in the streets, and it required 22,000 soldiers to return the college town to order. Though not an incident the administration

---

[216] Claude Sitton, "Alabama Admits Negro Students; Wallace Bows to Federal Force; Kennedy Sees 'Moral Crisis' in U.S.," *New York Times*, 12 June 1963, http://partners.nytimes.com/library/national/race/061263race-ra.html.
[217] Ibid.

would laud, looking back, it may have been a necessary evil, without which it is doubtful the situation in Alabama would have turned out the way it did. Wallace, more so than Barnett, understood this as well.

But in the midst of all this commotion, something else was happening. The fortunes of America's two major political parties were about to change; Wallace had done his part that day, but Kennedy would be required to oblige that evening.

Civil Rights Address to the Nation

Kennedy was watching the broadcasted events at the University of Alabama on his Oval Office television, and when he saw Wallace step aside on cue, Kennedy turned to Sorensen and said, "I think we better give that speech tonight."[218] In Sorensen's mind, the question must have rung out, *What speech?* as they didn't have anything on the table at the time. The speech would be a clarion call to the nation clearly outlining where the Kennedy Administration stood on civil rights for Negroes.

Until this point, the Kennedy Administration was viewed as trying to have it both ways on civil rights. They had won a close election in 1960 with the help of overwhelming Negro support. Kennedy had made the naive campaign promise that with the stroke of his pen he could secure equal rights for Negroes. But the president also sought to avoid sending any comprehensive civil rights legislation to Capitol Hill, unwilling to further alienate the Southern delegation that was not only a powerful block in Congress, controlling crucial committees in the House and Senate, but also key to his reelection hopes in 1964. But events on the ground were pulling the president away from the politically safe middle. Each year of his administration, the president pushed to take a firmer stand on civil rights.

In 1961, the Kennedy Administration sent federal marshals into Alabama to protect the Freedom Riders. In 1962, they sent the National Guard to protect James Meredith and keep order in Oxford. But in 1963, some eight and a half months after Oxford, events in

[218] Ted Sorensen interview with author, June 23, 2009.

140

Birmingham and in Tuscaloosa again forced the president to take action. He watched on television, along with millions of Americans, in disbelief of the brutality of Jim Crow, and he finally came to the conclusion that political considerations must now take a backseat to the moral direction of the country.

But the speech, like the administration's civil rights policy, was still in its formative stages. The policy would need weeks before it was ready to be sent to Congress; Sorensen would only have a few hours to put something together before Kennedy would address the nation.

As expected, many within the administration, particularly O'Brien and O'Donnell, urged the president not to give the speech, because the political downside was too great. And they advised that by no means should Kennedy send civil rights legislation that's doomed to fail to Congress—it was simply too high a price for his presidency to pay.

Sorensen fretted that he did not have enough time. The Kennedy–Sorensen team, long regarded as one of the best in presidential speechwriting history because of their symbiotic relationship, was under unique pressure to speak to the nation on a critical matter that had only recently gained national attention. The president had avoided taking on civil rights overtly, and now he had only a few hours to prepare to give the most significant speech on civil rights by any U.S. president in ninety-eight years. Recalling that night and their frantic preparation, Sorensen said, "It was the only time in my three years at the White House that JFK came to my office to ask about a speech."[219] In addition to Sorensen, the Assistant Attorney General Burke Marshall, who was head of the Civil Rights division, and the president himself, worked on the speech. But Vice President Lyndon Johnson may have given the most important contribution to the speech's success when he implored that civil rights was a "moral issue."[220]

---

[219] Ted Sorensen, *Counselor: A Life at the Edge of History* (New York: HarperCollins, 2008) 280.

[220] Alexander Tsesis, *We Shall Overcome: A History of Civil Rights and the Law* (New Haven, CT: Yale University Press), 244.

That night, the president opened the address by returning to the events at the University of Alabama that day:

This afternoon, following a series of threats and defiant statements, the presence of Alabama National Guardsmen was required on the University of Alabama to carry out the final and unequivocal order of the United States District Court of the Northern District of Alabama. That order called for the admission of two clearly qualified young Alabama residents who happened to have been born Negro. That they were admitted peacefully on the campus is due in good measure to the conduct of the students of the University of Alabama, who met their responsibilities in a constructive way.[221]

Kennedy then challenged the nation to reflect on its own values:

I hope that every American, regardless of where he lives, will stop and examine his conscience about this and other related incidents. This Nation was founded by men of many nations and backgrounds. It was founded on the principle that all men are created equal, and that the rights of every man are diminished when the rights of one man are threatened.[222]

Later in the speech, Kennedy uttered the most important statement: "We are confronted primarily with a moral issue. It is as old as the Scriptures and is as clear as the American Constitution."[223] And after making the moral appeal to the nation's conscience, Kennedy spoke specifically about the action proposed: "Next week I shall ask the Congress of the United States to act, to make a commitment it has not fully made in this century to the proposition that race has no place in American life or law."[224]

This speech was a far cry from Kennedy's earlier State of the Union Address, when he dedicated a scant sixty-five words to the issue

[221] John F. Kennedy, Civil Rights Address, 11 June 1963, http://www.americanrhetoric.com/speeches/jfkcivilrights.htm.
[222] Ibid.
[223] Ibid.
[224] Ibid.

of race, which was given the same day that Wallace made his "segregation now, segregation tomorrow, segregation forever" inaugural address. This speech instantly became the most important speech a president had made on civil rights since Abraham Lincoln.

Reaction to the speech fell down the predictable fault line of civil rights; where one stood on the issue on June 10, 1963, would determine how one received the president's words on June 11. Martin Luther King Jr. reportedly leaped to his feet and proclaimed, "Can you believe that white man not only stepped up to the plate, he hit it over the fence."[225] Members of the Southern congressional delegation, however, such as Georgia Senator Richard Russell, considered the civil rights bill to be a step toward Communism.[226]

This was arguably Kennedy's greatest moment as Commander in Chief. The John Kennedy who took the oath of office on January 20, 1961, was a very different person on the issue of race by June 11, 1963. Kennedy asked Americans to look within themselves as he was willing to do—and this is why that speech was so persuasive. Given that he had delivered the address at American University the day before, it is hard to argue for a comparable moment in presidential history, with two speeches of equal significance given on consecutive days.

The greatness of the speech, however, did not come simply in the context of words or its moral appeal. There was a political cost involved. To coin the phrase from his 1955 Pulitzer Prize–winning book, Kennedy's speech on civil rights was indeed a "profile in courage."[227] But O'Brien and O'Donnell's political considerations were not without merit. This is one of the reasons greatness is rare in

---

[225] Sorensen, 282.

[226] Taylor Branch, *Pillar of Fire: America in the King years 1963-1965* (New York: Simon& Schuster, 1999),,110.

[227] Term taken from the title of John F. Kennedy's 1957 Pulitzer Prize–winning book of short biographies describing acts of bravery and integrity by eight United States Senators throughout the Senate's history.

presidential politics. There is an aversion to taking risk inherent in the office.

Unlike the Cuban Missile Crisis, where Kennedy had to act against the Soviets and there was no political downside, he was not forced to give a speech on civil rights—the only thing that pressured him was his conscience, and he could no longer keep silent.

The president's speech and Wallace's stand at the University of Alabama earlier that day worked in tandem to mark the official beginning of the Democratic Party's decline, especially in the South. Then, in 1964 and 1965, President Lyndon Johnson would sign landmark civil rights legislation, and in 1968, Wallace would run for president as a third-party candidate. During Wallace's campaign, *Life* magazine cartoonist Ranan Lurie drew a telling image, and it ran on the front cover: the contiguous southern states shaped as a horse, with Wallace mounted atop it, Nixon attempting to feed it a carrot, and Reagan holding on to its tail. This depicted the development of what would be called the "Southern Strategy," the specific appeal to white voters in the South by using abstract "code language" to fan the flames of racial fears. This series of events allowed candidate Ronald Reagan—during his 1980 presidential campaign while in Philadelphia, Mississippi, the location of the murder of three civil rights workers in 1964—to say, without paying a political price, "I believe in states' rights." In this tacit remark Reagan sought to appeal to Southern white voters, which he did, and his followers would become known as "Reagan Democrats." The Republican Party enjoyed nearly thirty years of regional domination, and that legacy can be traced back to June 11, 1963.

Medgar Evers

Several hours after the president's address, this twenty-four-hour pendulum of hope across the nation would swing violently back to hostility in Mississippi, this time in the capital city of Jackson. Medgar Wiley Evers, the field secretary for the NAACP in Mississippi, was to become the movement's first high-profile martyr.

Born July 2, 1925, near Decatur, Mississippi, Evers grew up and attended school in his hometown until he was inducted into the army in 1943. He participated in the Battle of Normandy and was honorably discharged as a sergeant. After completing his service, Evers returned to Decatur, and along with his brothers and friends, he registered to vote. But on Election Day, the White Citizens' Council used intimidating tactics to prohibit him from voting. This became a life-changing experience for Evers; it became the moment that he committed his life to changing that status quo of segregation.

Evers enrolled at Alcorn College—now called Alcorn State University—and majored in business administration. While at Alcorn, he was a member of the debate team, the college choir, and the football and track teams, and he also held several student offices and was editor of the campus newspaper for two years.

It was at Alcorn that Evers met Myrlie Beasley, and they were married on December 24, 1951. Evers received his B.A. degree in 1952, and he and his wife moved to Mound Bayou, Mississippi. While working in the insurance business, Evers began to establish local chapters of the NAACP throughout the Delta, and he organized boycotts of gasoline stations that refused to allow blacks to use their restrooms. In 1954, the year a Supreme Court decision ruled school segregation unconstitutional, Evers applied to the University of Mississippi Law School, but his application was denied. His attempt to integrate into the state's oldest public university garnered the attention of the NAACP's national office. Later that year, Evers moved to Jackson and became the NAACP's first field secretary in Mississippi.

In 1955, Evers led a private investigation into the brutal murder of Emmett Till, a fourteen-year-old boy from Chicago who was savagely beaten beyond recognition and murdered in Money, Mississippi, for allegedly whistling at a white woman. Evers became the most visible face in the state while investigating, recruiting NAACP members, and organizing voter-registration efforts, demonstrations, and economic boycotts of white-owned companies that practiced discrimination.

In 1963, the civil rights struggle in Mississippi was no different than it was in other places in the South; it was a struggle for power. And the White Citizens' Council was leading the opposition.

The White Citizens' Council, also known as the "white-collar Klan" because many of its members were business executives and politicians, met openly and was seen as a legitimate organization. Though there were organized chapters throughout the South, the first known meeting was at Indianola, Mississippi, on July 11, 1954, roughly two months after the Supreme Court's *Brown v. Board of Education* ruling.

Unlike the Ku Klux Klan, the White Citizens' Council did not use violence or terrorism as their preferred means of maintaining the status quo. Instead they used punitive economic measures, such as foreclosing on an individual's mortgage, firing workers, or denying farm loans if it was suspected that one was sympathetic to integration. They were also effective at passing legislation to ensure white domination, and their commitment to the overarching principles of white supremacy ran just as deeply as the Klan's.

In 1962, in some counties in Mississippi, the population of Negroes outnumbered whites four to one.[228] And in many counties there was not a single Negro registered to vote. Though some Negroes were not necessarily discouraged by the prohibitive laws passed, they would realize that the Klan's violent arm still lurked close behind. Eviction, incarceration, and murder were among the punishments utilized when Negroes voted or attempted to vote.

By 1963, Evers had become the most visible symbol for Negro equality. He stood in support of James Meredith integrating into the University of Mississippi in 1962, and nine months later, he lead an economic boycott of stores in the state capital that supported the racial status quo. Evers was in effect countering the White Citizens' Council's punitive economic measures with community-based

---

[228] Brent Staples, "Sins of the Fathers," *New York Times*, 8 June 2003.

methods. For nearly a decade, Evers was the most well-known face in opposition to the second-class citizenship endured by the Negro.

Evers would implore demonstrators not to purchase anything on Capitol Street, one of the main streets in Jackson. He appealed to the Negro residents that until they were treated with dignity, the merchants on Capitol Street must also feel economic pain. Evers would often state publicly that they would continue the demonstration until "Freedom comes to Negroes in Jackson, Mississippi."

Evers's words inspired the determination of the demonstrators; it also increased the level of violence and overall tension in Jackson, which meant the situation became more dangerous for Evers. The economic tactics used by the White Citizens' Council were not effective in derailing Evers's determination and his ability to inspire others. It was clear that more drastic measures were required.

"It was simply in the air, you knew something was going to happen, and the logical person was Medgar," Evers's wife Myrlie recalled.[229] "I used to try and reassure him, 'nothing is going to happen to you, everybody know you, you're in the press, they wouldn't dare do anything to you.'"[230]

In the early morning of June 12, Evers pulled into his driveway, returning from a NAACP meeting. After emerging from his car, carrying NAACP T-shirts that read "Jim Crow Must Go," Evers was struck in the back with a bullet fired from a high-powered rifle, which then ricocheted into his home.[231] He staggered thirty feet before collapsing on the porch, where his wife found him.

Evers died at a local hospital fifty minutes later, just hours after President Kennedy's address to the nation in support of civil rights that ironically, if not prophetically, included the words "Those who do

---

[229] Clayborne Carson, ed., *Civil Rights Chronicle: The African American Struggle for Freedom* (Lincolnwood, IL: Publications International, Ltd., 2003), http://www.stanford.edu/group/King/pdfs/crc_238_239.pdf

[230] Ibid.

[231] "NAACP History: Medgar Evers," NAACP, http://www.naacp.org/pages/naacp-history-medgar-evers.

nothing are inviting shame, as well as violence. Those who act boldly are recognizing right, as well as reality."[232]

In some ways, Evers's death placed more of an exclamation point on Kennedy's address than the events at the University of Alabama earlier that day did. A man who had served his country in WWII, fighting for the liberation of Europe, was gunned down on his porch because he sought basic human rights for Negroes in a country that had already guaranteed those rights on paper—this was the height of absurdity.

The news of Evers's assassination reached the White House early in the morning. The president was told at breakfast, and he immediately released a statement that he was "appalled by the barbarity of this act."[233] Several days after Evers's assassination, Kennedy confided to historian and aide Arthur Schlesinger that the shooting challenged his views on Reconstruction. "I don't understand the South. I'm coming to believe Thaddeus Stevens was right. I had always been taught to regard him as a man of vicious bias. But when I see this sort of thing, I begin to wonder how else can you treat them."[234]

Thaddeus Stevens was one of the most vocal Republicans in the House of Representatives in opposition to Lincoln's Reconstruction plan. Viewing it as too lenient, Stevens called for a plan to treat the defeated southern states as "conquered provinces."[235]

Kennedy's statement, in this context, becomes an astonishing revelation. Just as Lincoln did not hold the same views on slavery in 1865 that he did in 1860, Kennedy indeed did not have the same opinion about civil rights in 1963 that he did when he entered the White House in 1961.

---

[232] John F. Kennedy, Civil Rights Address, 11 June 1963.

[233] Nick Bryant, *The Bystander John F. Kennedy and the Struggle for Black Equality* (New York: Basic Books, 2006), 424.

[234] Ibid.

[235] William Richter, *The A to Z of the Civil War and Reconstruction* (New York: Scarecrow Press, 2009), 489.

One month before Evers was murdered, Kennedy and his administration were critical of Martin Luther King using nonviolent civil disobedience, specifically his encouraging children to participate in demonstrations against Bull Connor's police dogs and fire hoses and not simply waiting for Albert Boutwell to assume office. After the Evers assassination, having just sandwiched Wallace's ceremonial stand at the University of Alabama between two incredible speeches, Kennedy had clearly moved from the middle, against the advice of key advisors, and had positioned his administration unquestionably as an advocate for civil rights.

Later that day, Kennedy sent a typewritten condolence letter to Myrlie Evers. "Although comforting thoughts are difficult at a time like this," the president wrote, "surely there can be some solace in the realization of the justice for which your husband gave his life." Below his signature the president added a hand written note: "Mrs. Kennedy joins me in extending her deepest sympathy."[236]

Not long after Evers died, a fingerprint on the murder weapon was found to belong to Byron De La Beckwith of Greenwood, Mississippi. He was a member of the Greenwood Episcopal Church of the Nativity, the Ku Klux Klan, and the White Citizens' Council. Though Beckwith claimed to be elsewhere when the shooting occurred, he did not hide his pleasure that Evers was dead.

At the time of Evers's assassination, those who knew De La Beckwith were not surprised that he was the accused. A member of the Greenwood Episcopal Church of the Nativity, while speaking to a *Time* magazine reporter in 1963, said of Beckwith, "He tried to inject racism into everything. If you talked about Noah and the Ark, he'd want to know if there were any Negroes in the Ark."[237] And the Mississippi political climate meant that Beckwith had his share of supporters. A local fund drive commenced to pay Beckwith's legal expenses. As one Greenwood resident declared, "I say the shooting of

---

[236] Bryant, 425.
[237] "Civil Rights: A Little Abnormal," *Time*, 5 July 1963, http://www.time.com/time/magazine/article/0,9171,875008-1,00.html

Evers was a patriotic act. If Delay pulled the trigger that night, he must have felt he was doing it for the South and the state."[238]

In 1964, Beckwith was tried twice for the murder of Evers, but both trials ended in mistrials because the all-white juries were unable to reach a verdict. The evidence seemed overwhelming against Beckwith. The murder weapon unquestionably belonged to Beckwith, his fingerprints were on the weapon, and a car matching the description of his had been seen by several witnesses near the Evers home on the night of the crime, but three policemen from Greenwood testified that he was playing cards with them roughly sixty miles from where the shooting occurred.

At one of the trials, former governor Ross Barnett appeared as Myrlie Evers was testifying. Barnett interrupted Evers's testimony to walk over and publicly shake Beckwith's hand. There couldn't have been a more tragic display of support for Beckwith—which was ultimately the very reason Evers was fighting for the civil rights cause.

For more than thirty years, Beckwith remained beyond the reach of justice, bragging almost to the point of admission that he was the one who shot Medgar Evers. Were it not for Myrlie Evers's dogged determination, Beckwith might very well have died a free man instead of taking his last breath behind bars as a convicted murderer.

The more immediate impact of Evers's death was realized in the days leading up to his funeral service. His organizing efforts and economic boycotts had struck a responsive chord with Negroes throughout Mississippi, but particularly in Jackson. On June 18, an estimated three thousand mourners were led by Martin Luther King Jr., Executive Secretary of the NAACP Roy Wilkins, and Nobel Prize recipient and diplomat Ralph Bunche. But tension flared in the nearly 100-degree heat, and Negro youth hurled stones at the police officers, shouting, "Where's the killer?"

As Jackson police prepared to replicate the tactics of Birmingham's Bull Connor with police dogs and fire hoses, Justice

---

[238] Kris Hollington, *Wolves, Jackals, and Foxes: The Assassins Who Changed History* (New York: Thomas, Dunne Books,2008), 74.

150

Department official John Dora placed himself between the mob and the police, pleading for order and reminding the demonstrators that their actions were not in keeping with the legacy of Medgar Evers and the cause for which he was willing to give his life.

The next day, Evers was buried at Arlington National Cemetery with full military honors. President Kennedy did not attend the burial service but did ask the attorney general to attend. Afterward, he invited Myrlie Evers and her two children to the White House. Kennedy offered his condolences and posed for photos. The president's very public displays of empathy for the cause of civil rights were not winning him political points in the South, but he had been reluctantly transformed by events on the ground.

The Streets of Saigon

The South had been predominate in shaping the twenty-four hours between June 11 and June 12, but it would be a different "South" that got Kennedy's morning started that same June 11. He was handed the morning paper as he sat in bed talking to the attorney general about their approach to the upcoming events at the University of Alabama, and the president reportedly interrupted their discussion with an emphatic, "Jesus Christ!"[239]

What altered Kennedy's focus was the self-immolation of Thich Quang Duc, a Vietnamese Buddhist monk, who, in a busy intersection of Saigon, protested South Vietnam President Ngo Dinh Diem's persecution of Buddhists by setting himself on fire. Kennedy would later remark, "No news picture in history has generated so much emotion around the world as that one."[240]

---

[239] James Douglass, *JFK and the Unspeakable: Why He Died and Why It Matters* (New York: Simon & Schuster, 2010), 148.

[240] Seth Jacobs, *Cold War Mandarin: Ngo Dinh Diem and the Origins of America's War in Vietnam, 1950–1963* (Lanham: Rowan & Littlefield, 2006), 149.

As Duc sat stoically burning, other monks and nuns passed out leaflets calling for Diem's government to show "charity and compassion" to all religions.

The report relayed that on June 10, a spokesperson for the Buddhists privately informed U.S. correspondents that "something important" would happen the following morning on the road outside the Cambodian embassy in Saigon.

The message had been widely disregarded, and only few journalists attended the following day. But among those who did attend were David Halberstam of the *New York Times* and Malcolm Browne, Saigon bureau chief for the Associated Press.

It was Browne's iconic photo that left Kennedy nearly speechless as he discussed the upcoming events at the University of Alabama with his brother later that day. The photo earned Browne a Pulitzer Prize. Halberstam also won a Pulitzer Prize for his reporting. He wrote:

I was to see that sight again, but once was enough. Flames were coming from a human being; his body was slowly withering and shriveling up, his head blackening and charring. In the air was the smell of burning human flesh; human beings burn surprisingly quickly. Behind me I could hear the sobbing of the Vietnamese who were now gathering. I was too shocked to cry, too confused to take notes or ask questions, too bewildered to even think . . . As he burned he never moved a muscle, never uttered a sound, his outward composure in sharp contrast to the wailing people around him.[241]

Halberstam's writing would not only earn him a Pulitzer; it would also draw the ire of Kennedy. In October 1963, Kennedy would place a call to *New York Times* publisher Arthur Ochs Sulzberger to have Halberstam removed from the Saigon bureau because he did not like Halberstam's Vietnam coverage.

---

[241] David Halberstam, *The Making of a Quagmire* (New York: Random House, 1965), 211.

152

The shock was felt primarily in the West. For centuries, self-immolation by Vietnamese monks was not an uncommon practice. The French colonial authorities tried unsuccessfully to ban it once they occupied Vietnam in the nineteenth century.

But the South Vietnam government's response to this suicide was to arrest thousands of Buddhist monks. By August, an additional five monks had committed suicide, also by self-immolation. Madame Nhu, Diem's sister-in-law and in effect South Vietnam's First Lady, cavalierly responded to these self-immolations by telling a newspaper reporter: "Let them burn, and we shall clap our hands."[242] She further offered to supply Buddhists who wanted to commit suicide with the necessary gasoline.

These statements reflected badly on the Kennedy Administration because they were supporting the South Vietnamese government. Kennedy was realizing he did not understand the southern region of America, and now the photos that greeted him on the morning of June 11, 1963, on the front page of the *New York Times* may have been the first major indicator that he did not understand the region of the world in which the United States had volunteered to stand proxy for the French. And each offhanded quote in response to the Buddhist monks or the heavy-handed tactics to quell the uprising was proof the Diem regime did not understand the ramifications of what was happening either. It was also an indication to the Kennedy Administration and the world that things would get worse in Vietnam before they improved.

24 Hours

It is hard to imagine that any president—or for that matter, an entire country—has or will experience a more transformative twenty-four hours. June 11, 1963, impacted the country both in the short term and long term on matters both foreign and domestic. It had dramatic

---

[242] Amy Davidson, "Madame Nhu's Match," http://www.newyorker.com/online/blogs/closeread/2011/04/madame-nhus-match.html (April 27, 2011).

moments of confrontation, political courage, senseless violence, and quiet examples that the country was indeed changing for the better. That single twenty-four-hour period would have a definitive impact on how politics would be conducted in America for more than a generation to follow, and it was significant in that it revealed a president moving from a political to a moral emphasis on civil rights. It also provided a glimpse into the window of the quagmire that ultimately would be known as the Vietnam War.

Cuban Prime Minister Fidel Castro and Soviet Premiere Nikita Khrushchev in Moscow (Associated Press)

Public Safety Commissioner for the City of Birmingham Theophilus Eugene "Bull" Connor" confronting civil rights protestors (Associated Press)

Buddhist monk, Thich Quang Duc's immolation on the streets of Saigon
(Associated Press)

Time Magazine superimposes the image of Governor George Wallace over the
blown out stained glass of the 16th Street Baptist Church bombing, linking the
governor to the most horrendous event in the battle for civil rights in 1963. (Time
Magazine)

Clarence Gideon, architect of the landmark case Gideon v. Wainwright

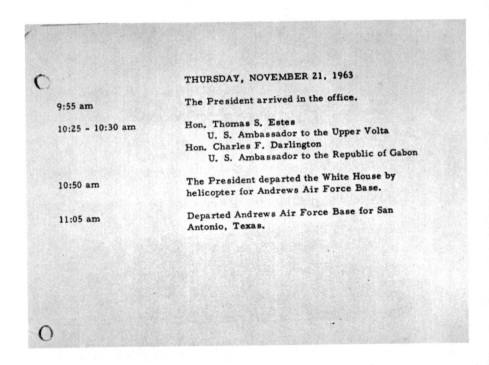

THURSDAY, NOVEMBER 21, 1963

9:55 am — The President arrived in the office.

10:25 - 10:30 am — Hon. Thomas S. Estes
U. S. Ambassador to the Upper Volta
Hon. Charles F. Darlington
U. S. Ambassador to the Republic of Gabon

10:50 am — The President departed the White House by helicopter for Andrews Air Force Base.

11:05 am — Departed Andrews Air Force Base for San Antonio, Texas.

President Kennedy's final itinerary (Associated Press)

The disbelief of November 22, symbolic of what the day did to us!
(Associated Press)

Chapter Six:

The Check Comes Back Marked "Insufficient Funds"

Perhaps no one did more to give voice for the modern civil rights movement than Asa Philip Randolph. Randolph was born in 1889 in Crescent City, Florida; he was the second son of the Rev. James William Randolph, a tailor and African Methodist Episcopal minister, and Elizabeth Robinson Randolph, a seamstress. Though his origins were humble, by 1919 the Woodrow Wilson Administration dubbed Randolph to be the "Most Dangerous Negro in America"[243] while segregating civil service; this same title would be given to Martin Luther King Jr. not long after the March on Washington in 1963.

In 1919, Randolph became president of the National Brotherhood Workers of America, a union of black shipyard dockworkers in Tidewater, Virginia. In June 1925, a group of Pullman porters, the all-black service staff of the Pullman sleeping cars, approached Randolph to lead their new organization, the Brotherhood of Sleeping Car Porters (BSCP). Randolph agreed to become its first president. Beyond

---

[243] "A. Phillip Randolph is Dead, Pioneer in Rights and Labor," http://www.nytimes.com/learning/general/onthisday/bday/0415.html (May 17,1979).

his knowledge and commitment to organizing, Randolph was known for his integrity.

For the next ten years, Randolph led the campaign to organize the Pullman porters, which resulted in the certification of the BSCP as the exclusive bargaining agent of the Pullman porters in 1935. Randolph called it the "first victory of Negro workers over a great industrial corporation."[244] For the first half of the twentieth century, Randolph was indeed the leading voice in the battle for equality and justice.

The First March on Washington

To fully appreciate the crescendo that was the March on Washington in 1963—a coalition of religious leaders, labor organizations, civil rights groups, and other concerned citizens—one must also appreciate the twenty-year history that led to its fruition.

In 1941, Randolph and Bayard Rustin organized the March on Washington Movement. The goal of Randolph's movement in 1941 was narrowly focused: he hoped to establish protections against racial discrimination in the defense industry. Randolph issued a "Call to Negro America to March on Washington for Jobs and Equal Protection in National Defense on July 1, 1941."[245] It was believed as many as 100,000 Negroes were planning to attend the march. On June 25, President Franklin Roosevelt issued Executive Order 8802 Fair Employment Act, prohibiting racial discrimination in the defense industry. Though it was not a law, it was the first federal action taken to curtail employment discrimination in the United States. As a result of Roosevelt's order, the march was called off.

Though Roosevelt managed to avoid the march, he did not dispel the reasons for conducting a demonstration in Washington. The coalition knew that a march would likely be held in the future, so the March on Washington Movement continued to meet annually,

---

[244] A. Phllip Randolph (1889–1979), http://www.aflcio.org/About/Our-History/Key-People-in-Labor-History/Asa-Philip-Randolph-1889-1979.
[245] Ibid.

discussing Negro desires for economic equality, though this fact is often forgotten in discussions of the August 28, 1963, march.

By 1963, the challenges facing America's Negro population had reached a point that a presidential executive order could not assuage. Moreover, the momentum for the movement was fueled by a strange coalition on Kennedy's right and left that ultimately left the president unable to sidestep the issue as Roosevelt had in 1941.

Momentum for the March on Washington, 1963

The coalition organized by Randolph and Rustin in 1941 had expanded to broader economic as well as civil rights concerns by 1963. The momentum for a march on Washington was further aided in that 1963 also marked the hundredth anniversary of the Emancipation Proclamation. But there were other unlikely elements that spurred the need for a march, in particular Alabama Governor George Wallace and Birmingham's Public Safety Commissioner Bull Conner.

In the first six months of 1963, through the medium of television, the nation watched as Wallace declared his commitment to segregation in his inaugural address in January, and many were horrified as Connor orchestrated his high-powered fire hoses and police dogs to attack nonviolent civil rights protesters. Many in the nation even witnessed Wallace keep his gubernatorial campaign promise by attempting to physically block the entrance as two Negro students entered the University of Alabama. One of the distinctive characteristics of 1963 is how the issues that define the year overlap. And in some cases, overlapping issues developed into outcomes that were the antithesis of what the nation expected.

On June 26, President Kennedy gave a speech in West Berlin that America's Negro citizens, sweltering under the heat of second-class citizenship, could only hope for at the time. Politically speaking, it was much easier for Kennedy to give an impassioned address in which he aligned himself with the people of Berlin than one in which he aligned himself with the Negro residents of Birmingham, Montgomery, or

Detroit. That's not to suggest that Kennedy's civil rights address to the nation on June 11, 1963, was not worthy of praise—it was probably the best civil rights speech by any president since Abraham Lincoln—but domestic politics being what they were, any U.S. president with ambitions for a second term could not speak as enthusiastically about Negroes as Kennedy did about Berliners.

In his civil rights address, Kennedy stated, "We are confronted primarily with a moral issue. It is as old as the Scriptures and is as clear as the American Constitution."[246] The president, whose voice was evolving on civil rights issues, began 1963 reluctant to even acknowledge the centennial anniversary of the Emancipation Proclamation, but six months later he had declared the civil rights of Negroes to be a moral issue. Kennedy also announced his intention to send a civil rights bill to Congress. What Kennedy didn't mention was that the moral issue that was so clear to him, based on the constitutional principle of equal protection under the law, was not as clear to others in Washington. Though Kennedy had managed to maneuver through the domestic opposition of Cold War politics, marvelously demonstrated by his "peace speech" at American University one day before his civil rights address to the nation, he had yet to truly find the passion he would display in his Berlin speech as millions of Negroes and others used 1963 to demonstrate to the nation their unwavering belief in the promises of America with blood, sweat, and tears.

Kennedy hit the right note in his June 11 address, but the issues of civil rights were new to him, relatively speaking. Until his presidency, Kennedy did not understand civil rights issues in a visceral way. At the beginning of 1963, the issues that were important to Negroes remained a second-term consideration for Kennedy. But Birmingham changed that. Kennedy, along with the rest of the nation, witnessed in disbelief atrocities conducted in America that had been conveniently reserved for third-world nations. He had witnessed fire

---

[246] John F. Kennedy, Civil Rights Speech, 11 June 1963, http://www.americanrhetoric.com/speeches/jfkcivilrights.htm.

hoses ripping the skin of nonviolent demonstrators and police dogs set on children, and after George Wallace stood in front of the University of Alabama as a symbolic attempt to block two Negro students from entering, Kennedy knew civil rights could no longer be set aside. But successfully challenging his critics on the best approach to confront the Soviet Union would prove easier than persuading members on Capitol Hill, especially those representing Southern states, to support his civil rights legislation. This forced Kennedy to attempt to do the right thing while minimizing any unnecessary political risk. Conversely, the mission of the Civil Rights Movement, led by Martin Luther King Jr., was to demonstrate to America that its demands were fait accompli, if not since 1787 when the Constitution was created then surely by 1868 with the approval of the Fourteenth Amendment and its guarantee of due process and equal protection clauses.

Eleven days after Kennedy addressed the nation on civil rights, he met with King at the White House. The meeting would offer the first indication that from the White House's perspective, a civil rights bill would come with an asking price. King first met with Assistant Attorney General Burke Marshall. Marshall took King aside to inform him that Communists had infiltrated the Southern Christian Leadership Conference and that King would need to distance himself from them immediately. The Administration cited Jack O'Dell and Stanley Levison. King's initial reaction to Marshall's comments was indifference. When King asked Marshall for hard evidence, Marshall asserted that concerns derived from the White House should serve as proof beyond doubt. King was not convinced, which meant his next meeting would be with Attorney General Robert Kennedy.

Like Marshall, the attorney general was unsuccessful in attempts to persuade King that Communism had tainted his organization. Though he had come to discuss what the movement meant in the annals of American democracy, King was met by an administration primarily committed to defeating Communism, and secondarily, depending on where the primary conversation went, the possibility of supporting civil rights legislation. It wasn't until the attorney general proved no more effective with King that he was finally admitted to meet with the president.

Kennedy took King out to the Rose Garden for a private conversation. He informed King that conservatives were worried about the proposed March on Washington and that FBI Director J. Edgar Hoover was concerned that Communists had indeed infiltrated the SCLC, specifically identifying O'Dell and Levison. According to King, the president placed his hand on King's shoulder in the intimidating surroundings of the White House and calmly suggested that King "get rid of Levison and O'Dell. They're communists."[247] The president went on to stress the international ramifications of King having two men close to him whose allegiance was ultimately to a foreign power. The administration's demands were incongruent—they were more concerned about Communist influence in King's organization than the federal government's inability to ensure that all its citizens were granted life, liberty, and the pursuit of happiness.

But after King's conversation with Kennedy, the quid pro quo was clear: White House support in exchange for firing O'Dell and Levison. The three-prong attack of Marshall, the attorney general, and the president must have been mesmerizing and confusing to King. His private sessions were not consistent with the way the Kennedy Administration had been in public—led by the president who had recently elevated the cause of civil rights concerns as a moral issue for the nation. But he told the larger gathering, "I may lose the next election because of this."[248] He then added, "I don't care."[249]

In the larger meeting with more civil rights leaders present, Kennedy made his concerns about a March on Washington known. He told those gathered that he did not want a "big show on the Capitol."[250] He was also concerned that a large demonstration could place

---

[247] Taylor Branch, *Parting the Waters: America in the King Years 1965–1963* (New York: Simon & Schuster, 1989), 837.

[248] Ibid., 839.

[249] Ibid.

[250] Ibid., 840.

164

members of Congress in a defensive posture, forcing them to act on civil rights legislation by the force of public opinion.

Through the lens of politics, Communism, and race in 1963, Kennedy's concerns were understandable. But he also feared, after the demonstrations in Mississippi and Birmingham, that if he did not support civil rights more actively, the movement would loose faith in his administration. On June 12, the morning after his civil rights speech to the nation, Kennedy received an apologetic phone call from Majority Leader Carl Albert. There were a number of Democratic defectors who opposed a $450 million section of the president's public works bill. As Albert explained his inability to keep his fellow Democrats in tow, Kennedy replied, "Civil rights did it."[251] Albert confirmed that a number of those members were more interested in matters that dealt with racial policy, especially legislation that threatened the existing status quo.

The president probably did not possess the worldview he needed to believe it was possible that a quarter million Americans with justifiable rage—many were experiencing the bitter taste of having their constitutional rights denied—could assemble in the nation's capital peacefully. He shared with the civil leaders at the meeting that since he proposed a civil rights bill during his nationally televised address, his approval rating dropped below 50 percent. This was a strange comment because after the Cuban Missile Crisis in October 1962 and until his death, no poll reported Kennedy below 56 percent approval. But high approval ratings were not enough for the president and his administration to forget that he won the election in 1960 by a razor-thin margin.

It is understandable, from a political perspective, having already given the most progressive speech on civil rights by any American president, that Kennedy would be opposed to the prospect of a major demonstration at the nation's capital. But in lieu of a march, the only plausible option the president and others could put forth was to be

---

[251] Nick Bryant, *The Bystander: John F. Kennedy and the Struggle for Black Equality* (New York: Basic Books, 2006), 425.

patient and allow the legislative process to take its course. But this felt too much like the words echoing from the Supreme Court's *Brown v. Board of Education* ruling, when states were ordered to end segregation with "all deliberate speed." In the twelve years since *Brown* was decided, it was clear that segregationists understood "all deliberate speed" differently than the Negroes who toiled under the systematic oppression.

But King suggested that both the march and the legislative process were actually working for the same goal. He then took direct aim at one of the president's chief concerns and said that the event "may seem ill-timed." But he explained, "Frankly, I've never engaged in a direct action movement that did not seem ill-timed."[252] Harking back to the administration's concerns about Project C in Birmingham several months earlier, King said, "Some thought Birmingham was ill-timed."[253]

Shortly after King's remarks, Kennedy summarized the difference in the two perspectives. While the leaders of the Civil Rights Movement had their immediate concerns of fairness of and justice, the president's concerns included Congress, the Soviet Union, and NATO. Kennedy left the meeting to prepare for his trip to Berlin. One thing Kennedy did not stress in his closing remarks, however, was that he and his administration were still very concerned about Communist influence within the movement.

Concerns about the March on Washington and the conversations about Communist infiltration were not rooted in the immorality of Jim Crow segregationists, but rather the amoral reality of politics. There is more than enough data to conclude that by June 1963, Kennedy clearly sided with the morality of the movement, intellectually. He had realized his moral voice in the civil rights address to the nation, but a potential march on Washington was approaching faster than he was willing or able to embrace. And fears of sending civil rights legislation to Congress on behalf of the lobbying efforts of organizations

---

[252] Branch, 840.
[253] Ibid.

allegedly influenced by Communism would label any civil rights bill as a "Communist bill."

The overarching demand by the Civil Rights Movement from its inception to its end was for America to live up to the promises it made to all of its people. It was one thing for Southern segregationists to label King and others as Communist—*Communist* was a euphemism for *nigger*. But the politics such as they were in 1963 made it easier for key members of the Kennedy Administration to ask King to fire any suspected Communist within his organization in exchange for support of civil rights legislation. And their Communist concern trumped their repeated commitment to those who sought to achieve equality by nonviolent civil disobedience.

As Kennedy made his triumphant trip to Berlin, highlighted by his electrifying speech, King participated in a march in Detroit with an estimated 125,000 participants. When the crowd reached Cobo Hall, King spoke for roughly forty minutes, calling for a march to Washington to show support for a civil rights movement, and he concluded by sharing his dream with the audience. This was definitely a precursor of greater things to come.

On June 26, King notified O'Dell that he should seek employment elsewhere. The price of O'Dell's head in exchange for having the support of the Kennedy Administration was one that King was willing to make. And the news was hardly a surprise to O'Dell— he was responsible for the voter registration direct mail fundraising for the SCLC, and he bluntly stated at a June 24 meeting, "[J. Edgar] Hoover can kiss my ass!"[254] King and his associates also understood that removing O'Dell would hardly placate the administration; such demands would merely give the administration more leverage over the movement. Moreover, O'Dell was exactly right to place FBI Director J. Edgar Hoover at the nexus of the witch hunt.

Hiding behind the veneer of Communist threats, leaders within the Civil Rights Movement became victims of Hoover's racism as he used the gamut of FBI resources to infiltrate and undermine their

---

[254] Branch, 845.

activities. This would be a common practice with Hoover throughout the remainder of the decade.

It was Hoover who initiated the requests to wiretap selected individuals within the movement. Hoover's motivation may have differed from John and Robert Kennedy's—they did at least overtly share a concern for Communist infiltration within King's organization. And this dynamic became clear in behind-the-scenes conversations between Hoover and the Kennedys.

In March 1962, Hoover made it known that he was aware of the president's romantic relationship with Judith Campbell. Campbell was also the alleged mistress of mob bosses Sam Giancana and John Rosselli. Hoover's not-so-subtle implication was that if he knew of this relationship, so too could the American people. It made Kennedy vulnerable to Hoover, and it placed Robert Kennedy in the bifurcated role of Attorney General and his brother's keeper.

Politics is an amoral enterprise, driven more by pragmatism than any compelling moral reasoning. It is equally prone to good as it is to evil. As theologian Reinhold Niebuhr opined, "Man's capacity for justice makes democracy possible, but man's inclination for injustice makes democracy necessary."[255] But it is another popular Niebuhrian adage through which someone living in a twenty-first-century democratic society must view Kennedy's situation in 1963. "Democracy," according to Niebuhr, "is a method for finding proximate solutions for insoluble problems."[256] One might do well to compare Kennedy's dilemma to seek a proximate solution to the crisis that was civil rights and Lincoln's dilemma with slavery in 1962. Recall that Lincoln's position on slavery in 1860 was not the same as his position in 1862 when he issued the Emancipation Proclamation,

---

[255] Arthur Schlesinger Jr. "Forgetting Reinhold Niebuhr," *New York Times*, 18 September 2005, http://www.nytimes.com/2005/09/18/books/review/18schlesinger.html?pagewanted=all&_r=0.

[256] Daniel Rice, *Reinhold Niebuhr: An American Odyssey* (New York: State University of New York Press,1993), 230.

and it had evolved even further by 1865 when he advocated voting rights for Negro men.

In addition, Kennedy still had to work with a slim margin in Congress, with some of that body's most powerful members representing Southern states. The problem was not insoluble, at least on the surface. That, however, did not diminish Kennedy's caution to find a proximate solution. He did not want to anger a voting block that had been key to the Democrats political fortunes since 1932.

After the actions of Wallace and Connor in Birmingham, King had successfully swayed Kennedy to take a public stand that sided with the movement. But in the amoral world of politics, it is not quite that simple. The moral leadership on civil rights issues that Kennedy had promised during his 1960 campaign was not as easy to implement once in office.

In June 1963, though the president had succumbed to the moral force of the Civil Rights Movement, the influence of Hoover on Kennedy's actions as they related to civil rights is also undeniable. It wasn't so much that Hoover would leak Kennedy's relationship with Campbell, but more so that race was very much an important factor in American politics for the North as well as the South. If Hoover could link fears of Communism to race, civil rights legislation could potentially become toxic.

Six years had passed since the second Red Scare occurred. During the post–WWII period, from 1947 to 1957, the Soviet Union was the unquestioned adversary of the United States, the Cold War had frozen itself into the psyche of Americans, and there was a fear of Communist espionage—and all this was symbolized by the rise and fall of Senator Joseph McCarthy, the Korean War, and the Berlin Blockade. There may have been a diminishing of American fear by 1963, but these issues had not been completely alleviated and wouldn't be for some time. Moreover, race made many of those participating in the Civil Rights Movement susceptible to the contradictory charges of Communism.

The charges were contradictory because the Civil Rights Movement was arguably the greatest demonstrated commitment to American values of the twentieth century. In the year 1963, individuals were prepared to be beaten, arrested, and in some cases die so that the words "We the People" would finally include every U.S. citizen. But some Americans believed that any second-class citizens automatically became vulnerable to foreign power and might place their allegiance elsewhere. Those were the fears on display when President Franklin Roosevelt issued Executive Order 9066 on February 19, 1942, giving the military broad powers to violate the civil liberties of Japanese Americans, appropriating land and uprooting entire communities. The Kennedys' concerns that Communists had infiltrated the SCLC may have, to some degree, come from a concern for King as the most visible face within the movement, but it was in large measure based on political apprehension. But Hoover's goal was nothing short of destroying King, and his concern would become something bordering on obsession.

Where King might have miscalculated was the amount of time he had to make any decisions about O'Dell and Levison. On June 30, slightly more than a week after his Rose Garden meeting with Kennedy, *Birmingham News* ran the following front page headline: "King's SCLC Pays O'Dell Despite Denial."[257]

King, having already assured Robert Kennedy and Marshall that O'Dell had resigned, now had to witness the rough side of his desire to have the administration's support. The article, relying heavily on information supplied by the FBI, offered specifics that portrayed King as having a lack of character on an issue important to the American psyche. Within a month after the Rose Garden meeting, the attorney general had approved Hoover's request to conduct extensive wiretapping on key members of the SCLC, including King. It was a

---

[257] Diane McWhorter, *Carry Me Home* (New York: Simon & Schuster, 2001), 468.

policy that would remain through two presidents, and three attorney generals, until the end of King's life.[258]

But in spite of the administration's charm offensive, wiretapping, cajoling, and overt pressure, Kennedy ultimately came to the conclusion to publicly endorse the march. The Nation of Islam and their national spokesperson, Malcolm X, denounced the endorsement as proof that the leaders of the march were the pawns of the Kennedy Administration. The president's support also created added pressure for the leaders to deliver a march that aligned with the concerns discussed at the June 22 meeting more so than their own vision. This responsibility would fall largely on the shoulders of Bayard Rustin.

Onward to Washington, D.C.

Quite simply, America's iconic moment that would be known as the March on Washington would most likely not have come to fruition were it not for the Herculean efforts of Bayard Rustin. Though the annals of history would rightly laud Rustin as the behind-the-scenes architect of the March on Washington, the decision that he would be the organizer of the event was not met with universal support.

As one of the movement's most eccentric and enigmatic figures, Rustin's social justice bona fides were well established; however, there were parts of his history that could have potentially caused irreparable harm. Roy Wilkins, the Executive Secretary of the NAACP (who would eventually become the organization's executive director), expressed his concerns about Rustin's history directly to Rustin. Because Rustin was a mentee of Randolph and a disciple of Gandhi's tactics of non-violent civil disobedience, and had influenced King on such practices during the Montgomery Bus Boycott in 1955, he was all ears while Randolph cited four reasons for his opposition.

During WWII, Rustin had been a conscientious objector, but on the floor of Congress he had been labeled a "draft dodger." Second,

---

[258] FBI surveillance on King (which lasted from 1958 until 1968) would amass more than 17,000 pages.

Rustin self-identified as a Socialist, and the practice of conflating Socialism with Communism was all too common. Third was Rustin's open admission that as a student at City College of New York in the 1930s, he was a member of the Young Communist League. The potential charges that the organizer of the March on Washington was an unpatriotic draft dodger whose allegiance aligned more with the Soviet Union than the United States was more than Wilkins was prepared to entertain. And this was before he outlined his fourth concern. Wilkins very calmly said to Rustin, "And then there's the whole business of your having been arrested in California on that sex charge."[259] The sex charge that Wilkins referred to offered tangible proof of what many suspected: that Rustin was homosexual.

The rumors began a few years earlier. In 1960, to refute planned civil rights marches at the Democratic Convention in Los Angeles because they could have been a public embarrassment, flamboyant Harlem Congressman Adam Clayton Powell Jr. threatened to accuse Martin Luther King Jr. and Bayard Rustin as being lovers. King canceled the planned protests, and Rustin resigned from the SCLC. But Wilkins was not referring to allegations, rumors, or leaks; rather, this matter was on the record. On January 21, 1953, Rustin and two other men were arrested after being discovered in the back of a parked car, and they were convicted in Pasadena, California, on a morals charge, resulting in thirty days in jail.

After relating his four concerns to Rustin, Wilkins simply asked, "Now do you think we ought to bring all that into the March on Washington?"[260] Wilkins's concerns, along with Hoover's obsessions and the administration's political fears, practically made Rustin's involvement the perfect excuse for those searching for a "legitimate" reason to justify their opposition to the proposed march.

On July 2, a meeting was held at the Roosevelt Hotel in New York between Randolph, King, Wilkins, Whitney Young of the Urban League, James Farmer of the Congress for Racial Equality (CORE),

---

[259] Branch, 846.
[260] Ibid.

and John Lewis of the Student Non-Violent Coordinating Committee (SNCC). At this meeting, a compromise would be reached that would assuage Wilkins's concerns about Rustin's participation. Randolph opened the meeting by sharing that the march had been an obsession of his for more than twenty years. Moreover, he wanted Rustin to lead it. Wilkins made his opposition to Rustin known. King and Farmer acknowledged that Rustin came with potentially damaging baggage, but they admitted that his skills would be an asset. The compromise was reached when it was agreed that Randolph would lead the march but that he would be free to select his deputy, and Randolph had already made it clear at the meeting that his deputy would be Rustin.

Though it was a public loss for Wilkins, none who attended the meeting doubted the legitimacy of his concerns. Several weeks before the march, the FBI intercepted a call between King and an associate, during which they expressed concerns about Rustin's background. King essentially held the same apprehensions as Wilkins. And ultimately, it would be only be a matter of time before Rustin's Communist associations and his morals conviction would be used against the movement by those in opposition to it.

In the recorded conversation, the associate said to King, "I hope Bayard don't take a drink before the march." King responded, "Yes, and grab one little brother. Cause he will grab one when he has a drink."[261] Hoover wasted little time distributing King's "little brother" remark to his key contacts, which included members of the administration and Capitol Hill. Soon after, South Carolina Senator Strom Thurmond, whose prior speeches had included Rustin's previous Communist affiliations, rose on the Senate floor to place a copy of Rustin's 1953 morals charge booking into the Congressional Record. But such revelations did not have the political or media traction many were hoping for; few newspapers carried Thurmond's latest allegations. But despite all these external pressures, Rustin organized the march, and with minimal resources, he and a ragtag coalition comprising a few paid staff and several hundred volunteers

---

[261] Branch, 861.

pulled off the largest rally for economic and civil rights that the nation's capital had seen to date.

A giant banner hung out of the window of Rustin's Harlem headquarters on West 130th Street that read: "March on Washington for Jobs and Freedom—August 28." The banner, in the simplest terms, indicated the expansion of Randolph's original vision in 1941. By linking jobs with freedom, the cause Randolph and Young had fought for was now married with what King, Wilkins, Lewis, and Farmer were fighting for. The task that lay before Rustin was simple: he had roughly sixty days to mobilize and organize a nonviolent march in Washington with an estimated 100,000 participants.

Some of the behind-the-scenes intrigue about the preparation was playing out on the front pages of many newspapers. The attorney general decided to prosecute a group known as the "Albany Nine." William G. Anderson, one of the leaders of the Albany Movement, was accused of obstruction of justice and perjury. In April, Anderson and others had picketed a grocery store owned by a white juror who had voted to acquit "Gator" Johnson, a local sheriff who allegedly shot a Negro man in custody at point-blank range in 1961. The Negro protestors had retaliated against the juror after Johnson was acquitted.

On August 10, Deputy Attorney General Nicholas Katzenbach held a press conference to announce the decision to prosecute. "Peaceful protest and demonstrations are not forbidden or discouraged by Federal law," he said. "The charges here, however, involve retaliation against a juror for his vote in a Federal case. Such conduct must become a matter of serious Federal concern."[262]

The timing may not have been the best for the administration in one sense, but the ramifications would have been great if they had not prosecuted. The level of frustration for the systematic injustice was understandable, but retaliating against a juror for his vote was the antithesis of the nonviolent civil disobedience that had come to symbolize the movement. But the news of the prosecution came as a

---

[262] Branch, 868.

surprise, especially to the youngest member of the leadership, SNCC's John Lewis.

Already frustrated by what was viewed as the administration's tepid response to civil rights, Lewis would demonstrate the militancy of youth as he prepared his remarks for the March on Washington. His speech was so incendiary and contradictory to the overarching goals of the march that many feared it would lead to violence. In his unedited final draft, Lewis used the word "revolution" no less than eight times. He referred to the Albany Nine indictments. And with words directed at the heart of Jim Crow segregation, Lewis said, "We won't stop now. All of the forces of [James] Eastland, [Ross] Barnett [George] Wallace, and [Strom] Thurmond won't stop this revolution. The time will come when we won't confine our marching to Washington. We will march through the South, through the heart of Dixie, the way Sherman did. We shall pursue our own scorched earth policy and burn Jim Crow to the ground—nonviolently."

It is doubtful, had he used those words, that many would have heard Lewis's nonviolent addendum to his scorched-earth proclamations. When an advanced copy of Lewis's remarks was sent to Washington Archbishop Patrick O'Boyle, who was scheduled to give the invocation, O'Boyle threatened to renounce his participation. The archbishop would also serve as the attorney general's conduit, updating him on the acceptability of Lewis's words. King and Rustin also urged Lewis to soften his language. And the speech that Lewis would ultimately give was substantially edited from his original "final" draft.

As the date grew near for the march, so did the momentum. King traveled across the country raising money, but much of the fundraising came by selling buttons at 25 cents each along with collecting small individual donations. King and others appeared on national television, where they were forced to constantly assuage fears of 100,000 militant Negroes descending on Washington; no one seemed to understand how it could be anything other than violent. In spite of assurances by King and others that the march was not a display based on anger but rather America's failed promise, the potential violence it could invoke was also a concern of Rustin's. He feared that some participants might become unruly, but also, what if those attending the march were brutally attacked, as the Freedom Riders Bus had been in 1961? Rustin became obsessed with deriving every possible scenario that could become violent.

As a result of Rustin's meticulous planning, the Washington Mall area was installed with several hundred portable toilets, twenty-one temporary drinking fountains, twenty-four first-aid areas, a check-cashing facility, and 80,000 cheese sandwiches for bag lunches. Rustin also made certain that the signs were high enough to be read by individuals in a crowd. He essentially was working with a fifteen-hour window, from sunrise to sunset, during which he had to get people in and out of Washington. Rustin also forewarned that speakers would be given a physical hook if their remarks exceeded the seven-minute time limit. Furthermore, the administration developed its own set of detailed plans.

In anticipation of the march, the FBI wanted every field agent to provide the names of the black activists who planned to attend. They were also concerned about George Lincoln Rockwell, head of the American Nazi Party, who had stated his plans to hold a counter march. That alone could produce a toxic and potentially uncontrollable situation. An estimated 150 agents from the FBI's office in Washington were assigned to mingle among the crowd. Washington, D.C., police were placed on the highest state of alert. In addition to the 1,900 D.C. officers, 2,400 National Guard members were sworn in as "special officers." Using emergency powers, the Washington, D.C., commissioner placed a twenty-four-hour ban on the sale of alcohol in stores, restaurants, and bars.

Government offices were shut down, and federal workers were asked to stay at home on the day of the march. Four military bases close to Washington were active on the day of the march, and Defense Secretary Robert McNamara was given orders to take "all appropriate steps" to disband the crowd should violence commence. This meant they would begin by brandishing unloaded rifles with bayonets and conclude with tear gas if necessary.

August 28, 1963

Though the president had gone on record as supporting the march, the politics, being what they were, would not allow him to grant a request from civil right leaders for a meeting with him before the march; he also denied the appeal to send a written statement to be read to those in attendance.

But history would demonstrate that the day did not require the formal approval from the president. It was a day when an estimated 250,000 Americans—mostly black, but quite a few whites—placed their own stamp of approval on the movement. It was a day when folk singers Peter, Paul, and Mary; Joan Baez; and Bob Dylan would sing "Blowin' in the Wind." Marian Anderson and Mahalia Jackson would stir the souls of those who stood joyously in the sweltering sun to be reminded of America's promise.

It was a day when individuals who weren't certain how they would make it to Washington would not only make it, but would also be part of an assembly that included some of the world's leading entertainers. All were there based on an idea that was much larger than the sum of the collective assembly. The hope symbolized on August 28, 1963, was rivaled only by similar feelings on June 26 of that same year in Berlin, when the president said that he too was a Berliner.

And television was there to cover it, riding the crest that began in Birmingham that would ultimately make it the invaluable medium by which most Americans would get their news.

The day was granted a symbolic passing of the torch, as it was announced that William Edward Burghardt Du Bois had died in Accra, Ghana, one day prior to the march. He was the first African American to earn a doctorate at Harvard University, and he was a historian, a civil rights activist, and one of the founding members of the NAACP. As biographer David Levering Lewis wrote, "In the course of his long, turbulent career, W. E. B. Du Bois attempted virtually every possible solution to the problem of twentieth-century racism, scholarship, propaganda, integration, self-determination, human rights, cultural and economic separatism, politics, international Communism, and third-world solidarity."[263]

Though it could be argued at the time of his death that Du Bois had amassed as many detractors as supporters, there was no doubting his lifetime of commitment. That commitment, along with Lewis's observation that Du Bois had attempted every possible solution, which included his embracing Communism, led Du Bois to write upon the death of Soviet leader Joseph Stalin:

Joseph Stalin was a great man; few other men of the twentieth century approach his stature. He was simple, calm and courageous. He seldom lost his poise; pondered his problems slowly, made his decisions clearly and firmly; never yielded to ostentation nor coyly refrained from holding his rightful place with dignity. He was the son of a serf but stood calmly before the great without hesitation or nerves. But also—and this was the highest proof of his greatness—he knew the common man, felt his problems, followed his fate.[264]

The ten years that had passed was not enough time to forget the adulation that Du Bois held for Stalin. Given the existing speculation of Communist infiltration within the organizations that led the march, it would have been understandable if the death of Du Bois were only announced through mere murmurs within the crowd. Appropriately, it was Wilkins who made the announcement to the crowd, deftly stating as he led them into a moment of silence, "Now regardless of the fact that in his later years Dr. Du Bois chose another path, it is incontrovertible that at the dawn of the twentieth century, his was the voice that was calling to you to gather here today."[265]

[263] W. E. B. Dubois,
http://www.princeton.edu/~achaney/tmve/wiki100k/docs/W._E._B._Du_Bois.html
[264] W. E. B Dubois, "One Stalin," *National Guardian* (March 16, 1953).
[265] Mass Movement,

The Dream

The seminal moment of the day came when it was time for the featured speaker to step up to the microphone. It fell upon Randolph to make the introduction.

The seventy-four-year-old Randolph, who had labored for decades for the march, introduced the thirty-four-year-old King as "The moral leader of our nation."[266] It was a role that, if King had not already accepted it, would be granted to him almost by unanimous consent roughly seventeen minutes after being introduced by Randolph.

Over the decades since King's speech, it has become colloquially titled "I Have A Dream." But it is important to distinguish its two parts. The second part of the speech, in which King tells the world about his "dream," is a four-minute-and-fifty-seven-second glimpse into the prophetic tradition of the historical black church, of which King was a product. But it was the first eleven minutes and three seconds of the speech that answered the question, "Why we are here today?"

King's opening remarks captured the symbolism of speaking at the Lincoln Memorial while taking the nation back to January 1, 1963, and the centennial of the Emancipation Proclamation becoming law. He began:

Five score years ago, a great American, in whose symbolic shadow we stand today, signed the Emancipation Proclamation. This momentous decree came as a great beacon light of hope to millions of Negro slaves who had been seared in the flames of withering injustice. It came as a joyous daybreak to end the long night of their captivity.[267]

---

http://www.massmoments.org/moment.cfm?mid=122.

[266] Drew Hanson, The Dream (New York: HarperCollins, 2003), 50.

[267] Martin Luther King: "I Have a Dream,"
http://abcnews.go.com/Politics/martin-luther-kings-speech-dream-full-text/story?id=14358231#.UciSlOChDFI.

King then quickly pivoted on the axis of history in order to critique where the Negro stood in that moment: "But one hundred years later," he said, "the Negro still is not free."[268] He then used repetition both to amplify his point, by illustrating that Negroes were forced to live in America, and also to begin the process of drawing in the crowd so that by the end of the address, they became equal partners in the creation of an oratory masterpiece:

One hundred years later, the life of the Negro is still sadly crippled by the manacles of segregation and the chains of discrimination. One hundred years later, the Negro lives on a lonely island of poverty in the midst of a vast ocean of material prosperity. One hundred years later, the Negro is still languishing in the corners of American society and finds himself an exile in his own land. So we have come here today to dramatize a shameful condition.[269]

By methodically moving the crowd from a listening audience to active participants, complete with the call-and-response cadence of the black church tradition, King was now ready to fully reveal the reason they were there this day:

In a sense we have come to our nation's capital to cash a check. When the architects of our republic wrote the magnificent words of the Constitution and the Declaration of Independence, they were signing a promissory note to which every American was to fall heir. This note was a promise that all men, yes, black men as well as white men, would be guaranteed the unalienable rights of life, liberty, and the pursuit of happiness. It is obvious today that America has defaulted on this promissory note insofar as her citizens of color are concerned. Instead of honoring this sacred obligation, America has given the Negro people a bad check, a check which has come back marked "insufficient funds."[270]

But the dire reality that King offered was then countered by his unwavering belief in America:

---

[268] Ibid.
[269] Ibid.
[270] Ibid.

180

But we refuse to believe that the bank of justice is bankrupt. We refuse to believe that there are insufficient funds in the great vaults of opportunity of this nation. So we have come to cash this check—a check that will give us upon demand the riches of freedom and the security of justice.[271]

Before he announced his dream, King wove into his remarks the hope and hostility that had come to symbolize civil rights in 1963. He spoke of the "fierce urgency of now"[272] and explained that 1963 "is not an end but a beginning."[273]

He reminded the crowd, "Those who hope that the Negro needed to blow off steam and will now be content will have a rude awakening if the nation returns to business as usual."[274] He then tapered into a topic he defined as "The marvelous new militancy,"[275] which was a warning to Negroes along with an appeal to inclusivity.

King stated that the frustration of the Negro community must not lead "to a distrust of all white people, for many of our white brothers, as evidenced by their presence here today, have come to realize that their destiny is tied up with our destiny. They have come to realize that their freedom is inextricably bound to our freedom. We cannot walk alone."[276]

As with most iconic moments, King's speech was made famous due to precise planning as well as the good fortune of providence and timing. As King was concluding his prepared remarks, urging the crowd to "Go back to Mississippi, go back to Alabama,"[277] Mahalia Jackson reportedly stood nearby, urging him, "Tell them about your dream, Martin, tell them about the dream."[278] Clarence Jones, King's attorney and advisor, who helped with the prepared remarks, was also

---

[271] Ibid.
[272] Ibid.
[273] Ibid.
[274] Ibid.
[275] Ibid.
[276] Ibid.
[277] Ibid.
[278] Author's interview with Clarence B. Jones.

close by. He heard what Jackson said, and as King pushed his papers aside and grabbed the podium, he remarked, "These people don't know it, but they are about to go to church."[279]

For many in attendance and those watching on television, including the president, this would be the first time they heard King speak beyond a sound bite. Kennedy was reportedly riveted by Kings remarks. He turned to Lee White, an advisor on civil rights, and said, "He's good. He's damned good!"[280]

On the heels of a successful event that did not warrant the preemptive caution that the government exhibited, Kennedy warmly greeted the civil rights leadership. He greeted King particularly with a warm smile that showed his respect for King's great oratory.

Unlike Lincoln's Gettysburg Address—or for that matter, Kennedy's address at American University—it would not require historians to revisit King's speech sometime later to be aware of its greatness. The following day, James Reston of the *New York Times* wrote that until King appeared, "the pilgrimage was merely a great spectacle."[281] He added, "Dr. King touched all the themes of the day, only better than anybody else. He was full of symbolism of Lincoln and Gandhi and the cadence of the Bible. He was both militant and sad, and he sent the crowd away feeling the long journey had been worthwhile."[282]

As "I Have a Dream" continues into the present day to serve as the statement that is simultaneously used and misused to characterize the King legacy, many maintain that the speech was not King's best work of 1963. That honor is given to his Letter from Birmingham Jail. But the keynote address, which was originally called "A Canceled Check," was his most important work. The importance was based on

[279] Ibid.

[280] Bryant, 10.

[281] James Reston, "I Have a Dream: Peroration by Dr. King Sums Up a Day the Capital Will Remember," *New York Times*, 29 August 1963.

[282] Ibid.

the fact that his stage was not the Lincoln Memorial but the ideals of America, and television was there to capture the moment.

Naturally, most remember King and his unforgettable words. But it was King's attorney and advisor Clarence B. Jones, who assisted with the prepared remarks that day, who some fifty years later, in his book *Behind the Dream*, may have developed the most eloquent statement that captured the speech's importance. Jones wrote:

A quarter of a million people, human beings who generally had spent their lives treated as something less, stood shoulder to shoulder across that vast lawn, their hearts beating as one. Hope on the line. When hope was an increasingly scarce resource. There is no dearth of prose describing the mass of humanity that made its way to the feet of the Great Emancipator that day; no metaphor that has slipped through the cracks waiting to be discovered, dusted off, and injected into the discourse a half century on. The March on Washington has been compared to a tsunami, a shockwave, a wall, a living monument, a human mosaic, an outright miracle.[283]

September 15, 1963

But eighteen days after the March on Washington that Jones had accurately described as "hope on the line," there would be hostility— perhaps more accurately, hatred—that would brutally serve notice to the nation that the euphoria felt at the Lincoln Memorial was not shared universally.

In the aftermath of Project C, the images of Bull Connor's police dogs and high-powered fire hoses still dominated the thoughts of many when thinking of Birmingham. What was clear was that the eloquence of King's prophetic dream, when he stated, "One day right there in Alabama, little black boys and black girls will be able to join hands

---

[283] Clarence B. Jones and Stuart Connelly, *Behind the Dream: The Making of a Speech that Transformed a Nation* (United Kingdom: Palgrave MacMillan, 2011), xiv.

with little white boys and white girls as sisters and brothers,"[284] was still a fantasy and could not yet be realistically implemented across the Alabama state line.

There was a federal court order in Birmingham to admit five Negro students into three public schools. On September 9, when the schools were scheduled to open, Wallace, under the shroud that he was concerned about an increase in violence, sent the National Guard to block the students from entering. The next day, Kennedy federalized the National Guard, ordering them to withdraw, allowing the students to enter. But the climate of racial tension remained.

Sunday, September 15, was Youth Day at the Sixteenth Street Baptist Church. Founded in 1873, it was the first organized black Baptist church in Birmingham. It also served as the epicenter for the Project C campaign. At approximately 10:22 AM, nineteen sticks of dynamite exploded just outside the basement, killing four girls, Addie Mae Collins, Carole Robertson, Cynthia Wesley, and Denise McNair. Twenty-two others were injured. The explosion reportedly brought hundreds of angry Negroes pouring into the streets. Some attacked the police with stones, which resulted in more death.

Johnny Robinson, a sixteen-year-old Negro, was shot in the back and killed by a policeman with a shotgun that afternoon. Officers said the victim was among a group that had hurled stones at white youths driving through the area in cars flying Confederate battle flags. Virgil Wade, a thirteen-year-old Negro, was also shot and killed just outside Birmingham while riding a bicycle. The Jefferson County sheriff's office indicated that Wade's death also was related to the bombing earlier that day.

The Sixteenth Street Baptist Church in Birmingham had been used as a central meeting place for the Birmingham campaign in the spring. It was the location where those willing to stand on the front lines of nonviolent civil disobedience were trained, including the members of the Children's Crusade. The campaign to register Negroes to vote in Birmingham was also initiated there. In this context, perhaps

---

[284] See "I Have a Dream"

a modicum of public opinion might have turned had the bombing occurred on any other day. But there were no civil rights meetings planned, no nonviolent civil disobedience trainings scheduled, and no voter registrations being held on the morning of September 15. It was the Sabbath. And the victims of the barbarity were not outside agitators, but four local girls preparing for worship service. It was the third bombing that had occurred in eleven days, and it was unquestionably the worst in terms of the symbolic nature and the innocence of the victims.

The *New York Times* queried in an editorial, "How long can such barbaric abuses go on without a mass uprising by men and women who see the forces of law and order only a shield for their bloodstained oppressors?" [285] Other newspapers, nationally and internationally, offered similar sentiments.

The bombing of the Sixteenth Street Baptist Church stood in stark contrast to King envisioning on the Washington Mall, less than three weeks earlier, the time when his "Four little children would one day live in a nation where they would not be judged by the color of their skin but by the content of their character."[286]

The Justice Department immediately sent Burke Marshall to Birmingham. The president issued a statement on September 16, read by Press Secretary Pierre Salinger, where he laid the blame on Wallace for instigating the violent climate in Birmingham. "It is regrettable that public disparagement of law and order has encouraged violence, which has fallen on the innocent," he said.[287]

Wallace, on behalf of the city, offered a $5,000 reward for the arrest and conviction of the perpetrators. A tepid response indeed, given there had been approximately fifty bombings of Negro-owned property in Birmingham since WWII and not one had resulted in a conviction. King sent Wallace a telegram, stating, "Your irresponsible

---

[285] Bryant, 449.

[286] See "I Have a Dream."

[287] John F. Kennedy, American Presidency Project, http://www.presidency.ucsb.edu/ws/?pid=9410.

and misguided actions have created in Birmingham and Alabama the atmosphere that has induced continued violence and now murder."[288]

United Press International reported that police patrols, augmented by three hundred State troopers sent into Birmingham by Wallace, quickly broke up all protests in the aftermath of the bombing. Wallace also ordered five hundred National Guardsmen to stand by at Birmingham armories.

That evening, King arrived in Birmingham and immediately joined a conference with Reverend Fred Shuttlesworth about what actions should be taken. The City Council held an emergency meeting to discuss safety measures for the city, but they rejected proposals for a curfew.

Dozens of persons were injured when the bomb went off in the church, which held four hundred Negroes at the time, including eighty children. This was unquestionably one of the worst the worst crimes committed during the civil rights era. Innocent children preparing for Sunday morning worship became the public symbols of the hatred within the Jim Crow South. Wallace had received what he desired, but not in the manner he would have preferred. Eight months after his "segregation forever" inaugural address, and three months after he stood in the doorway to symbolically block two Negroes from entering the University of Alabama, he was labeled the governor of the state where such a heinous and unfathomable crime could occur. The church bombing made Alabama the unofficial citadel of segregation. The September 27 edition of *Time* magazine featured Wallace on its cover, and behind him was the stained glass window of the Sixteenth Street Baptist Church, with the face of Jesus blown out as a result of the bombing.

Three days after the bombing and exactly three weeks since the March on Washington, King eulogized three of the four young girls.

---

[288] "Six Dead After Church Bombing," United Press International, 16 September 1963,
http://www.washingtonpost.com/wp-srv/national/longterm/churches/archives1.htm.

The Robertson family maintained their desire to grieve privately, resisting the temptations to participate in a mass funeral.

"These children—unoffending, innocent, and beautiful—were the victims of one of the most vicious and tragic crimes ever perpetrated against humanity,"[289] King said during the eulogy. "Yet they died nobly. They are the martyred heroines of a holy crusade for freedom and human dignity."[290] He went on to issue a blanket challenge:

And so this afternoon in a real sense they have something to say to each of us in their death. They have something to say to every minister of the gospel who has remained silent behind the safe security of stained-glass windows. They have something to say to every politician who has fed his constituents with the stale bread of hatred and the spoiled meat of racism. They have something to say to a federal government that has compromised with the undemocratic practices of southern Dixiecrats and the blatant hypocrisy of right-wing northern Republicans. They have something to say to every Negro who has passively accepted the evil system of segregation and who has stood on the sidelines in a mighty struggle for justice. They say to each of us, black and white alike, that we must substitute courage for caution. They say to us that we must be concerned not merely about who murdered them, but about the system, the way of life, the philosophy which produced the murderers. Their death says to us that we must work passionately and unrelentingly for the realization of the American dream.[291]

In three weeks, America went from being electrified by King on the steps of the Lincoln Memorial to being forced to make sense of a level of hostility so blind that it could not see the humanity of children. This cowardly act, following the successful March on Washington, brought worldwide attention and condemnation. It served as a black

---

[289] "Eulogy for Martyred Children,"18 September 1963, http://mlk-kpp01.stanford.edu/index.php/encyclopedia/documentsentry/doc_eulogy_for_the_m artyred_children.

[290] Ibid.

[291] Ibid.

eye for the Kennedy Administration, which looked hypocritical, no matter how good their intentions, speaking of freedom and democracy abroad while such heinous crimes were conducted at home. Within the span of three weeks, America was granted a front-row seat to the hope and hostility that symbolized the year. But as brutal and unfathomable as the Sixteenth Street Bombing may have been, America and the world had not yet experienced the most shocking act of 1963.

Chapter Seven:

"In the Final Analysis, It's Their War"

On June 11, 1963, Americans awoke to the ghastly image of Thich Quang Duc, a seventy-three-year-old Buddhist monk, as he immolated himself while sitting calmly in the lotus position in a busy intersection in Saigon. The photo conveyed many messages, but it was perhaps the most compelling evidence to date that the United States had invaded a country that it knew very little about. Duc's protest was the emergence of something that imperial politicians dread, but as history shows, they often remain stuck despite incidents like these, arrogantly believing in their own abilities rather than ever trying to understand the will of the indigenous people of the invaded country. The photos that appeared in the *New York Times* and elsewhere left Americans, including President Kennedy, in a state of bewilderment. This much-publicized act of defiance placed Vietnam in the public discourse in ways that it had not been before.

Before the Gulf of Tonkin Resolution, the My Lai Massacre, or the Tet Offensive became part of the Vietnam lexicon, there was this simple act, and it was beyond anything most Americans could comprehend. It sent the first official signal that the U.S.-backed individual in the Vietnam conflict, South Vietnamese President Ngo Dinh Diem, might be ill-fated.

Vietnam was the most unpopular and most controversial U.S. war of the twentieth century. When the last troops left Vietnam in 1975, nearly 60,000 Americans had made the ultimate sacrifice, along with an estimated 2 million Vietnamese. How did the conflict incur so many deaths when Defense Secretary Robert McNamara knew by 1965 that the war was not winnable militarily?[292] For those who participated directly, those who somehow managed to avoid service, and those who engaged in public protests, Vietnam continues to be a dark and somewhat unresolved chapter of American history, as the opinion of the war in the twenty-first century is that it was a moral failure, a necessary war, and everything in between those two extremes.

The lion's share of blame for what Vietnam became lies at the feet of President Lyndon Johnson. There is no doubt Johnson escalated the effort that led to an untenable policy position. In 1963, at the end of the Kennedy Administration, there were roughly 16,000 troops in Vietnam, and by the end of the Johnson Administration, in 1968, there were 537,000 troops.

The opposition to Vietnam seemingly grew in proportion to Johnson's systematic escalation of the conflict, and the chants of "Hey, hey, LBJ, how many kids you kill today?" grew louder, contributing greatly to Johnson becoming the permanent historical face of the Vietnam disaster. While it is understandable that this became Johnson's fate, events in 1963 may have placed him in a box impossible to escape. This was of course the year the led to the title of David Halberstam's 1965 book, *The Making of a Quagmire*.

With each passing day after the Buddhist monk's public self-immolation, it became clearer to the policymakers of the Kennedy Administration that they had backed themselves into a dilemma. The U.S.-backed anti-Communist South Vietnam remained in the throes of

---

[292] Robert McNamara, interview by Jim Lehrer, MacNeil and Lehrer Newshour, "Robert McNamara's War Reflections," April 17, 1995.

a civil war against the Communist guerrillas, who were backed by North Vietnam. But U.S. policy, designed by Cold War fears and blindly supporting whoever claimed anti-Communist bona fides, could no longer be ignored when it came to Diem.

Between 1961 and 1963, the Kennedy Administration consistently increased its levels of military aid in Saigon. In 1962, the CIA described Vietnam as a "slowly escalating stalemate." But Vietnam did not have Kennedy's primary focus during these years, not with the Bay of Pigs, the Cuban Missile Crisis, the Berlin Wall, and civil rights dominating the White House's attention. Kennedy was also more concerned about Soviet Premiere Nikita Khrushchev than North Vietnam leader Ho Chi Minh, but members of the press corps began identifying the inconsistencies with the president's statements about Vietnam and the realities of the policy. In addition to Halberstam at the *New York Times*, United Press International's Neil Sheehan and Peter Arnett of the Associated Press served vital roles by lifting the veil from the narrative preferred by the Kennedy Administration—that Vietnam was a minor irritant that was under control with victory on the horizon—revealing that the conflict was potentially malignant and that the outcome was unknown.

The Formation of Disaster

There are so many places one could begin to chronicle the chain of events that became known as the Vietnam conflict. July 1954 certainly marks a key moment in America's Vietnam saga.

Beginning on April 26 to July 20, foreign ministers representing the Soviet Union, Britain, France, and the United States met in Geneva seeking a peaceful solution to the conflicts in Korea as well as the Indochina war between France and the Vietminh. These negotiations included the following agreements:

Vietnam would be divided. Ho Chi Minh would rule North Vietnam and Diem would rule South Vietnam. France would withdraw its troops from North Vietnam, the Vietminh would withdraw from

South Vietnam, the Vietnamese could freely choose to live in the North or South, and a general election for the whole of Vietnam would be held before July 1956, under the supervision of an international commission.

Ho Chi Minh agreed to these conditions because he believed the election would produce Communist leadership. This was a position shared by then President Dwight Eisenhower. The president would write to his brother Edgar, "I have never talked or corresponded with a person knowledgeable in Indochinese affairs who did not agree that had elections been held at the time of the fighting, possibly 80 per cent of the population would have voted for the Communist Ho Chi Minh."[293] The prospect of a free election resulting in transforming a united Vietnam into a Communist-led country dampened the possibility of elections in Vietnam and strengthened U.S. support of Diem.

Diem was born in the Huế province of Vietnam in 1901. His ancestors reportedly converted to Catholicism in the seventeenth century, so Diem was educated in French Catholic schools. He contemplated following his older brother Ngo Dinh Thuc, who would become Vietnam's most popular bishop, by becoming a priest. Instead Diem studied at the School of Public Administration and Law in Hanoi. After he graduated, he was trained as an administrator for the French authorities in Vietnam. At the age of twenty-five he became a provincial governor. During the French–Indochina War, Diem received permission to leave Vietnam, and he traveled to Rome for the Holy Year celebrations at the Vatican in 1950.

Once outside Vietnam, Diem's travels took him to Japan, where he met Wesley Fishel, an American academic who supported anti-Communist and anti-colonial polices. Fishel, who was reportedly impressed with Diem, proved instrumental in connecting him to individuals in the United States who would be supportive of an anti-colonial and anti-Communist leader in Vietnam. The importance that

---

[293] "The American Involvement in Vietnam,"
http://rationalrevolution.net/war/american_involvement_in_vietnam.htm.

timing played in these affairs cannot be overlooked. This saga occurred in the midst of the Korean War and the rise of Senator Joseph McCarthy and McCarthyism.

Through the contacts made in the United States, Acting Secretary of State James Webb held a reception for Diem at the State Department. It was reported that Diem was unimpressive, as his brother Thuc, who did the majority of the talking during the reception, which temporarily quelled further meetings with potentially supportive audiences. But Diem also met Cardinal Francis Spellman, a politically powerful priest, who proved to be a valuable ally.

Spellman had studied with Thuc in Rome, and he managed to get Diem an audience with Pope Pius XII. Afterward, Diem lobbied across Europe before returning to the United States. In 1951, Diem met with Secretary of State Dean Acheson, and he lived as Spellman's guest in Lakewood Township, New Jersey. Over the next three years, with Spellman's assistance, Diem began to amass strong support among U.S. right-wing Catholic circles, and Senator McCarthy became one of his backers. Diem was on the college lecture circuit, and in his lectures he advocated that only a government that was anti-Communist and anti-colonial, sponsored by the United States, could save Vietnam.

Diem was also appointed as a consultant to Michigan State University's Government Research Bureau, where Fishel was affiliated, to administer U.S.-sponsored programs to assist Cold War allies. In 1953, along with Fishel, Diem would lay the groundwork for what would eventually be called the Michigan State University Vietnam Advisory Group.

The Michigan State University Vietnam Advisory Group was a nation-building effort that would provide technical assistance to South Vietnam. From 1955 to 1962, under contract to the International Cooperation Administration in Washington and the Vietnamese government in Saigon, the group of Michigan State University faculty and staff advised and trained Vietnamese personnel in the disciplines of public administration, police administration, and economics. It even participated in the writing of the country's new constitution. And it worked autonomously from most U.S. government agencies.

As the French's war efforts declined, Diem's popularity rose in America. Dien Bien Phu fell in 1954, which essentially ended French involvement in Indochina. The Dien Bien Phu victory, which was led by Ho Chi Minh, was significant because it was a non-European, anti-colonial movement that began as a guerilla effort, and it defeated its colonial occupiers. This only served to heighten Communist fears in the United States. With the support of the Eisenhower Administration and the opposition of the French (who viewed Diem as incompetent), Diem was named Prime Minister of South Vietnam.

Aided by a CIA propaganda campaign and the Navy's Operation Passage to Freedom, roughly one million Vietnamese refugees, mostly Catholic, fled to the South. Signs were posted in North Vietnam that read, "Christ has gone South," and, "The Virgin Mary had departed from the North." These not-so subtle attempts to label Ho Chi Minh as anti-Catholic were effective, but they were also meant to solidify Vietnam as the election approached. But South Vietnam becoming solidified required a preliminary step.

Impact of Potsdam

Though the peace accords in Geneva named Diem Prime Minister, Bao Dai was still Head of State of South Vietnam. Like Diem, Dai was also born in the in Huế province in 1913. After being educated in France, Dai succeed his father as emperor in November 1925. He reigned under the Regency of Ton-Thai Han until he came of age in September 1932.

In September 1940, the Japanese army invaded Indochina. With Paris already occupied by the Germans, the French quickly surrendered to Japan. After Japan surrendered to the allies in August 1945, the Viet Minh, under Ho Chi Minh, had set their sights on taking control of Vietnam. The following month, the Vietminh formed the Democratic Republic of Vietnam. But U.S. President Harry Truman,

British Prime Minister Winston Churchill, and Soviet Union General Secretary Joseph Stalin had independently decided Vietnam's post-war future at Potsdam.

At Potsdam, these leaders agreed that Vietnam would be divided into two, the northern half under the control of the Chinese and the southern half under the British. And on September 22, the British released 1,400 French soldiers from former Japanese internment camps, along with an estimated 20,000 French citizens living there, commenced riots, killing Viet Minh suspects and ordinary Vietnamese civilians in Saigon. The Viet Minh responded by calling a national strike and organized a guerrilla campaign against the French. By October, 35,000 French soldiers arrived in South Vietnam to restore French rule. The Viet Minh immediately began a guerrilla campaign while the French began expelling the Viet Minh from Saigon.

In what would be the underpinnings of the Indochina war, Dai was largely absent. He went into exile in Hong Kong in March 1946. He signed an accord that recognized Vietnamese national unity within the French Union. He returned to Vietnam in June 1948. The following year the French installed him as a puppet Head of State.

These were the choices before the South Vietnamese on Election Day in 1955: Dai the puppet leader of the French, or Diem the quasi puppet leader of the United States. But when it came time to vote, those supportive of Dai were subjected to violence, and their ballots were thrown away. Diem claimed he received 98.2 percent of the vote, though he was warned by American advisors to lower the results of his victory. Diem refused to comply, and his overwhelming victory, with the aid of dubious methods, ultimately served to undermine his authority.

When Diem was reminded by the North Vietnamese that the general election for the whole of Vietnam was scheduled for July 1956, he balked. He began arresting his opponents. Communists and Socialists were the primary targets, but others who might be in opposition to the Diem regime were also included, such as journalists, members of trade unions, and leaders of religious groups. Primarily non-Catholics were imprisoned, but so were children who were found writing anti-Diem messages on city walls. At this point, Diem's political opponents began to consider alternative methods of obtaining their goals, which included violence in order to convince him to agree to the terms of the 1954 Geneva Conference.

Under the pretense of excessive communist influence, Diem canceled the election to unify Vietnam. In 1957, following the cancelled elections, there was an increase in the numbers of individuals who opted for guerilla warfare against the South Vietnamese Army. The first attempt made on Diem's life occurred on February 22, 1957. Ha Minh Tri, a South Vietnamese Communist, attempted to assassinate Diem at an economic fair in Ban Me Thuot. Tri was able to fire at close range but missed, hitting the Secretary of Agrarian Reform instead. Tri was overpowered before he could get off another shot, and Diem was unharmed.

But in the months following Diem's election victory over Dai, U.S. policy was clearly on the side of Diem. Walter S. Robertson, the Assistant Secretary of State for Far Eastern Affairs, delivered an address to the American Friends of Vietnam stating the following:

And finally Vietnam today, in mid-1956, is progressing rapidly to the establishment of democratic institutions by elective processes, its people resuming peaceful pursuits; its army growing in effectiveness, sense of mission, and morale; the puppet Vietnamese politicians discredited; the refugees well on the way to permanent resettlement; the countryside generally orderly and calm; the predatory sects eliminated and their venal leaders exiled or destroyed. Perhaps no more eloquent testimony to the new state of affairs in Vietnam could be cited than the voice of the people themselves as expressed in their free election of last March. At that time the last possible question as to the feeling of the people was erased by an overwhelming majority for President Diem's leadership. The fact that the Vietminh was unable to carry out its open threats to sabotage these elections is impressive evidence of the stability and prestige of the government. The United States is proud to be on the side of the effort of the Vietnamese people

196

under President Diem to establish freedom, peace, and the good life. The United States wishes to continue to assist and to be a loyal and trusted friend of Vietnam.[294]

Robertson's words served as an accurate reflection of U.S. policy in 1956—which would continue until 1963—but he also ignored the blatant gulf between his glowing commendation of Diem and the realities on the ground.

One word drove the direction of U.S. foreign policy more than any other word during this Cold War period: anti-Communist. Diem's commitment to anti-Communism blinded the U.S. government to other atrocities that would ensue, just as the United States supported proclaimed anti-Communist Francois Duvalier in Haiti, Augusto Pinochet in Chile, and Anastasio Somoza Debayle in Nicaragua while ignoring obvious human-rights atrocities in those regions.

Diem's leadership was composed of two fundamental problems that would ultimately serve to be his undoing. Firstly, he ran South Vietnam with a religious bias. As a devout Catholic, he overtly mistreated the overwhelming majority of Buddhists in Vietnam, revealing the disgraceful underbelly that would become the hallmark of the Diem regime. Catholicism had become synonymous with Vietnam's former occupiers—the French. Roman Catholics made up slightly over 10 percent of the population in South Vietnam, but under Diem, they held a privileged position. The Catholic Church was the largest landowner in the country, and most of the country's administrative officials who helped with French communications were Catholic. Moreover, tensions continued to grow because Diem was unwilling to repeal several anti-Buddhist laws that had been instituted by the French, specifically the "private" status that was imposed on

[294] "United States Policy with Respect to Vietnam," address by the Assistant Secretary of State for Far Eastern Affairs, Walter S. Robertson, Washington, 1 June 1956. Delivered to the American Friends of Vietnam at the Willard Hotel in Washington, D.C., https://www.mtholyoke.edu/acad/intrel/willard.htm.

Buddhism, which meant that any public Buddhist activities required official government permission. Diem also instituted many pro-Catholic policies that upset South Vietnam's Buddhist population. For example, Catholics were often promoted in public service and military positions. It was reported that a number of Buddhist military officers converted to Catholicism in hopes of enhancing their careers. Likewise, though firearms were distributed so that villages could defend themselves from the Vietcong, they were primarily given to Catholics. There were also Catholic priests in charge of private armies, which fostered looting and the destruction of Buddhist pagodas. When it occurred, Buddhist conversion to Catholicism was based more on self-preservation than an act of faith.

Diem oversaw a two-tiered society in South Vietnam: one for Catholics and another for Buddhists—separate and unequal. His land reforms placed more property in Catholic control than in Buddhist control. U.S. aid was disproportionately directed to Catholic villages. Moreover, Catholics were essentially exempt from the mandatory labor that the government obliged all citizens to perform. In many ways, the Diem regime was an eight-year extension to the previous sixty-seven years of French occupation.

The Buddhists were the majority, yet they were second-class citizens in a land where they had once been dominant. Catholics were better educated, wealthier, and better trained. Assuming South Vietnam was to follow a Western model more so than a Communist one, these factors led to the creation of a privileged class.

Though a fledgling nation might place an overreliance on its wealthiest and most educated population, in South Vietnam, the wealthy and educated were vivid reminders of the French who had just left and the Americans who were now supporting the oppression. In addition, the devoutly Catholic president and his two Catholic brothers, one the leader of the intimidation tactics and the other a high-profile Catholic archbishop, were committed to combining their religious and political understanding into a single writ for all of Vietnam to follow—Catholic and non-Catholic alike.

Externally, Vietnam was viewed through the lens of the Cold War's domino theory, but the internal tension was due to religion, which has assumed the same role in many conflicts throughout human history. It was the religious tension that galvanized support, albeit for different reasons, against Diem and brought global condemnation against his regime—and the United States for backing him.

The strain on Buddhist–Catholic relations became apparent soon after the peace agreements in Geneva divided the country between North and South. Several thousand Catholic refugees, fearing reprisal from the Communist in the North, found a friend in Diem. Already predisposed to be suspicious of non-Catholic inhabitants of South Vietnam, Diem reciprocated the trust of the small minority of Catholics by placing them in positions of influence throughout the country. Priests served as mediators in Diem's land development reforms, which disproportionately benefited Catholics. As land development centers forced the uprooting of entire Buddhist villages in some cases, Catholic villages went undisturbed. Moreover, there were reports that these practices against Buddhists turned violent.

Diem's second fundamental problem was his commitment to nepotism. Ngo Dinh Nhu, Diem's brother, was the most trusted and most powerful member of his cabinet, though he did not hold any official position. Nhu was leader of the primary pro-Diem Can Lao political party, in which he orchestrated Diem's intimidation tactics. An admirer of Adolph Hitler, Nhu reportedly based many of his torture tactics on Nazi practices. Diem's oldest brother, Thuc, was the Archbishop of Huế. Moreover, Thuc, Nhu, and Madame Ngo Dinh Nhu, Nhu's wife, lived with Diem in the Presidential Palace. Because Diem never married, Madam Nhu was seen as South Vietnam's titular First Lady.

For eight years, the U.S.-backed regime in South Vietnam was at war against Ho Chi Minh in North Vietnam, but also, through divisive pro-Catholic policies, South Vietnam had an antagonistic and oppressive relationship internally with much of the South Vietnamese population.

Diem is best understood in the dominating light of Cold War fears. His proclamations of being an anti-Communist blinded the United States to other obvious shortcomings.

During this time period, Diem was not the only leader backed by the United States that turned out to be a mistake. In 1953, a CIA-backed coup helped to replace an Iranian-elected government with the Shah of Iran. Though it would take much longer for the gravity of these mistakes in policy to materialize than the Vietnam fiasco did, in 1953, the United States had direct access to Iranian oil reserves, and they were able to keep the Soviet Union out. But events beginning in May 1963 forced the reluctant Kennedy Administration to become irretrievably weary of Diem's leadership.

The events leading up to May 1963, if taken in isolation, may be viewed as minor, but collectively they formed a perfect storm that led to the Buddhists' revolt and Diem's demise. The revolt ironically originated in Diem's hometown of Hué. Several days before the revolt, Diem's brother Thuc was honored for his twenty-fifth anniversary as bishop. Diem attended the festivities while government as well as Vatican flags flew from churches. The latter was a violation of government policy—only the South Vietnam flag was allowed to fly in public.

A few days later was the commemoration of Buddha's 2,587[th] birthday. The Buddhists of Hué wanted to fly their Buddhist flags, but they were reminded of the ordinance. The government also denied the request by a Buddhist leader to speak on the local radio. This oppression caused thousands of militant Buddhists to engage in mass protests, and the government was called in to suppress the demonstrations. In the aftermath, nine people were killed.

After hastily burying the victims without performing autopsies, the government initially reported that the Vietcong was responsible for the killings, claiming one of its agents had hurled a grenade into the crowd. But numerous eyewitness reports, including some by Americans, contradicted the government's version of the story and sided with the Buddhist's recollections of the events. Charley Mohr,

200

Time magazine's Hong Kong Bureau Chief, succinctly captured the essence of the problem when he suggested to Halberstam, "Diem can't admit he's wrong so the government will pretend it didn't happen, and make a hell of a lot of people angry."[295]

Whether intentional or unintentional, a sort of tone-deafness was part of Diem's leadership style. Underlings unwilling or unable to tell Diem a fact that might challenge his preconceived notions greatly fostered this process. Even after the Minister of Interior investigated the deaths of the nine Buddhists during the Huế incident and found the government's version of the story to be incorrect, he reportedly returned to Saigon, and, fearful of Diem, reassured the president that the Vietcong were indeed the malefactors. Blinded by his reliance on nepotism, Diem transformed the presidential palace into a self-contained Shangri-La, allowing him to see South Vietnam as a mystical harmonious valley, removed from the ensuing chaos. Disconnected from reality, Diem enjoyed the false luxury to think and believe whatever he wanted. But Diem's government had unwittingly hit a hornet's nest in Huế.

Unlike Buddhists in other parts of the country, Buddhists in Huế were organized and militant. Huế was also at the heart of Buddhist thought in the country. These Buddhists were the first to publicly demonstrate on a large scale the anti-government feelings that would soon be exemplified by a majority of the country.

The Huế massacre instigated demonstrations throughout South Vietnam. Buddhist delegations in Saigon demanded the removal of restrictions on their religion and the discriminatory laws imposed against them. But the government arrested many of these demonstrators. The tension then escalated, and during a Buddhist protest in Huế, the government responded by dispersing troops and using tear gas. Sixty-seven people were taken to hospital with chemical burns.

---

[295] David Halberstam, *The Making of a Quagmire* (New York: McGraw Hill, 1965), 118.

In spite of protest by the Kennedy Administration and Diem's supposed willingness to heed those concerns, discriminations against the Buddhists continued. There was an increase of Buddhist arrest. Pagodas were shut down and in some cases attacked. The police also engaged in torture against the Buddhists. And as this religious chaos flourished in the summer of 1963 in South Vietnam, South Vietnamese Catholics and Buddhists fought in solidarity against the Communist-led North Vietnamese.

In July, Kennedy appointed his former Massachusetts nemesis and the 1960 Republican nominee for Vice President, Henry Cabot Lodge, as Ambassador to South Vietnam. Speculation as to why Kennedy selected Lodge ranges from Lodge's well-documented public service to the cynical viewpoint that if Vietnam went bad, there would be a Republican in a key position to assume a portion of the blame.

That said, the possibility of Vietnam going bad was not lost on Kennedy. In late 1962, he sent Senate Majority Leader Mike Mansfield to Vietnam to assess the situation. When Mansfield returned, he offered a sobering report, concluding that the resources committed by the United States ($2 billion in seven years) had changed very little in the way of progress. Laying fault with Diem regime as well as U.S. policy, Mansfield recommended a clear assessment of U.S. interest, stating, "It's their country, their future that's at stake, not ours. To ignore that reality will not only be immensely costly in terms of American lives and resources, but it may also draw us inexorably into some variation of the unenviable position in Vietnam that was formerly occupied by the French."[296]

The first public statement that U.S. support was shifting against Diem came in March 1963, when Mansfield submitted his report to the Senate Foreign Relations Committee. The report portrayed Diem as isolated, and it called for him to introduce democratic reforms.

---

[296] Stanley Karnow, *Vietnam: A History* (New York: Penguin Books, 1997), 285.

Before Lodge arrived, Kennedy sent Diem a personal message of confidence by way of Ambassador Nolting. But this effort changed nothing. If anything, it merely intensified the brutality. Under the guise of Communist influence among the Buddhists, the secret police force became more brutal as they instituted policies that could be described in no other terms than outright religious persecution.

On September 2, Kennedy sat down with CBS News Anchor Walter Cronkite at the president's family compound in Hyannis Port, Massachusetts. When the subject of Vietnam came up, Kennedy provided a rather free-flowing and somewhat contradictory response that has offered historians on both sides of the Vietnam ledger fodder for their position:

Cronkite: The only hot war we've got running at the moment is of course the one in Vietnam . . . What can we do in this situation, which seems to parallel other famous debacles dealing with unpopular governments of the past?

Kennedy: Well in the first place we ought to realize Vietnam has been at war for twenty-five years . . . The war is still going, in many ways its going better, but that doesn't mean, however, the events of the last two months aren't very ominous. I don't think that unless a greater effort is made by the government to win popular support the war can be won out there. In the final analysis, it's their war. They are the one's who have to win it or lose it. We can help them, we can give them equipment, we can send our men out there as advisors, but they have to win it—the people of Vietnam against the Communists. We're prepared to assist them, but I don't think the war can be won unless the people support the effort. In my opinion, in the last two months, the government has gotten out of touch with the people. The repressions against the Buddhists, we felt were very unwise. All we can do is to make it very clear we don't think this is the way to win. It's my hope this would become increasingly obvious to the government that they would take steps to try to bring back popular support for this very essential struggle. But these people who say we ought to withdraw from Vietnam are wholly wrong. Because if we withdrew from Vietnam the Communists would control Vietnam, pretty soon Thailand, Cambodia, Laos, Malaysia would go and all of Southeast Asia would be under the control of the Communists and the domination of Chinese. And India, Burma would be the next targets. So I think we should stay, we should make it clear, as Ambassador Lodge is now making it clear, that while we want to help, we don't see successful end to this war unless the people support it. And the people will not support the effort if their government continues to follow the policies of the past two months.[297]

In this portion of Kennedy's response lies proof of his belief in the domino theory, an argument for not getting bogged down in Vietnam, as well as a commitment to stay. Kennedy is critical of Diem, but he cites the problem as being one of two months rather than approaching nearly nine years. Kennedy's public concerns that Diem must have public support belie his private knowledge that only South Vietnam's Catholic minority falls into that category. But Kennedy then sends another contradicting message when he goes on to say, in that same response to Cronkite:

I hope that [ending the policies developed over the last two months] will be clear to the government—it should be; after all, they've been conducting this struggle for ten years. I admire what the president has done. He's been counted out a number of times—I am hopeful he will come to see that [he and the South Vietnamese people] have to reestablish their relationship. We ought to remember they're the ones who are dying by the thousands and they're the ones who have to win this war or they are the ones who will lose it. We can't do either; we can assist it, and we can warn them against losing it.[298]

---

[297] The American Presidency Project: Transcript of Broadcast With Walter Cronkite Inaugurating a CBS Television News Program, 2 September 1963, http://www.presidency.ucsb.edu/ws/?pid=9388.
[298] Ibid.

Immediately following his tepid support of Diem, Kennedy then went on to say something that in hindsight would demonstrate just how dramatically the policy would change in the years following 1963: "We don't have troops en masse dying by the thousands,"[299] Kennedy said, referencing the number of casualties sustained by the South Vietnamese.

Cronkite followed up by asking Kennedy, "Do you think this government still has time to regain the support of the people?"[300] And Kennedy responded:

Kennedy: I do, with changes in policy and perhaps with personnel, I think it can. If it doesn't make those changes, I would think the chances of winning it would not be very good.

Cronkite: Hasn't every indication from Saigon been that President Diem has no intention of changing his pattern?

Kennedy: If he doesn't change it, of course that his decision, he's been there ten years. As I say, he has carried this burden when he's been counted out on a number of occasions. Our best judgment is he can't be successful on this basis. We hope that he comes to see that. But in the final analysis, it is the people and the government themselves that have to win or lose this struggle. All we can do is help . . . But I don't agree with those who say we should withdraw—that would be a great mistake; that would be a great mistake. I know people don't like Americans to be engaged in this type of effort; forty-seven Americans have been killed in combat with the enemy. But this is a very important struggle even though it's far away.[301]

In that brief exchange with Cronkite, Kennedy clearly provides ammunition for historians to support whatever theory they may have about Vietnam and the role his administration played. What is not

---

[299] Ibid.
[300] Ibid.
[301] Ibid.

present in the interview is the fact that during the Eisenhower Administration, the United States had systematically developed an eight-year "sink or swim" policy with Diem that Kennedy now wished to change. Based on the actions already undertaken that year, the Kennedy Administration's immediate plan was to commit itself deeper into the affairs of Vietnam. Nine days prior to Kennedy's interview with Cronkite, his administration had sent out what is commonly referred as Cable 243.

Cable 243

Cable 243, the Kennedy Administration's most significant policy decision on Vietnam, occurred under the most inauspicious circumstances—the most significant members of the Kennedy Administration were absent. How could a policy that in effect changed U.S. policy in South Vietnam begin with the administration's key players away from Washington?

On August 24, Roger Hilsman, Head of the State Department's Far East Bureau, sent the following memo to Lodge:

It is not clear whether military proposed martial law or whether Nhu tricked them into it; Nhu took advantage of its imposition to smash pagodas with Police and Tung's Special Forces, loyal to him thus placing onus on military in eyes of [the] world and Vietnamese people. The Government cannot tolerate [a] situation in which power lies in Nhu's hands. Diem must be given [a] chance to rid himself of Nhu and his coterie and replace them with [the] best military and political personalities available. If, in spite of all your efforts, Diem remains obdurate and refuses, we must face the possibility that Diem himself cannot be preserved.[302]

The message was clear: Diem must jettison his brother or face the reality that a similar fate awaits him. Hilsman went on to instruct

[302] Department of State, Cable 243, http://www.gwu.edu/~nsarchiv/NSAEBB/NSAEBB101/vn02.pdf.

Lodge to inform the dissident generals of the administration's new direction. He also told Lodge that he "should urgently examine all possible alternative leadership and make detailed plans as to how we might bring about Diem's replacement if this should become necessary."[303]

Cable 243 and Kennedy's statement to Cronkite—"It's their war"—are somewhat inconsistent. If Lodge had been sent a memo to support the overthrow of an ally (at least by Cold War definitions), it was not "their war," as Kennedy proclaimed, but the United States' war. Though the memo to Lodge may have been clear in articulating the strong possibility of America's change of direction in South Vietnam, what remains less clear is the chain of events that led to the memo.

Hilsman drafted Cable 243, but there are several competing versions as to how the memo came to be. What's not in dispute is that Hilsman, along with Under Secretary of Political Affairs Averell Harriman, who collaborated with Hilsman on the memo, tracked down Under Secretary of State George Ball for his approval while he was on the ninth hole of a Washington country club. Ball supported it, but he instructed Hilsman and Harriman to contact Kennedy, who was in Hyannis Port for the weekend. Hilsman contended that the president received the entire memo via Teletype. Ball claims that the "relevant passages"[304] were read to Kennedy over the phone. It seems unlikely that Kennedy could believe all his key advisors signed off on the document. Secretary of State Dean Rusk was in New York and Secretary of Defense Robert McNamara was on vacation. Rusk gave it his approval believing that Kennedy supported it. Roswell Gilpatric, acting defense secretary in McNamara's absence, approved largely because he thought Kennedy and Rusk approved, but he later informed the Chair of the Joint Chiefs of Staff, Maxwell Taylor, of his doubts.

The following Monday, with most of the key administration officials back in Washington, a series of meetings began with

[303] Ibid.
[304] Kranow, 303.

opposing sides lobbying for their perspectives. Kennedy was reportedly critical of Hilsman, Harriman, and Ball for their hasty approach. Vice President Lyndon Johnson, Defense Secretary McNamara, and CIA Director John McCone were opposed to overthrowing Diem. But the more senior members of the administration, in spite of the madcap manner in which Cable 243 came into fruition, were unable to impede its progress. Soon, it would be the new policy of the Kennedy Administration. Quite a turnaround, given that just two years prior, Vice President Johnson was in South Vietnam lauding Diem with comparisons to Winston Churchill.

The speed in which Cable 243 became the policy of the United States was evident at the National Security Council meeting held August 31, 1963. Paul Kattenburg, chairman of the Vietnam Working Group, who had recently visited Saigon, opposed the overthrow of Diem, advocating instead a total American withdrawal from Vietnam: "It would be better for us to make the decision to get out honorably," he said.[305] Kattenburg's travels between the 1950s and early 1960s convinced him that Diem would not survive and that North Vietnam would ultimately prevail. Kattenburg shared the opinion that the Kennedy Administration could not continue to support Diem, offering that the existing policy had a shelf life of no more than six months. But those in the room, which included Rusk and McNamara, roundly dismissed his alternative for withdrawal.

With withdrawal off the table, the only hope that Cable 243 offered was a disingenuous condition—because of Diem and his leadership style—that was impossible for him to accept. Diem would not distance himself from his brother, leaving only one possible outcome. Diem's rigid family loyalty, his blind eye to the corruption within his regime, and the loss of confidence from the majority in South Vietnam contributed to his demise, but those factors without the involvement of the Kennedy Administration working against him would not have been enough to topple him.

---

[305] Interview with Paul Kattenburh, WGBH, "Open Vault," 1981.

After several months of speculating whether a potential coup would actually take place, the on-again-off-again status was finally set for the early hours of November 1. The coup was well organized so that only a single guard defended Diem when it commenced. Moreover, the Kennedy Administration assured the generals behind the coup that they would not interfere. At 4:30 PM, with the palace completely surrounded, Diem telephoned Lodge. The exchange made it clear that Lodge, as representative of the administration's Vietnam policy, was not about to change the direction that the coup had taken:

Diem: Some units have made a rebellion, and I want to know what is the attitude of the United States.

Lodge: I do not feel well enough informed to be able to tell you. I have heard the shooting but I'm not acquainted with all the facts. Also, it is 4:30 AM in Washington and the U.S. government cannot possibly have a view.[306]

The brief exchange moved to Diem's safety, but the president was still focused on preserving order:

Lodge: If I can do anything for your physical safety, please call me.

Diem: I am trying to establish order.[307]

Several hours would pass after Lodge and Diem's exchange before reality set in. Diem's attempts to reach key supporters went in vain. Along with his brother Nhu and two aides, Diem slipped out of the palace through a secret passage, maneuvered through the curfew on the streets, and ended up at St. Francis Xavier church. At approximately 6:00 AM the next day, he contacted the insurgents to negotiate his resignation. The final agreement was for Diem to resign and then leave Vietnam. At that point, Diem disclosed his location so

---

[306] Kranow, 322.

[307] Kranow, 323.

that a car could pick him, Nhu, and the aides up. Diem and Nhu were placed in the back of an armored car and were handcuffed. By the time the armored car arrived at the insurgent's headquarters, the dead bodies of Diem and Nhu were riddled with bullets and knife wounds.

When the news of Diem's death reached Washington, Kennedy, who was in a meeting, reportedly leaped from his chair in disbelief, and Ted Sorensen confirmed this account.[308] According to Sorensen, "President Kennedy never thought that Diem would be assassinated."[309]

Assuming the accuracy of Sorensen's comments, his statement offers insight into the disharmony that existed as Cable 243 was contemplated. In a reactionary posture, the Kennedy Administration essentially doubled down on the actions of the Eisenhower Administration seven years earlier. Just as Eisenhower failed to insist that Diem conduct elections to unify Vietnam in 1956 per the Geneva Agreement in 1954, due in large measure to the potential of an unfavorable outcome, so did Kennedy, with Cable 243, set in motion a policy to manipulate the outcome of a foreign government based on an uncooperative ally who failed to bend to the administration's will.

Two days after Diem's assassination, Kennedy dictated some candid thoughts from the Oval Office: "Monday, November 4, 1963, over the weekend the coup in Saigon took place—culminated three months conversations about a coup, conversations which divided the government here and in Saigon."[310] The president then chronicled those within his cabinet who supported and opposed the operation to overthrow Diem, and after, he offered this sobering reflection:

I feel we must bear a great deal of responsibility for it, beginning with our cable of early August in which we suggested a coup. In my judgment that wire [Cable 243] was badly drafted, should have never been sent on Saturday. I should have not given my consent to it

[308] Ted Sorensen, interview with the author, June 23, 2009.
[309] Ibid.
[310] Kennedy Dictates His Thoughts on Vietnam Coup, http://www.youtube.com/watch?v=eo_HQVP5KRI

without a roundtable conference in which McNamara and Taylor presented their views.[311]

Whatever lessons Kennedy may have learned from the Bay of Pigs experience that informed him during the Cuban Missile Crisis seemed unavailable to the president roughly thirteen months later. How could such crucial policy position gain so much traction without the president's vehement support? Kennedy followed up this dictation with a November 6 memo to Lodge, which reveals U.S. involvement and the first stages of what history will prove to be an untenable quagmire:

Now that there is a new Government which we are about to recognize, we must all intensify our efforts to help it deal with its many hard problems. As you say, while this was a Vietnamese effort, our own actions made it clear that we wanted improvements, and when these were not forthcoming from the Diem Government, we necessarily faced and accepted the possibility that our position might encourage a change of government. We thus have a responsibility to help this new government to be effective in every way that we can, and in these first weeks we may have more influence and more chance to be helpful than at any time in recent years.[312]

The administration had reached this point because of Diem's inflexible nature and his mistreatment of the Buddhists, but they were also here because of what Eisenhower believed to be true in 1954 (conveyed in a letter to his brother) and what Kennedy conveyed to Cronkite in 1963. Though Kennedy had his misgivings about the coup against Diem, Cable 243, regardless of the disjointed nature that led to its fruition, was the policy going forward, and Lodge was committed

---

[311] Ibid.

[312] "November 6, 1963 Cable from President Kennedy to Ambassador Lodge in Saigon, Discusses U.S. Policy in Light of Recent Coup," http://mcadams.posc.mu.edu/viet10.htm

to seeing it through. There was now the ominous possibility of a Communist takeover.

In 1963, this may have been the greatest of all unexamined assumptions. If a Communist takeover were inevitable, what would have been the purpose of expending additional resources? Could the United States exist with a Communist-led Vietnam? Though years of hindsight can greatly assist the clarity by which we view such questions, it was not as clear in the moment. But there is little evidence these were questions seriously entertained by either the Kennedy Administration or its immediate predecessor or successor.

As Eisenhower prepared to leave the White House in 1961, it was the situation in Laos that occupied his last days more so than Vietnam. Among the states formerly known as French Indochina (Cambodia, Vietnam, and Laos), Laos was viewed as key to the rest of Southeast Asia. The Soviet Union's involvement in the Laotian civil war enhanced domino theory fears. But Kennedy, who early in his political career was supportive of French participation in Indochina and later of Diem's administration, failed to share Eisenhower's concern for Laos.

Perhaps the Bay of Pigs invasion and his first meeting with Soviet leader Nikita Khrushchev, which occurred only months after Kennedy assumed the presidency, led to his focus on Vietnam. On the heels of that meeting in Vienna, where Khrushchev reportedly pushed Kennedy around, Kennedy told the *New York Times'* James Reston, "Now we have a problem in making our power credible, and Vietnam is the place."

Later that year Kennedy sent General Taylor on a two-week tour of Vietnam. In October 1961, Taylor produced a report, heavily affected by the domino theory, explaining that losing Vietnam would make it difficult to hold on to the Southeast Asia region, which would result in a loss of U.S. credibility with the Communists, so he advocated for an increase in military advisors and helicopter squadrons. Taylor also presented Kennedy with a memo that called for an initial commitment of 8,000 combat troops disguised as "logistical legions" to combat the floods in the Mekong Delta. When the Kennedy

Administration began in January 1961, there were 675 military advisors already in Vietnam, and by the end of 1962, that number had increased to 11,000, along with 300 aircraft, and 120 helicopters. By the time Kennedy was assassinated, there were 16,700 advisors.

With the makings of a military escalation and ostensibly a quagmire already in place in Washington by 1962, it was U.S. support for the overthrow of the Diem regime in 1963 that was clearly a turning point in the Vietnam conflict. But it was a turning point that went largely unnoticed at the time for several reasons.

Less than one hundred soldiers had been killed at the time Diem was overthrown. The Communist threat was felt much more through Cuba and the Soviet Union than Indo-China; television had not yet garnered the influence it would come to have—the type of influence it was having in the Civil Rights Movement—and November 22 had not yet occurred.

The fall of Diem formally transferred the Vietnam situation from a war in which the United States assisted the South Vietnamese government in their struggle against the North Vietnamese to an enterprise that would be wholly owned by the U.S. government.

The decisions made in 1963 by the Kennedy Administration, right or wrong, were based on the belief that South Vietnam would be defeated by North Vietnam under Diem's leadership, thereby opening the door for the region to be dominated by the Communist Ho Chi Minh. With hindsight, could Vietnam circa 1963 be understood void of the Korean War, the domino theory, or the Geneva Accords in 1954?

To suggest the Kennedy Administration involved itself in the internal affairs of a duly elected foreign government by supporting the overthrow of Diem is true on the surface, though it misses a central point. When Diem reneged on the 1956 elections (as negotiated at Geneva) to consolidate North and South Vietnam, his government ceased to be duly elected. The United States' failure to step in, demanding that Diem go through with what was agreed, made his administration a puppet government. Likewise, the Eisenhower Administration did not have much to say in response when Diem, through violence and intimidation, obviously rigged the election against Bao Dai in 1955.

Though Eisenhower and Kennedy based their actions on the premise that South Vietnam was responsible for their own defense, U.S. policy increasingly placed the United States on a trajectory that led to increased involvement. It was a policy that aimed to take a divided nation with competing ideologies and transform it into a unified democracy. But this is only true in theory; the practical application of the policy was to stop the Communist threat from spreading. The United States had no problem, at least judging by its overt behavior, when Diem demonstrated no intention to hold the elections as negotiated at Geneva. Diem was hardly moving toward anything that resembled a democracy, but from 1954 to 1963, he was the United States' pawn in that region of the Cold War, the one whose mission was to stop the dominos from falling into the lap of Communist China.

Many who served in the Kennedy Administration hold to the belief that had Kennedy lived, he would have withdrawn troops after his reelection in 1964. Ted Sorensen certainly intimated as much. But the timing of Kennedy's tragic death, along with the decisions made in 1963, placed Lyndon Johnson in a situation for which there was no viable exit strategy. Ironically, given the existing political climate in 1963, only Eisenhower and Kennedy—because of their established anti-Communist bona fides—could have avoided Vietnam being the tragic mistake that it ultimately became, even though they were responsible for getting the United States so deeply involved in the Vietnam struggle.

The instability of Vietnam began as a cancerous growth at Geneva in 1954, and it was allowed to spread for nine years. It was only after a malignancy was acknowledged, already having destroyed any chance for a democratic Vietnam or the North and South living in harmony, that the United States made the decision made to remove Diem.

But the coup to overthrow Diem did not improve conditions in Vietnam. The new leaders in South Vietnam ushered in an era of a never-ending power struggle. Saigon quickly deteriorated, and the United States intensified its commitment to the struggle, though this ultimately lead the Vietnamese to explain to the United States government that there was no compelling reason for U.S. involvement. Johnson had inherited a policy that began at Potsdam, which was refined by the Korean War and fortified by more than a decade of Cold War thinking, and it would take an additional twenty years to undo. It was Cold War realpolitik that allowed first the Eisenhower Administration and subsequently the Kennedy Administration to ignore the glaring weaknesses in Diem's leadership.

Johnson simply could not have pulled out of Vietnam sooner than he did—not given who he was and the state of the nation at that time. Had he pulled out in 1965 or 1966 after McNamara told him the conflict was not winnable, he would have been the first U.S. president to lose a war, and this was unacceptable for a commander in chief that still harbored visions of reelection in 1968. In 1964, in the midst of a presidential campaign, political adversaries were waiting to demagogue Vietnam and label Johnson as an appeaser who followed the tradition of British Prime Minister Neville Chamberlain. [313] Moreover, the appearance of any U.S. president to be "soft" on Communism would be unacceptable, with the memories of WWII still fresh in the nation's consciousness along with Cold Wars fears.

Johnson lamented his Vietnam dilemma to biographer Doris Kearns Goodwin after he left the Oval Office:

I knew from the start that I was bound to be crucified either way I moved. If I left the woman I loved—Great Society—in order to get involved with that bitch of a war on the other side of the world, then I would lose everything at home. All my programs. All my hopes to feed the hungry and shelter the homeless. All my dreams to provide

---

[313] In 1938, Chamberlain signed the Munich Agreement with Adolph Hitler, conceding the Sudetenland region of Czechoslovakia to Germany. But Hitler's advance into Poland led to Britain declaring war on Germany on September 3, 1939.

education and medical care to the browns and blacks and the lame and poor. But if I left that war and let Communists take over South Vietnam, then I would be seen as a coward and my nation would be seen as an appeaser, and we would both find it impossible to accomplish anything for anybody anywhere on the entire globe.[314]

In addition, Johnson's post-1963 actions would be, to some degree, hampered by the looming shadow of a martyred president and a grieving nation. Johnson would be forced to assume the role of armchair quarterback, naively and myopically discussing how Kennedy might have done it differently. This does not excuse Johnson for proclaiming during the 1964 presidential campaign that he would not send U.S. soldiers on a mission that could only be carried out by South Vietnamese soldiers while simultaneously approving plans to escalate the conflict. Furthermore, his aforementioned quote to Kearns reveals his belief in the domino theory, which also motivated his predecessors Eisenhower and Kennedy to support Diem for nearly a decade.

The events of 1963, which ultimately led to the fall of Diem, serve as the dividing line between the United States hiding behind a nine-year policy that was never achievable and overtly replacing the French, though with far more tragic outcomes.

As civil rights burst onto the nation's conscience in 1963, opinions about Vietnam were still moving at a snail's pace. Print media was still responsible for the majority of reporting in Vietnam, and as shocking as the photos of Thich Quang Duc immolating himself were, they were merely an indicator as to how little the U.S. government understood about this region of the world. Television had not yet begun to cover the situation in Vietnam the way it had in Birmingham. There were no body bags arriving to Dover AFB shown on the evening news, there were no broadcasted anti-war protests that

[314] Doris Kearns Goodwin, *Lyndon Johnson and the American Dream* (New York: Harper and Row, 1976), 251.

would later play a role in defining the decade, and Cronkite had yet to tell the American people that any measurement of military success was not achievable. In 1963, it was only print reporters, like David Halberstam, who were in Saigon offering a different narrative than the one preferred by the Kennedy Administration, trying to help the American people understand the gravity of what was being attempted.

In hindsight, it is easy to see how the fall of Diem was inevitable, though the fact that the United States didn't see it coming can be summed up in Kennedy's words to Cronkite: "In the final analysis, it's their war." By the end of 1963, that honor would belong to the United States.

Chapter Eight:

"Something Has Happened in the Motorcade Route"

On Friday, November 22, 1963, Sam Pate, a reporter for KBOX Radio, was on the Stemmons Freeway in a mobile news cruiser covering President Kennedy's trip to Dallas. Here is an excerpt of his now famous coverage of that fateful day:

The president's car is now turning onto Elm Street and [it will] only be [a] matter of minutes before he arrives at the Trade Mart. I was on Stemmons Freeway earlier, and even the freeway was jam-packed with spectators waiting [for] their chance to see the president as he made his way toward the Trade Mart. It appears as though something has happened in the motorcade route, something, I repeat, has happened in the motorcade route![315]

These were the famous, infamous, and haunting words that described much more than the tragedy in Dealey Plaza at approximately 12:30 PM, CST. Something had indeed happened in the motorcade route, and it was much more than a youthful president, full

---

[315] KBOX 1480-Dallas, http://www.youtube.com/watch?v=if4KPjlBz_w.

of vigor, being struck down in the prime of life. It was a severe blow to the nation that made it difficult for Americans to entertain hope and see possibility the same way.

When Kennedy's body arrived back from Dallas, columnist Mary McGrory described his mournful friends as "leaderless men of the New Frontier" as they "picked up their inexpressible burden" of the young president's coffin.[316] McGory's words were also true for a nation now uncertain of its direction, as it unexpectedly found itself toiling under the weight of "inexpressible burden."

November 22, 1963, is one of those indelible dates in American history alongside December 7, 1941, and September 11, 2001. Those who were alive and conscious could never forget what they were doing the moment they received the news that the president had been shot.

Just twenty days prior, South Vietnam's President, Ngo Dinh Diem, had been assassinated in a coup. But that was to be expected— not that there were a cadre of individuals predicting Diem's demise, but Vietnam had not yet reached the level of democratic sophistication of the U.S., so a violent outcome was less surprising. But what happened in the motorcade route seemed less "American"—it was not who we were, and it was not what we do, at least not in theory. It had been sixty-two years since a president had been assassinated. But suddenly, and without warning, it had once again become who we were, as First Lady Jacqueline Kennedy's blood-splattered pink Chanel suit bore witness when she disembarked from the back of Air Force One behind her husband's coffin.

Furthering our dilemma, the Kennedy assassination remains the greatest unsolved murder in the twentieth century. The fact may be that the accused assassin, Lee Harvey Oswald, did indeed act alone, but unresolved questions—the key to any conspiracy theory—remain even today. If there ever was a breaking point when more than a fractured few began to distrust the government, it was upon the release

---

[316] "Mary McGory, 85, Longtime Washington Columnist, Dies, Amazing," *New York Times*, 23 April 2004.

of the President's Commission of the Assassination of President Kennedy, more commonly referred to as the Warren Commission. The 888-page final report concluded that Oswald acted alone, but it failed to answer key questions and thereby created a cottage industry of conspiracy theories that remain to the present day. Moreover, it would be eleven years after the Warren Commission was released before the Zapruder Film, the 8mm home movie taken by Abraham Zapruder that shows the actual assassination, would be shown on national television. Its premiere viewing along with subsequent others did more to raise questions than to quell suspicions. The mere physics of the shot that killed the president as it appeared on the Zapruder Film make it difficult for many to believe that Oswald was the lone gunman, and from then on, more than one person would qualify the assassination as a conspiracy. But even if it was a conspiracy, the Kennedy assassination remains one of the best-kept secrets in American history.

Stepping aside from the tragedy itself, the assassination of John F. Kennedy is the primary reason that the events of 1963 have not been as appreciated as they should be. It is instead 1968 that is generally viewed as the monumental year of change. November 22, 1963, represents the sum total of events for the year, and even today that belief holds true. What happened in the motorcade route has simultaneously been viewed as the postlude for the image we hold of the 1950s and the prelude for how we would come to identify with the 1960s—but this leaves out entirely the opus that was the hope and hostility of 1963. But in America's attempt to make sense of the absurd, it has been convenient for us to mark November 22 as the day we eulogize the 1950s and welcome the 1960s with its unpredictability.

Though many Americans today may be hard pressed to recall any major events in 1963 besides the Kennedy assassination, there was in fact a major occurrence nearly every month of the year, as this book chronicles. Domestically and internationally, the country was changing. And the metamorphosis did not happen overnight, but the America of January 1961 was not the same America of November

1963, just as Kennedy was not the same the day he assumed the presidency as the day he was murdered.

The Kennedy assassination led to the first nationally televised live murder, when nightclub owner Jack Ruby shot Lee Harvey Oswald. It also gave us our first taste of what twenty-four-hour news would look and feel like. Though it would be twenty-seven years before CNN became a household name, there was now round-the-clock coverage that the country looked to, and needed, to aid them in the monumental task of making sense out of absurdity. ABC, CBS, and NBC suspended normal programming for four days and instead recalled the brief Kennedy Administration and repeated the coverage of the crime, attempting to understand who Lee Harvey Oswald was and why Kennedy went to Dallas.

Perhaps in part because of the events in Dallas, 1963 became the year when television would establish itself as the preeminent medium for communicating events across the nation. In September 1963, the nightly network news, led by Walter Cronkite at CBS, expanded from fifteen minutes to thirty minutes, and two months later it became the primary source by which people tried to make sense of a seemingly nonsensical tragedy. And of course, television also played a key role in transforming the nation's attitude about civil rights that year.

Ironically, it may have been an untelevised event that caused the most stir during that tragic November weekend. Former National Football League Commissioner Pete Rozelle would come to lament his decision to not cancel the games the weekend of the assassination even though Rozelle had been urged not to cancel them by his former classmate and Kennedy Press Secretary Pierre Salinger. The American Football League postponed their games, which made Rozelle appear callous to a nation that had not endured such mourning since the death of Lincoln.

Nothing that happened in 1963 could compare with the JFK assassination—it took all the oxygen out of the room and replaced it with a suffocating cynicism that Americans have yet to relinquish. What happened in the motorcade route has blinded us to Martin Luther

King Jr.'s greatest moment, not just of 1963, but perhaps of his illustrious career—his Letter from Birmingham Jail. It has prohibited us from recognizing the impact of the twenty-four hours between June 11 and June 12. The courage of John Doar standing between protestors and Jackson Mississippi police to quell rioting during the services for Medgar Evers, and the bravery of Nicholas Katzenbach confronting George Wallace is lost on us. We've forgotten the fact that Vivian Malone needed an accounting degree from an accredited institution of higher learning more than she needed to be a freedom fighter.

It has been easier to conclude that 1968 was the more eventful year, and it still may be, but the totality of transformative events in 1963 dwarf those in 1968, and certainly nothing shocked the nation in 1968 like November 22, 1963, did—including April 4 and June 5, 1968.[317] If anything, what happened in the motorcade route made the assassinations of King and Robert Kennedy conceivable.

Perhaps another reason 1968 is widely viewed as the more significant year is that most of the noteworthy events that define the year are negative. The year is marred by the assassinations of Martin Luther King Jr. and Robert Kennedy, the war in Vietnam, and the Democratic Convention in Chicago. The increasing influence of television that began in 1963 only served to enhance those negative events five years later. Contrarily, 1963 was a mixed bag of hope and hostility that has unfortunately been engulfed by a single day of tragedy that still remains beyond our comprehension.

It is presumptuous to conclude that any year is more significant than another. No years exist in isolation. And in the words of historian David McCullough, "History is who we are and why we are the way we are."[318] It is therefore a mistake to view 1963 as superior to any other year because the events that occurred were influenced by events from other years. The significance of Kennedy attempting to normalize relations with Castro in 1963 must been seen through the prism of the

---

[317] April 4 1968 and June 5, 1968 are the dates that Martin Luther King Jr. and Robert Kennedy were assassinated respectively.

[318] "What is History?" http://www.dur.ac.uk/4schools/History/default.htm.

Bay of Pigs in 1961 and the Cuban Missile Crisis in 1962. Likewise, Kennedy's speeches at American University and in Berlin, which lead to the signing of the Limited Nuclear Test Ban Treaty in October 1963, have 1961 at their foundations, one of the worst foreign policy years for any U.S. president. And George Wallace and University of Alabama in 1963 is linked with Ross Barnett and the University of Mississippi in 1962.

Though myriad authors have examined every event chronicled in this book, none have examined them through the prism of a single monumental year—a year that began with George Wallace declaring, "Segregation today, segregation tomorrow, segregation forever," and concluded with Martin Luther King Jr. being *Time* magazine's "Man of the Year."

In naming King as the recipient of the prestigious award, *Time* captured in the moment the hope and hostility that has since been forgotten. An excerpt from the article read:

In 1963, the centennial of the Emancipation Proclamation, that coalition of conscience insatiably changed the course of U.S. life. Nineteen million Negro citizens forced the nation to take stock of itself in the Congress as in the corporation, in factory and field and pulpit and playground, in kitchen and classroom. The U.S. Negro, shedding the thousand fears that have encumbered his generations, made 1963 the year of his outcry for quality, of massive demonstrations, of wins and speeches and street fighting, of soul searching in the suburbs and psalm singing in the jail cells.[319]

The country was changing, internationally and domestically, and 1963 bore the obvious fruits of this transformation. And what happened in the motorcade route could not disrupt the uncomfortable change that the country was destined to undergo.

Even with November 22, 1963, Kennedy's legacy on civil rights was not derailed, as Lyndon Johnson masterfully completed what JFK

---

[319] Martin Luther King: 1963, http://www.time.com/time/specials/packages/article/0,28804,2019712_201971 1_2019683,00.html.

started. But would the nation be as politically divisive today had November 22 not occurred? If the 1964 campaign is any indication, with the country still grieving from its fallen president and in no mood for having a third president within the span of one year, voters still showed indication of regional change.

In 1960, one of the closest elections in history, Kennedy carried Louisiana, Mississippi, Georgia, and South Carolina. He won the popular vote in Alabama, but split the eleven electoral votes (five to six) with Virginia Senator Harry Byrd. In 1964, Johnson won a landslide victory against Arizona Senator Barry Goldwater, winning forty-four of fifty states. Johnson, a Southerner, only lost Louisiana, Mississippi, Alabama, Georgia, South Carolina, and Arizona, Goldwater's home state. The only tangible effect that could account for the switch was the civil rights legislation signed by Johnson on July 2, 1964, and articulated to the nation by Kennedy on June 11, 1963.

It was an impressive victory for Johnson and the Democrats, and it was also the initial indicator that the country was shifting. The solid South that had been part of Democratic presidential dominance since FDR was gone. The first threat the South would leave the party was 1948, when South Carolina Governor Strom Thurmond ran as the States Rights Democratic Party presidential nominee and won thirty-nine electoral votes—all in the South, and based almost exclusively on a platform that maintained racial segregation. If the 1948 election represented the trial separation, the 1964 election, driven by the events in 1963, began what would become evidence of irreconcilable differences between the Democratic Party and the South.

Assuming it was Kennedy and not Johnson who ran in 1964, would Kennedy have begat Nixon, who begat Ford, who begat Carter, who begat Reagan, and so on? Did what happen in the motorcade route lead to George Wallace becoming one of the most influential politicians since 1963?

Wallace was one of America's grotesque political animals. Though he does not stand alone in this unfortunate category, what he accomplished, beginning in 1963, became a trademark for future politicians, particularly members of the Republican Party.

Wallace's infamous declaration never to be "out-niggered again" was what Wallace circa 1963 was prepared to do. But the cynic could say the same about the repentant Wallace circa 1979, who apologized to civil rights leaders by stating that standing at the door of the University of Alabama was wrong. Politics was Wallace's orthodoxy, but the nation paid a huge price for it. What Wallace had unleashed, beginning in 1963, could not be put back in the bottle so easily.

In 1963, George Wallace unveiled a blueprint for electoral politics that would be followed into the twenty-first century by appealing to white voters propelled by racial undercurrents, primarily, but not limited to, those living in the South. *Life* magazine's August 1968 cover, the cartoon of Wallace riding the horse made up of the contiguous Southern states, masterfully illustrates the Wallace influence.

The 1968 "Southern Strategy," a term popularized by Nixon aide Kevin Phillips, had Wallace circa 1963 at its foundation. In a 1970 *New York Times* article, Phillips wrote:

From now on, the Republicans are never going to get more than 10 to 20 percent of the Negro vote and they don't need any more than that . . . but Republicans would be shortsighted if they weakened enforcement of the Voting Rights Act. The more Negroes who register as Democrats in the South, the sooner the Negrophobe whites will quit the Democrats and become Republicans. That's where the votes are. Without that prodding from the blacks, the whites will backslide into their old comfortable arrangement with the local Democrats.[320]

What happened on the motorcade route also meant the end for Malcolm X and his association within the Nation of Islam. Malcolm X, a Muslim minister and human rights activist, had been portrayed in

---

[320] James Boyd, "Nixon's Southern Strategy: It's All in the Charts," 17 May 1970, *New York Times*, http://www.nytimes.com/packages/html/books/phillips-southern.pdf.

the public conversation as the antithesis to Martin Luther King. King's nonviolent approach to civil disobedience was the preferred method of change among the mainstream, whereas the Nation of Islam preached self-defense. And it had no better spokesperson than Malcolm X.

On December 1, Malcolm X described the Kennedy assassination as a case of the chickens coming home to roost. He cited the murders that year of Medgar Evers, Congo leader Patrice Lumumba, and the four girls bombed in the Birmingham church, emphasizing 1963's climate of violence. But he also added in his comments, "Chickens coming home to roost never did make me sad; they've always made me glad."[321]

The violence and the racial overtones in 1963 that Malcolm X referred to were undeniable, but his timing was poor. Nine days after America had lost its young president to violence, it was unable and unwilling to hear such a stinging critique from a man that on the surface appeared somewhat pleased about the news.

November 22 gave rise to the Kennedy Camelot metaphor. For several decades, this metaphor made it more difficult for Americans to view the Kennedy Administration honestly. We were collectively blinded by the images of Kennedy's youthful and charismatic eloquence along with the massive shadow created by his death. What happened on the motorcade route led more to the eulogizing of the Kennedy Administration than detached examination. It shadowed Johnson's presidency before it even began, as many viewed his accomplishments and failures through the subjective lens of a martyred and beloved president.

If Johnson proved to be the right person for the hope of the Civil Rights Movement, as the landmark legislation in 1964 and 1965 demonstrate, he would equally serve as the wrong person to face the

---

[321] Malcolm X Scores U.S. and Kennedy; Likens Slaying to 'Chickens Coming Home to Roost.'" 2 December 1963, *New York Times*, http://select.nytimes.com/gst/abstract.html?res=FB0812FE35541A7B93C0A9 1789D95F478685F9.

hostility of Vietnam, which came to define the counterculture of the 1960s. Vietnam may be the topic of the greatest "what-if" question formulated after the assassination.

Kennedy's interview with Walter Cronkite in September 1963 offers fodder to both sides engaged in the speculation of what the outcome of Vietnam would have been had Kennedy lived. In the interview, Kennedy said, "In the final analysis it's their war." This is perhaps the strongest argument for those who feel Kennedy was already prepared to pull out of Vietnam and that it was simply a matter of wining the 1964 election. But Kennedy followed that statement with the contradictory offering, "I don't agree with those who say we should withdraw, that would be a great mistake."

Kennedy's statements to Cronkite are somewhat inconsistent, but they reflect the division and tension within his administration as well as the growing complexity that Vietnam was becoming.

Those who argue that Kennedy would have conducted the war similarly to Johnson, with massive troop buildups, cite that it was Kennedy's people who orchestrated the effort that Johnson undertook; Dean Rusk was Secretary of State, McGeorge Bundy was National Security Advisor, and, most notably, Robert McNamara was Secretary of Defense. These key people, who advised Johnson, were appointed by Kennedy, and furthermore, they orchestrated the Diem overthrow and assassination. Because the Vietnam situation was spiraling out of control so rapidly and the overall Cold War climate was so heavy before Kennedy's assassination, perhaps the outcome of Vietnam would have turned out very similarly had Kennedy lived. David Halberstam's book *The Making of a Quagmire* is a very compelling resource for this argument.

The first part of Kennedy's statement to Cronkite, "It's their war," suggests Vietnam would have turned out differently had Kennedy survived. The quote displays the pragmatism that was very much of a part of Kennedy's political philosophy, which was tempered by the lessons he learned from the disaster of the Bay of Pigs and the success of the Cuban Missile Crisis.

During the Bay of Pigs, Kennedy did not want to appear soft on Communism, so he gave his initial blessing and depended too much on the advice of his military and the CIA. But the mission failed and resulted in the reverse effect: it made Kennedy appear weak as a leader. Fortunately, Kennedy learned several positive lessons from this otherwise disastrous enterprise.

It was immediately following the Bay of Pigs when Kennedy famously opined: "Victory has a thousand fathers; defeat is an orphan."[322] After the Bay of Pigs, Kennedy placed more trust in his own instincts and less in the military, and this trust was evident during the Cuban Missile Crisis—the naval blockade that was ultimately decided was the not the Joint Chief's first response. But his leadership after the Cable 243 memo was left undeterminable.

Would McNamara's role under Kennedy have differed from his role under Johnson? It most likely would have, especially with Robert Kennedy at the Justice Department and serving as de facto Chief of Staff, whose raison d'etre at the time was the success of his brother's presidency.

Kennedy was perceived has having stared down and winning against Khrushchev during the Cuban Missile Crisis. At this point, he was not burdened with proving whether or not he was tough on Communism, which may have given him the freedom to act in ways Johnson could not.

The Cuban Missile Crisis also allowed Kennedy to make the speech at American University, where he called for peace between the United States and the Soviet Union, and it could have allowed him to possibly negotiate a peace without being viewed as having "lost" Vietnam. Johnson possessed no background, beyond any anti-Communist rhetoric, of standing firm against the perceived threat. This made Johnson vulnerable to charges of being "soft" if he sought the path of a negotiated peace over the escalation of conflict. Even the

---

[322] Arthur M. Schlessinger Jr., *A Thousand Days* (New York: Ballantine Books, 1965), 289.

strong anti-Communist stands that Kennedy took in the annals of history did not take place without charges by his Republican counterparts that he was actually seeking appeasement. When one factors in this political climate, it begs the question: What were Johnson's options in Vietnam?

What happened after the motorcade route was not an example of the "butterfly effect," which is when a small change in a nonlinear system results in large differences later on. Instead, it was the convergence of tsunami-like waves that caused displacement of many of America's values. The country, without warning, was forced to redefine who it was as a society.

With Kennedy's death and the deaths of Robert Kennedy and Martin Luther King Jr. in 1968, America's sense of what was possible was permanently changed by the end of the decade—and this stood in stark contrast to of the original promise symbolized by JFK's inaugural address in 1961.

What happened in the motorcade route opened the door to the overt distrust that would continue to permeate America's body politic into the present day. The work of the Warren Commission was far from perfect or as transparent as it needed to be.

The president's top aide, Kenny O'Donnell, who was riding in the car behind Kennedy, told the Warren Commission that the shots came from the rear, which would be consistent with the lone-gunman theory. But he later told his friend, former Speaker Tip O'Neil, that he was under pressure by the FBI to say what he did and that he actually believed the shots came from in front of the motorcade. O'Donnell's second account is supported by Dave Powers, who also was seated in the car behind Kennedy. O'Donnell's recollection of what happened in the motorcade route does not prove a conspiracy, but it reflects the type of inconsistency from which notions of conspiracy can flourish. Whether or not Oswald did in fact act alone, the Warren Commission had glaring omissions that sewed the seeds of doubt.

Though that distrust was temporarily shifted to Vietnam in the late 1960s and Watergate in the early 1970s, it never strayed too far from the conclusions drawn by many in the court of public opinion about the Warren Commission. And though no evidence has been presented to date that conclusively debunks the Warren Commission's findings, distrust remains. It remains because the notion of Oswald acting alone does not fit the magnitude of the crime.

Historian William Manchester, writing in the *New York Times*, outlined the fundamental problem in accepting Oswald as the lone assassin:

Those who desperately want to believe that President Kennedy was the victim of a conspiracy have my sympathy. I share their yearning. To employ what may seem an odd metaphor, there is an esthetic principle here. If you put six million dead Jews on one side of a scale and on the other side put the Nazi regime—the greatest gang of criminals ever to seize control of a modern state—you have a rough balance: greatest crime, greatest criminals.

But if you put the murdered President of the United States on one side of a scale and that wretched waif Oswald on the other side, it doesn't balance. You want to add something weightier to Oswald. It would invest the President's death with meaning, endowing him with martyrdom. He would have died for something. A conspiracy would, of course, do the job nicely.[323]

Not only did November 22 change the course of history, but also it has limited our ability to only serve the otherwise transformative events of 1963 à la carte.

The years since the assassination have given us more than enough unanswered questions, a plethora of conspiracy theories, the meticulous pouring over the Warren Commission in search of the key evidence not yet revealed, and the accumulated distrust that we've transferred to other events.

Three days after the centennial anniversary of Lincoln's Gettysburg Address, the nation was again torn asunder. It was not severed geographically as it was during Lincoln's day, but it was

---

[323] William Manchester, "To the Editor" *New York Times*, 5 February 1992.

ripped apart nevertheless by what happened in the motorcade route. Invoking Lincoln's words at Gettysburg, the world would little note nor long remember what was said in Dallas on November 22, 1963, but it can never forget what was done there.

What happened in the motorcade route managed to place a period on what would otherwise be a semi-colon on the amazing metamorphous of John F. Kennedy as president. The young Commander in Chief who had perhaps the worst inaugural foreign policy year of any president in the twentieth century clearly learned from his miscues. He used what he learned from the Bay of Pigs, his unsuccessful summit with Khrushchev, and the construction of the Berlin Wall in 1961 to then stare down the Soviet leader during the Cuban Missile Crisis in 1962 and to sign the Nuclear Test Ban Treaty in 1963.

In 1960, candidate Kennedy was naive, as was a majority of the nation, about the severity of civil rights as an issue domestically as well as internationally. But the leadership of Martin Luther King Jr. along with those on the front lines of the movement in Birmingham and elsewhere, the political ambitions of George Wallace, and the brutality of Bull Connor moved Kennedy from the safe confines of political promises. He went from simplistically offering a "stroke of his pen" to eradicate something the nation had struggled with since its inception if elected in 1960 to declaring on June 11, 1963: "We are confronted primarily with a moral issue. It is as old as the Scriptures and is as clear as the American Constitution." Though the beginning of 1963 might have hosted what appeared to be a failed effort on the part of the leadership of the Civil Rights Movement to get Kennedy to be more vocal in the commemoration of the centennial anniversary of the Emancipation Proclamation, by the middle of 1963, the United States had witnessed the most powerful speech on civil rights by any U.S. president since Lincoln. Those who criticize Kennedy for his seemingly lukewarm approach to civil rights must also praise him for the boldness of the speech that rose above the politics of the moment.

What happened in the motorcade route has caused us to focus almost exclusively on the tragedy that fell upon a 46-year old man who was at the apex of life. In the age of television, America saw Kennedy grow into the presidency, demonstrating tremendous leadership, home and abroad. In 1963, the presidency and John F. Kennedy fit like hand in glove. No American president in the twentieth century experienced a month of meaningful oratory like Kennedy had in June 1963. Over the span of seventeen days, Kennedy humanized the Soviet Union; the next day made civil rights a moral issue; and with a mangled German phrase he fluently spoke to the superiority of freedom to the people of West Berlin.

But that man, if he were alive today—though it seems doubtful given his documented health challenges—would have been 96. He has been cryogenically frozen in our minds. His charm, confidence, youth, and vitality (at least publicly) have caused us to ignore another group that warrants our commiseration.

The assassination in Dallas began a systematic following of a family who has endured enormous tragedy. In addition to Dallas, we grieved when shots rang out at the Ambassador Hotel.[324] We did likewise roughly a year later when Mary Jo Kopechne drowned at Chappaquiddick Island.[325] Some even believed that the man who was driving when Kopechne died could be president even though he failed to provide Roger Mudd with a cogent response when simply asked, "Senator why do you want to be president?" in 1980.

We remember the image of a young child, barely old enough to comprehend the magnitude of the moment, saluting his father's flag-draped coffin as it passed by. How could that moment not emotionally invade the lymph nodes of our soul? We placed our hopes, no matter

---

[324] Site of the Assassination of Robert F. Kennedy.

[325] On July 18, 1969, Mary Jo Kopechne was a passenger of U.S. Senator Edward M. "Ted" Kennedy, and was killed when he accidentally drove his car off a bridge and into channel off Chappaquiddick Island. Kennedy swam free and left the scene, not reporting the accident for nearly nine hours, but Kopechne died in the vehicle.

how fleeting, in the Kennedy name for more than a generation. Maybe, just maybe, Camelot could make a return performance. Such thoughts were misleading because Camelot was the melancholy longings from a post Dallas creation. But we so desperately wanted to believe it, if only to assuage our own unexamined pain.

The unintended consequence of our grief has led to the inability to examine what November 22 did to us. It was a blow to the nation's solar plexus, leaving us in excruciating pain, but also causing arrested development and acute cynicism.

Dallas made the inconceivable possible. Before J. R. Ewing became a pop culture icon, Dallas was a euphemism for unfathomable shock. That is not to suggest we have not been stunned by subsequent tragic events, but for those living on November 22, 1963, America would never be the same. The decade that began with the Kennedy campaign running on the Frank Sinatra theme of "High Hopes" would later be defined more by Dr. Timothy Leary's nonconforming idiom: "Turn on, tune in, drop out." With brief exceptions, America has been overtly dominated primarily by an "us versus them" ethos that seems unwilling to forgo its suffocating grip on our democracy.

For those who believe that conspiracy theorists are a cabal of crackpots searching for a platform, it is reflective, however, of a fifty-year odyssey that continues to leave holes in the official explanation.

But cynicism does not occur overnight. In retrospect, the sleepy stereotypes that were held for the 1950s could not camouflage the obvious: cynicism was already there, lying dormant, waiting for the opportune moment. What led to the Vietnam protests later in the 1960s was created by decades of presidential leadership methodically kicking the can down the road. Vietnam was a mess before Lyndon Johnson was granted the opportunity to add his own tragic decisions to the equation. Civil rights did not begin in 1963, but that was the year it grabbed the nation's attention.

Therefore, 1963, in many ways, served as an incubator for cynicism yet unborn. Whatever cynicism may have dwelled beneath the surface, it was unleashed in Dallas. It immobilized the nation in

233

such a way that it has been unable look back on this year that for 365 days neatly wove hope and hostility into a single garment of possibility and pain.

What happened in the motorcade route changed the people, but elected leaders were slow to catch up, engrossed more in their traditional playbook than what was occurring in the hearts and minds of many Americans. But it was too late. On November 22, 1963, at approximately 12:30 PM CST, the memo went out from Dallas that change was on the horizon and there was no turning back.

Author's Note:

I was just old enough at the time of the assassination to include it in my personal lexicon of important events. Though I was only four years old, I remember it like it was yesterday. I was playing in the living room of my aunt's house; she was on the phone talking with a church friend. The game show *Concentration* was on the television. Suddenly, my aunt gave out a loud scream—an operator had come on the line asking her to clear it because the "president had been shot." My dad came home early from work. Even at four, I knew he came home the same time every day, but on November 22, he was early.

My interest in politics had already begun to take shape. I remembered JFK as president, and I knew Johnson was the new president, and I watched the events of that day and evening right along with my dad. But what I remember more than anything else that day were the tears that rolled down my dad's face as he watched the president's casket return to Washington, D.C., after being taken off Air Force One. It was the first and definitely the most memorable time I saw my father cry. It was at that moment, like Sam Pate, I knew, though I did not have the words to express it, that something had happened in the motorcade route.

Chapter Nine:

It Was Indeed a Year of Hope and Hostility

It could be argued that 1963, politically and culturally, was the midwife for what America has become in the twenty-first century. Though human history is ultimately a yarn forged by competing and often contradictory interests, could there be a more persuasive example of a year of hope and hostility since 1963?

This was the year that saw a governor ascend to the national platform on a foundation of race and hatred; it saw a young president inspire the people of Berlin and challenge his own nation before being struck down in Dallas. It was a year marred by violence on the streets of Birmingham, with its church bombing, police dogs, and high-powered fire hoses. But it was Birmingham that demonstrated that hatred could not trump hope. It was the jails of Birmingham that proved solitary confinement would not bring on writer's block but rather the inspiration for a 6,000-word epistle for the ages. And it was the streets of Birmingham that exhibited to the world that there was a type of internal fire that no amount of water could consume, no matter how powerfully the pressure was applied. And not even the heinous death of four children as they prepared for Sunday worship could erase from the minds of Americans the "dream" that was articulated in the nation's capital several weeks earlier.

But it was the tragedy in Dallas that officially placed an end to the 1950s. The 1960s—commonly associated with hippies, psychedelic music, the "summer of love," Vietnam protests, and urban unrest—was in essence a six-year odyssey that began in 1964. So was 1963 the end of the 1950s or the beginning of the 1960s? Perhaps it was both, and its uniqueness lies in its duality. 1963 was a year where two opposing forces, hope and hostility, lived in proximity—often intertwined. Kennedy, King, and Wallace are intertwined in 1963 as much as Birmingham is linked to Saigon, and all these elements serve to define that unique 365-day journey in the American experiment.

Another tragic irony from 1963 is that the main protagonists from this year—Kennedy, King, and Wallace—all met with violence. Of the three, only Wallace survived the 1960s, though he was confined to a wheelchair for the last twenty-six years of his life. And it was Kennedy, the most powerful and best protected of the three, who was the first to meet tragedy. The Kennedy assassination along with its years of subsequent conspiracy theories has prevented us from viewing 1963 on an even keel. Moreover, the systematic mythologizing of Kennedy and King in the aftermath of their deaths has somewhat blurred the lines between reality and idealism. Wallace's tangible influence may have been the most significant of the three. Though Wallace does not stand alone as America's only overly ambitious political animal, what he accomplished beginning in 1963 became a trademark for future politicians, particularly the members of the Republican Party.

The landmark civil rights legislation passed in 1964 and 1965 was fueled by the valiant efforts of those who took to the streets in nonviolent civil disobedience as well as the disharmony created by the brutality captured on television in 1963. The years after 1963 were marred by urban unrest, and the Vietnam protests enhanced fear, particularly among many white voters. Wallace tapped in to the age-old secret that reflects the potential shortcomings of a democracy:

When the stark choice is presented between people's hopes or people's fears, fear invariably triumphs. As Wallace stated in 1963, "The South is going to decide who the next president is; whoever the South votes for will be the president. You can't win without the South. You're going to see that the South is going to be against some folks."[326]

Wallace's not-so-subtle observation did not deafen Americans to the dog whistle of race and what would ultimately be the Southern Strategy. In the aftermath of the Civil Rights Act of 1964, many disaffected white voters found a new home in the Republican Party. Georgia Senator Richard Russell reportedly warned Johnson that his strong support for the civil rights bill "will not only cost you the South, it will cost you the election."[327] Though passage of the civil rights bill did not cost Johnson the election in 1964, the pendulum of momentum was swinging toward the Republican Party. Tapping into the fears of white voters in the South, Wallace's 1968 third-party presidential candidacy was the most successful since Theodore Roosevelt's in 1912. But self-appointed surrogates would continue the journey Wallace began in 1963.

In 1980, Ronald Reagan would successfully continue to use Nixon's Southern Strategy. Immediately following his the Republican nomination for president, Reagan made his first campaign stop at Neshoba County Fair, a few miles in Philadelphia, Mississippi. Philadelphia was the site where in 1964 the Ku Klux Klan murdered three civil rights workers. It was there that Reagan told the crowd, "I believe in states' rights."[328] For many of the whites in Mississippi and the surrounding areas who heard those words, the battle cry of Dixie had been granted an affirmation by the Republican nominee for president. With those five words, the cause of the Confederacy that split the nation lived on, the Supreme Court ruling *Plessy v. Ferguson* that upheld racial segregation lived on, and so did the valiant efforts of

---

[326] HBO, "A President to Remember: In the Company of John F. Kennedy," January 20, 2011.

[327] Taylor Branch, *Pillar of Fire* (New York: Simon & Schuster, 2006), 187.

[328] http://www.onlinemadison.com/ftp/reagan/reaganneshoba.mp3.

Southern governors, like Wallace, who wanted to prohibit black students from enrolling in public institutions of higher learning.

Many have debated whether this episode means Reagan was a racist, most notably *New York Times* columnist David Brooks. Brooks argued that most of Reagan's speech focused on the economy. He also pointed out that Regan courted the Urban League for their support, which suggests he was not racist.[329] But there is no way of knowing what was in Reagan's heart. There is certainly more historical evidence to suggest he was a not racist than to conclude otherwise, but this misses the point.

Regardless of what Reagan believed, the subtext of his words, based on this nation's history, was race. "I believe in states' rights" was a signal to white voters, and it is one that realizes its origins in some of America's darkest moments. It is difficult to believe that whoever wrote those words for Reagan was unaware of the racial overtones that find their genesis in the legacy of George Wallace circa 1963. Moreover, examining whether or not Reagan was racist downplays the fact that his words caused pain in the African American community. Intent has long been the false refuge of the perpetrator. When placing more emphasis on the victimizer's heart, there is a tendency to not hear the cries of the victim with the requisite sense of urgency.

Reagan is hardly alone in this nefarious waltz with evil and ambition. Other infamous examples such as the "Willie Horton" commercial during the 1988 presidential race and the Jesse Helms "hands" commercial in 1990 served to stoke white fears. But as late as 2006, the formula honed by Wallace still possessed a pulse in the veins of Republican electoral politics, as the Tennessee senatorial campaign proved.

The race between Republican Bob Corker and Democrat Harold Ford was one of the most competitive in the 2006 mid-term elections.

[329]David Brooks, "History and Calumny," *New York Times*, 9 November 2007.

But roughly two weeks before the election, the Republican National Committee aired a television ad titled "Who Hasn't?" In the controversial ad, a white woman says she met Ford (who is African American) at the Playboy Mansion. The ad concludes with the woman, as she winks to the camera, asking Ford to "call [her]."[330] Corker called the ad "distasteful"[331] and told MSNBC that it should come down.

There was, however, just enough truth in the ad to at least provide Republicans with an aura of cover. Ford, by his own admission, had attended a Super Bowl Party at the Playboy Mansion. But the undeniable subtext fueled the white fears tragically portrayed in D. W. Griffith's *Birth of a Nation* in 1915, Strom Thurmond's decision to leave the Democrats to run as a third-party presidential candidate in 1948, Wallace's commitment to never be "out-niggered," Nixon's Southern Strategy, and Reagan's belief in states' rights.

In 2005, Republican National Committee Chairman Ken Mehlman spoke at the NAACP annual convention, stating, "Some Republicans gave up on winning the African American vote, looking the other way on trying to benefit politically from racial polarization. I come here as Republican Chairman to tell you: We were wrong."[332]

As with Reagan, there is no way of knowing what was in Mehlman's heart. The words he spoke to the NAACP seemed heartfelt, but they also were in direct contradiction to the negative ad his party ran against Ford in 2006, along with his initial resistance to take it down. It would be presumptuous to assume the ad cost Ford the Tennessee senate race, but forty-three years after Wallace burst onto the national stage on a platform of race, there was still a belief lingering somewhere in Republican circles that such practices—

---

[330] Harold Ford, "Call Me," http://www.youtube.com/watch?v=24rM3--lIv8.

[331] M. Alex Johnson "Tennessee Ad Ignites GOP Squabble," NBC (October 25, 2006) http://www.nbcnews.com/id/15403071/ns/politics/t/tennessee-ad-ignites-internal-gop-squabbling/#.UcZUIODRfdk.

[332] Richard Bernedetto, "GOP: "We Were Wrong to Play Racial Politics," *USA Today*, http://usatoday30.usatoday.com/news/washington/2005-07-14-GOP-racial-politics_x.htm?csp=34 (July 14, 2005)

regardless of their vehement public denials, disassociations, and claims of ignorance as to the racial impact—still possessed a shelf life in their political arsenal.

The final word on this dubious display I leave to the late Republican political consultant Lee Atwater. In a 1981 interview, Atwater explained how abstract the racial coding had become:

You start out in 1954 by saying, "Nigger, nigger, nigger." By 1968 you can't say "nigger"—that hurts you, backfires. So you say stuff like, uh, forced busing, states' rights, and all that stuff, and you're getting so abstract. Now, you're talking about cutting taxes, and all these things you're talking about are totally economic things and a byproduct of them is, blacks get hurt worse than whites . . . "We want to cut this," is much more abstract than even the busing thing, uh, and a hell of a lot more abstract than "Nigger, nigger."[333]

There were also long-term negative ramifications for the Democratic Party. In 1960, when Lyndon Johnson sought the presidency, no Southerner had been elected since Zachary Taylor in 1848. From 1963 to 2008, three Democrats had been elected president—all from the South (Johnson, Carter, Clinton). During that same period, it was a commonly held belief that Democrats were weak on issues related to defense. This was the residue of the Vietnam quagmire and the ensuing anti-Vietnam protests.

What lessons have we learned from Vietnam? The policy decisions that led to the war in Vietnam were cemented in 1963. This can only be disputed by speculation based on what would have happened if Kennedy were not murdered on November 22. In the ensuing international conflicts, it would appear the greatest lesson learned was how to properly market the government's war effort.

[333]Rick Perlstein, "Lee Atwater's Infamous 1981 Interview on the Southern Strategy," *The Nation*, http://www.thenation.com/article/170841/exclusive-lee-atwaters-infamous-1981-interview-southern-strategy#axzz2X0ByGj5D

To diminish the protests that were symbolic of the 1960s, our presidential leaders have conveniently made war policy and support for the soldiers synonymous. Without a draft that would ensure a larger swath of Americans' participation, the all-volunteer armed forces are seductively used, through the manipulation of history, so that the Vietnam protests are now seen as America having turned its back on its soldiers. This places the emphasis on the soldiers rather than the policy. The problems with Vietnam were policy-oriented.

Since Vietnam, we've been systematically denied video footage of the fallen soldiers returning to Dover Air Force Base. In lieu of honest assessments, particularly with the conflicts in Afghanistan and Iraq in 2001 and 2003 respectively, Americans were rewarded with tax breaks—this was unprecedented in U.S. history. Today, simplistic catchphrases are preferred over honest debate, creating an unhealthy climate of nationalism. The nation becomes blind through the belief that it is on the side of good, seeing only the inerrancies of the mission.

But the successful marketing of a pain-free war cannot mask the pain that American soldiers have endured. If war changes people, what is the impact of multiple tours of duty in order to minimize the number of soldiers participating?

Could it be, in the attempt to maintain a pain-free war, that recent presidential leadership has become an exaggerated version of that which they claim to guard against? If the marketing efforts are in reaction, in part, to how the veterans of Vietnam were treated when they returned home, can one offer that the treatment of today's troops, who have endured multiple tours of duty in Afghanistan and Iraq, have improved?

Though the government has been successful in minimizing dissent and prolonging support, life after war for many soldiers has been challenging. It is impossible to return to the life that was; and for some, it is even more challenging to come to terms with the new life. The divorce rate, addiction, and depression prevalent in the larger society have taken a greater toll in the small community of soldiers and their families trying to reclaim the life they once had.

Though support for war inevitably comes with an expiration date, the successful marketing, based on the Vietnam experience, managed to expand the efforts in Afghanistan, resulting in the longest military effort in U.S. history.

Not enough Americans have a clear understanding of why the war in Vietnam happened. It is almost unfathomable to consider, given the number of lives lost and the staggering amount of money spent, that the country does not have a collective understanding of how it all began. It remains a sad commentary that beyond political public relations, very little has been absorbed. As a result, the failure to learn lessons from Vietnam will allow this generation to offer little more than a shrug to its posterity.

To define 1963 by what went wrong is to do a disservice to history. It makes sense that King's moral clarion call would be challenged, taken as they were, by Wallace's political ambition, Bull Connor's overt evil, and Kennedy's pragmatic desires to govern and to be reelected. But 1963 did not merely transform domestic and international political policy; it was also the year that Sidney Poitier won the Academy Award for best actor. This was the first time a black person was awarded this prestigious honor, reflecting a glimpse of hope that blacks could be viewed with the equality guaranteed by the Constitution. Unlike Hattie McDaniel, the first African American to win an Academy Award, for her portrayal as Mammy in *Gone with the Wind*, the significance of Poitier's victory was not simply that a black man won, but also the role he played. In addition to Poitier, A-list actors such as Paul Newman or Steve McQueen could have very easily portrayed Homer Smith because it was a role based on being a good person and it was not dependent on one's race. Poitier defeated an impressive list of Hollywood luminaries for the award, including Rex Harrison for *Cleopatra*, Paul Newman for *Hud*, Richard Harris for *The Sporting Life*, and Albert Finney for *Tom Jones*.

Hollywood, like the rest of America, has a history marred by the stench of racism, from *Birth of a Nation* to countless demeaning stereotypical portrayals of blacks in movies, reflecting much of the prevailing ethos of the times. But Poitier was different. He consistently played roles that ran counter to these depictions. By 1967, Poitier would star in three highly acclaimed movies, *To Sir, with Love*; *Guess Who's Coming to Dinner*; and *In the Heat of the Night*, making Poitier the most successful actor at the box office that year.

Poitier's body of work, and in particular the fact that he was acknowledged by his peers as delivering the best performance by a male actor, is further testimony to the hope that marked this transformative year.

It could also be argued that 1963 spawned the legacy of Walter Cronkite, who is often cited as "the most trusted man in America." In addition to his being the first to expand the nightly news coverage from fifteen minutes to a half hour, millions watched pensively as Cronkite told the nation, "From Dallas Texas, the flash apparently official, President Kennedy died at 1:00 PM, Central Standard Time."[334] Cronkite then glanced up at the clock, visibly fighting back tears, and continued, "two o'clock, Eastern Standard Time, some thirty-eight minutes ago."[335] But Cronkite had another iconic moment several weeks later, which was less significant at the time: he may have been the first to give the Beatles national attention.

On December 10, Cronkite ran a story about the growing Beatlemania phenomenon that was sweeping the United Kingdom, featuring their hit song "She Loves You." After seeing the report, Marsha Albert, a fifteen-year-old from Silver Spring, Maryland, wrote a letter to disc jockey Carroll James at radio station WWDC in the nation's capital. She asked, "Why can't we have music like that here in America?"[336] On December 17, James had Albert introduce the Beatles' next single, "I Want To Hold Your Hand," live on the air for

---

[334] JFK Assassination (CBS Coverage), Part 8 of 10, CBS News, November 22, 1963. http://www.youtube.com/watch?v=dzsYntj_YWk

[335] Ibid.

[336] Bruce Spizer, "Walter Cronkite Jumpstarted Beetlemania in America," http://www.beatlesnews.com/news/the-beatles/200907201306/how-walter-cronkite-jumpstarted-beatlemania-in-america.html.

its American debut. What ensued would be known as the "British Invasion." Over the next several years, in addition to the Beatles, Dusty Springfield, Herman's Hermits, The Kinks, The Animals, The Who, and the Rolling Stones would become household names.

The hope of conservation, as we know it today, can also trace its inception to this year of hope and hostility. Freshman Senator Gaylord Nelson from Wisconsin made environmental protection a priority upon entering office in 1963. He was the lone voice who introduced legislation to ban dichlorodiphenyltrichloroethane (DDT). It wouldn't be until 1972, when DDT was banned in the United States, that other members of Congress would come to understand Nelson's concerns.

But the freshman senator was determined to spur the nation's conscience on matters of conservation. In a White House letter dated May 16, 1963, the president wrote:

Dear Gaylord:

Arthur Schlesinger tells me you that have some thoughts about possible new initiatives in the field of conservation. I would be most interested in any suggestions that you might have to amplify our program.[337]

Nelson urged President Kennedy to go on a five-day, eleven-state "conservation tour," and Nelson accompanied him when he agreed. The tour did not immediately produce political fanfare. The press was more occupied with asking the president questions about the Nuclear Test Ban Treaty and the Soviet Union; ultimately, the tour left Nelson somewhat disappointed. But he remained committed to making the nation cognizant of conservation. Six years after the conservation tour, Nelson decided there should be a single day focused on environmental issues. Along with the momentum of local organizations across the country, Nelson took out a full-page ad in the *New York Times* in January 1970 to announce the inaugural Earth Day would be held on April 22.

---

[337] Letter from President Kennedy to Senator Gaylord Nelson (May 16, 1963), http://www.nelsonearthday.net/collection/conserv-environ/nelson_231-16_nelson-kennedy_correspondance_re_trip.pdf.

It was in this year of hope and hostility that the United States Supreme Court ruled unanimously, in the landmark decision of *Gideon v. Wainwright*, that state courts are required under the Sixth Amendment of the Constitution (which guarantees that in all criminal prosecutions, the accused shall enjoy the right to a speedy and public trial by an impartial jury of the State) and the Fourteenth Amendment (which guarantees equal protection under the law) to provide legal counsel for criminal cases.

On June 3, 1961, a burglary occurred at the Bay Harbor Pool Room in Panama City, Florida. The contents taken were approximately $5 in cash, along with several beers and sodas. A witness reported that Clarence Earl Gideon was in the poolroom at around five thirty that morning and that he left with a wine bottle and money in his pockets. The time Gideon was allegedly in the poolroom was within the timeframe the crime was believed to have occurred. This single eyewitness testimony was enough for police to arrest Gideon, charging him with breaking and entering with the intent to commit petty larceny.

Gideon was unable to afford legal representation and was forced to represent himself. The jury returned a guilty verdict, sentencing Gideon to five years in prison. Undeterred by his verdict, he continued his fight while incarcerated. With no formal legal training, Gideon wrote in pencil one of the most important pleas to the Supreme Court in history. Among the estimated thousands of pleas the Court receives annually, it chose to hear Gideon's case. On March 18, 1963, the Court ruled in favor of Gideon. The failure to receive counsel was a violation of the Sixth and Fourteenth Amendments of the Constitution. The Court agreed unanimously that everyone, regardless of his or her income status, is entitled to a lawyer when facing serious criminal charges.

Later that year, Attorney General Robert Kennedy would opine of the extremely extraordinary circumstances that led to this historic decision:

If an obscure Florida convict named Clarence Earl Gideon had not sat down in prison with a pencil and paper to write a letter to the Supreme Court, and if the Supreme Court had not taken the trouble to look for merit in that one crude petition among all the bundles of mail it must receive every day, the vast machinery of American law would have gone on functioning undisturbed. But Gideon did write that letter. The Court did look into his case and he was retried with the help of a competent defense counsel, found not guilty, and released from prison after two years of punishment for a crime he did not commit, and the whole course of American legal history has been changed.[338]

In 1963, Gideon opened the door to other landmark Sixth Amendment cases in that decade: *Massiah v. United States* (1964), in which the Court ruled the Sixth Amendment prohibits the government from eliciting statements from defendants about themselves after the point that the Sixth Amendment right to counsel attaches; and *Miranda v. Arizona*, where the court held that statements made in response to interrogation by a defendant in police custody will be admissible at trial only if the prosecution can show the defendant was informed of the right to consult with an attorney before and during questioning along with the right against self-incrimination. So much of what we now take for granted today in terms of civil and legal rights realized its genesis in 1963.

What does 1963 in its totality teach us? The overall importance of 1963 is the overall importance of history. It is another cog that tells the ongoing saga of who we are and how we came to be, while providing some insight on where we go from here. Just as our present health is influenced by our past, the same holds true for history. The more we can examine that history through the dispassionate lens of what happened, the more we can grow from it.

---

[338] *Clarence Earl Gideon v. Wainwright*, November 11, 1963, http://www.nelsonearthday.net/collection/conserv-environ/nelson_231-16_nelson-kennedy_correspondance_re_trip.pdf

246

This year of hope and hostility also provided a future president with two profound and life-changing moments. On July 24, the American Legion Boys Nation visited the White House. As a high school student and delegate to the American Legion Boys Nation, a sixteen-year-old Bill Clinton met President Kennedy in the White House Rose Garden. The iconic photograph and footage of the current and future presidents shaking hands embodied Kennedy's words at his inaugural address: "The torch has been passed to a new generation of Americans."[339]

By Clinton's own admission, the other event was King's eloquent address at the Washington Mall. On the thirty-fifth anniversary of King's speech, Clinton said, "I remember weeping uncontrollably during Martin Luther King's speech. And I remember thinking, when it was over, my country would never be the same and neither would I."[340]

In 1960, former President Harry Truman was concerned about Kennedy's lack of experience and urged him to wait to run for president until he was more seasoned. But Kennedy responded in part by saying, "The world is changing. The old ways will not do."[341] Kennedy did not know how right he was.

This year of hope and hostility demonstrates that the world was indeed changing. It is so easy in our twenty-first century context to view the national and international events of 1963 through our contemporary lens. But in the 1960s, the nation was going through the

---

[339] John F. Kennedy Inaugural Address, January 20, 1961, http://www.bartleby.com/124/pres56.html

[340] Editorial, "In Clinton's Remarks: A Focus on Interdependence and Forgiveness," New York Times, 28 August 1998,
http://www.nytimes.com/1998/08/29/us/in-clinton-s-remarks-a-focus-on-interdependence-and-forgiveness.html?pagewanted=all&src=pm

[341] John F. Kennedy Accepting the Democratic Party Nomination, Memorial Coliseum, Los Angeles, July 15, 1960,
http://www.presidency.ucsb.edu/ws/?pid=25966.

early stages of civil rights puberty, coming to terms with the dangers of the Cold War, and formulating a hopeless quagmire, the impact of which we have yet to fully understand. Moreover, the role of history is not to examine what should have happened, but to observe what actually happened and investigate the lessons to be learned from it.

The year 1963 was amazing. One day it was civil rights, the next it was the Cold War, the next Vietnam, and on a single day in June it was an unprecedented combination of all three. But one of the important lessons that can be garnered from 1963 is that change never occurs as quickly as it is hoped by those who desire it. The year of hope and hostility did not solve civil rights, the Cold War, or Vietnam. But 1963 revealed that America was a far more complex nation than it was prepared to concede. And in that sense, not much has changed.

Appendix:

Key Speeches and Writing from 1963

1963 Inaugural Address
of Governor George C. Wallace

January 14, 1963
Montgomery, Alabama

OPENING REMARKS

Governor Patterson, Governor Barnett, from one of the greatest states in this nation, Mississippi, Judge Brown, representing Governor Hollings of South Carolina, members of the Alabama Congressional Delegation, members of the Alabama Legislature, distinguished guests, fellow Alabamians:

Before I begin my talk with you, I want to ask you for a few minutes patience while I say something that is on my heart: I want to thank those home folks of my county who first gave an anxious country boy his opportunity to serve in State politics. I shall always owe a lot to those who gave me that <u>first</u> opportunity to serve.

I will never forget the warm support and close loyalty at the folks of Suttons, Haigler's Mill, Eufaula, Beat 6 and Beat 14, Richards Cross Roads and Gammage Beat . . . at Baker Hill, Beat 8, and Comer, Spring Hill, Adams Chapel and Mount Andrew . . . White Oak, Baxter's Station, Clayton, Louisville and Cunnigham Place; Horns Crossroads, Texasville and Blue Springs, where the vote was 304 for Wallace and 1 for the opposition . . . and the dear little lady whom I heard had made that one vote against me . . by mistake . . because she couldn't see too well . . and she had pulled the wrong lever . . . Bless her heart. At Clio, my birthplace, and Elamville. I shall never forget them. May God bless them.

And I shall forever remember that election day morning as I waited . . . and suddenly at ten o'clock that morning the first return of a box was flashed over this state: it carried the message . . . . Wallace 15, opposition zero; and it came from the Hamrick Beat at Putman's

Mountain where live the great hill people of our state. May God bless the mountain man . . . his loyalty is unshakeable, he'll do to walk down the road with.

I hope you'll forgive me these few moments of remembering . . . but I wanted them . . and you . . to know, that I shall never forget.

And I wish I could shake hands and thank all of you in this state who voted for me . . and those of you who did not . . for I know you voted your honest convictions . . . and now, we must stand together and move the great State of Alabama forward.

I would be remiss, this day, if I did not thank my wonderful wife and fine family for their patience, support and loyalty . . . . and there is no man living who does not owe more to his mother than he can ever repay, and I want my mother to know that I realize my debt to her.

This is the day of my Inauguration as Governor of the State of Alabama. And on this day I feel a deep obligation to renew my pledges, my covenants with you . . . the people of this great state.

General Robert E. Lee said that "duty" is the sublimest word on the English language and I have come, increasingly, to realize what he meant. I SHALL do my duty to you, God helping . . . to every man, to every woman . . . yes, to every child in this state. I shall fulfill my duty toward honesty and economy in our State government so that no man shall have a part of his livelihood cheated and no child shall have a bit of his future stolen away.

I have said to you that I would eliminate the liquor agents in this state and that the money saved would be returned to our citizens . . . I am happy to report to you that I am now filling orders for several hundred one-way tickets and stamped on them are these words . . . "for liquor agents . . . destination: . . . out of Alabama." I am happy to report to you that the big-wheeling cocktail-party boys have gotten the word that their free whiskey and boat rides are over . . . that the farmer in the field, the worker in the factory, the businessman in his office, the housewife in her home, have decided that the money can be better spent to help our children's education and our older citizens . . . and they have put a man in office to see that it is done. It shall be done. Let me say one more time . . . . no more liquor drinking in your governor's mansion.

I shall fulfill my duty in working hard to bring industry into our state, not only by maintaining an honest, sober and free-enterprise climate of government in which industry can have confidence . . but in going out and getting it . . . so that our people can have industrial jobs in Alabama and provide a better life for their children.

I shall not forget my duty to our senior citizens . . . so that their lives can be lived in dignity and enrichment of the golden years, nor to our sick, both mental and physical . . . and they will know we have not forsaken them. I want the farmer to feel confident that in this State government he has a partner who will work with him in raising his income and increasing his markets. And I want the laboring man to know he has a friend who is sincerely striving to better his field of endeavor.

I want to assure every child that this State government is not afraid to invest in their future through education, so that they will not be handicapped on every threshold of their lives.

Today I have stood, where once Jefferson Davis stood, and took an oath to my people. It is very appropriate then that from this Cradle of the Confederacy, this very Heart of the Great Anglo-Saxon Southland, that today we sound the drum for freedom as have our generations of forebears before us done, time and time again through history. Let us rise to the call of freedom-loving blood that is in us and send our answer to the tyranny that clanks its chains upon the South. In the name of the greatest people that have ever trod this earth, I draw the line in the dust and toss the gauntlet before the feet of tyranny . . . and I say . . . segregation today . . . segregation tomorrow . . . segregation forever.

The Washington, D.C. school riot report is disgusting and revealing. We will not sacrifice our children to any such type school system--and you can write that down. The federal troops in Mississippi could be better used guarding the saftey of the citizens of Washington, D.C., where it is even unsafe to walk or go to a ballgame--and that is the nation's capitol. I was safer in a B-29 bomber over Japan during the war in an air raid, than the people of Washington are walking to the White House neighborhood. A closer example is Atlanta. The city officials fawn for political reasons over school integration and THEN build barricades to stop residential integration--what hypocrisy!

Let us send this message back to Washington by our representatives who are with us today . . that from this day we are standing up, and the heel of tyranny does not fit the neck of an upright man . . . that we intend to take the offensive and carry our fight for freedom across the nation, wielding the balance of power we know we possess in the Southland . . . . that WE, not the insipid bloc of voters of some sections . . will determine in the next election who shall sit in the White House of these United States . . . That from this day, from this hour . . . from this minute . . . we give the word of a race of honor that we will tolerate their boot in our face no longer . . . . and let those certain judges put that in their opium pipes of power and smoke it for what it is worth.

Hear me, Southerners! You sons and daughters who have moved north and west throughout this nation . . . . we call on you from your native soil to join with us in national support and vote . . and we know . . . wherever you are . . away from the hearths of the Southland . . . that you will respond, for though you may live in the fartherest reaches of this vast country . . . . your heart has never left Dixieland.

And you native sons and daughters of old New England's rock-ribbed patriotism . . . and you sturdy natives of the great Mid-West . . and you descendants of the far West flaming spirit of pioneer freedom . . we invite you to come and be with us . . for you are of the Southern spirit . . and the Southern philosophy . . . you are Southerners too and brothers with us in our fight.

What I have said about segregation goes double this day . . . and what I have said to or about some federal judges goes TRIPLE this day.

Alabama has been blessed by God as few states in this Union have been blessed. Our state owns ten percent of all the natural resources of all the states in our country. Our inland waterway system is second to none . . . and has the potential of being the greatest waterway transport system in the entire world. We possess over thirty minerals in usable quantities and our soil is rich and varied, suited to a wide variety of plants. Our native pine and forestry system produces timber faster than we can cut it and yet we have only pricked the surface of the great lumber and pulp potential.

With ample rainfall and rich grasslands our live stock industry is in the infancy of a giant future that can make us a center of the big and growing meat packing and prepared foods marketing. We have the favorable climate, streams, woodlands, beaches, and natural beauty to make us a recreational mecca in the booming tourist and vacation industry. Nestled in the great Tennessee Valley, we possess the Rocket center of the world and the keys to the space frontier.

While the trade with a developing Europe built the great port cities of the east coast, our own fast developing port of Mobile faces as a magnetic gateway to the great continent of South America, well over twice as large and hundreds of times richer in resources, even now awakening to the growing probes of enterprising capital with a potential of growth and wealth beyond any present dream for our port development and corresponding results throughout the connecting waterways that thread our state.

And while the manufacturing industries of free enterprise have been coming to our state in increasing numbers, attracted by our bountiful natural resouces, our growing numbers of skilled workers and our favorable conditions, their present rate of settlement here can be increased from the trickle they now represent to a stream of enterprise and endeavor, capital and expansion that can join us in our work of development and enrichment of the educational futures of our children, the opportunities of our citizens and the fulfillment of our talents as God has given them to us. To realize our ambitions and to bring to fruition our dreams, we as Alabamians must take cognizance of the world about us. We must re-define our heritage, re-school our thoughts in the lessons our forefathers knew so well, first hand, in order to function and to grow and to prosper. We can no longer hide our head in the sand and tell ourselves that the ideology of our free fathers is not being attacked and is not being threatened by another idea . . . for it is. We are faced with an idea that if a centralized government assume enough authority, enough power over its people, that it can provide a utopian life . . that if given the power to dictate, to forbid, to require, to demand, to distribute, to edict and to judge what is best and enforce that will produce only "good" . . and it shall be our father . . . . and our God. It is an idea of government that encourages our fears and destroys our faith . . . for where there is faith, there is no fear, and where there is fear, there is no faith. In encouraging our fears of economic insecurity it demands we place that economic management and control with government; in encouraging our fear of educational development it demands we place that education and the minds of our children under management and control of government, and even in feeding our fears of physical infirmities and declining years, it offers and demands to father us through it all and even into the grave. It is a government that claims to us that it is bountiful as it buys its power from us with the fruits of its rapaciousness of the wealth that free men before it have produced and builds on crumbling credit without responsibilities to the debtors . . . our children. It is an ideology of government erected on the encouragement of fear and fails to recognize the basic law of our fathers that governments do not produce wealth . . . people produce wealth . . . free people; and those people become less free . . . as they learn there is little reward for ambition . . . that it requires faith to risk . . . and they have none . . as the government must restrict and penalize and tax incentive and endeavor and must increase its expenditures of bounties . . . then this government must assume more and more police powers and we find we are become government-fearing people . . . not God-fearing people. We find we have replaced faith with fear . . . and though we may give lip service to the Almighty . . in reality, government has become our god. It is, therefore, a basically ungodly government and its appeal to the psuedo-intellectual and the politician is to change their status from servant of the people to master of the people . . . to play at being God . . . without faith in God . . . and without the wisdom of God. It is a system that is the very opposite of Christ for it feeds and encourages everything degenerate and base in our people as it assumes the responsibilities that we ourselves should assume. Its psuedo-liberal spokesmen and some Harvard advocates have never examined the logic of its substitution of what it calls "human rights" for individual rights, for its propaganda play on words has appeal for the unthinking. Its logic is totally material and irresponsible as it runs the full gamut of human desires . . . including the theory that everyone has voting rights without the spiritual responsibility of preserving freedom. Our founding fathers recognized those rights . . . but only within the framework of those spiritual responsiblities. But the strong, simple faith and sane reasoning of our founding fathers has long since been forgotten as the so-called "progressives" tell us that our Constitution was written for "horse and buggy" days . . . so were the Ten Commandments.

Not so long ago men stood in marvel and awe at the cities, the buildings, the schools, the autobahns that the government of Hitler's Germany had built . . . just as centuries before they stood in wonder of Rome's building . . . but it could not stand . . . for the system that built it had rotted the souls of the builders . . . and in turn . . . rotted the foundation of what God meant that men should be. Today that same system on an international scale is sweeping the world. It is the "changing world" of which we are told . . . it is called "new" and "liberal". It is as old as the oldest dictator. It is degenerate and decadent. As the national racism of Hitler's Germany persecuted a national minority to the whim of a national majority . . . so the international racism of the liberals seek to persecute the international white minority to the whim of the international colored majority . . . so that we are footballed about according to the favor of the Afro-Asian bloc. But the Belgian survivors of the Congo cannot present their case to a war crimes commission . . . nor the Portuguese of Angola . . . nor the survivors of Castro . . . nor the citizens of Oxford, Mississippi.

256

It is this theory of international power politic that led a group of men on the Supreme Court for the first time in American history to issue an edict, based not on legal precedent, but upon a volume, the editor of which said our Constitution is outdated and must be changed and the writers of which, some had admittedly belonged to as many as half a hundred communist-front organizations. It is this theory that led this same group of men to briefly bare the ungodly core of that philosophy in forbidding little school children to say a prayer. And we find the evidence of that ungodliness even in the removal of the words "in God we trust" from some of our dollars, which was placed there as like evidence by our founding fathers as the faith upon which this system of government was built. It is the spirit of power thirst that caused a President in Washington to take up Caesar's pen and with one stroke of it make a law. A Law which the law making body of Congress refused to pass . . . a law that tells us that we can or cannot buy or sell our very homes, except by his conditions . . . and except at HIS descretion. It is the spirit of power thirst that led the same President to launch a full offensive of twenty-five thousand troops against a university . . . of all places . . . in his own country . . . and against his own people, when this nation maintains only six thousand troops in the beleagured city of Berlin. We have witnessed such acts of "might makes right" over the world as men yielded to the temptation to play God . . . but we have never before witnessed it in America. We reject such acts as free men. We do not defy, for there is nothing to defy . . . since as free men we do not recognize any government right to give freedom . . . or deny freedom. No government erected by man has that right. As Thomas Jefferson said, "The God who gave us life, gave us liberty at the same time; no King holds the right of liberty in his hands." Nor does any ruler in American government.

We intend, quite simply, to practice the free heritage as bequeathed to us as sons of free fathers. We intend to re-vitalize the truly new and progressive form of government that is less that two hundred years old . . . a government first founded in this nation simply and purely on faith . . . that there is a personal God who rewards good and punishes evil . . . that hard work will receive its just deserts . . . that ambition and ingenuity and incentiveness . . . and profit of such . . are admirable traits and goals . . that the individual is encouraged in his spiritual growth and from that growth arrives at a character that enhances his charity toward others and from that character and that charity so is influenced business, and labor and farmer and government. We intend to renew our faith as God-fearing men . . . <u>not</u> government-fearing men nor any other kind of fearing-men. We intend to roll up our sleeves and pitch in to develop this full bounty God has given us . . . to live full and useful lives and in absolute freedom from all fear. Then can we enjoy the full richness of the Great American Dream.

We have placed this sign, "In God We Trust," upon our State Capitol on this Inauguration Day as physical evidence of determination to renew the faith of our fathers and to practice the free heritage they bequeathed to us. We do this with the clear and solemn knowledge that such physical evidence is evidently a direct violation of the logic of that Supreme Court in Washington D.C., and if they or their spokesmen in this state wish to term this defiance . . . I say . . . then let them make the most of it.

This nation was never meant to be a unit of one . . . but a united of the many . . . . that is the exact reason our freedom loving forefathers established the states, so as to divide the rights and powers among the states, insuring that no central power could gain master government control.

In united effort we were meant to live under this government . . . whether Baptist, Methodist, Presbyterian, Church of Christ, or whatever one's denomonation or religious belief . . . each respecting the others right to a separate denomination . . . each, by working to develop his own, enriching the total of all our lives through united effort. And so it was meant in our political lives . . . whether Republican, Democrat, Prohibition, or whatever political party . . . each striving from his separate political station . . . respecting the rights of others to be separate and work from within their political framework . . . and each separate political station making its contribution to our lives . . . .

And so it was meant in our racial lives . . . each race, within its own framework has the freedom to teach . . to instruct . . to develop . . to ask for and receive deserved help from others of separate racial stations. This is the great freedom of our American founding fathers . . . but if we amalgamate into the one unit as advocated by the communist philosophers . . then the enrichment of our lives . . . the freedom for our development . . . is gone forever. We become, therefore, a mongrel unit of one under a single all powerful government . . . and we stand for everything . . . and for nothing.

The true brotherhood of America, of respecting the separateness of others . . and uniting in effort . . has been so twisted and distorted from its original concept that there is a small wonder that communism is winning the world.

We invite the negro citizens of Alabama to work with us from his separate racial station . . as we will work with him . . to develop, to grow in individual freedom and enrichment. We want jobs and a good future for BOTH races . . the tubercular and the infirm. This is the basic heritage of my religion, if which I make full practice . . . . for we are all the handiwork of God.

But we warn those, of any group, who would follow the false doctrine of communistic amalgamation that we will not surrender our system of government . . . our freedom of race and religion . . . that freedom was won at a hard price and if it requires a hard price to retain it . . we are able . . and quite willing to pay it.

The liberals' theory that poverty, discrimination and lack of opportunity is the cause of communism is a false theory . . . if it were true the South would have been the biggest single communist bloc in the western hemisphere long ago . . . for after the great War Between the States, our people faced a desolate land of burned universities, destroyed crops and homes, with manpower depleted and crippled, and even the mule, which was required to work the land, was so scarce that whole communities shared one animal to make the spring plowing.

There were no government handouts, no Marshall Plan aid, no coddling to make sure that <u>our</u> people would not suffer; instead the South was set upon by the vulturous carpetbagger and federal troops, all loyal Southerners were denied the vote at the point of bayonet, so that the infamous, illegal 14th Amendment might be passed. There was no money, no food and no hope of either. But our grandfathers bent their knee only in church and bowed their head only to God.

Not for a single instant did they ever consider the easy way of federal dictatorship and amalgamation in return for fat bellies. They fought. They dug sweet roots from the ground with their bare hands and boiled them in iron pots . . . . they gathered poke salad from the woods and acorns from the ground. They fought. They followed no false doctrine . . . they knew what the wanted . . and they fought for freedom! They came up from their knees in the greatest disply of sheer nerve, grit and guts that has ever been set down in the pages of written history . . . and they won! The great writer, Rudyard Kipling wrote of them, that: "There in the Southland of the United States of America, lives the greatest fighting breed of man . . . in all the world!"

And that is why today, I stand ashamed of the fat, well-fed whimperers who say that it is inevitable . . . that our cause is lost. I am ashamed <u>of</u> them . . . . and I am ashamed <u>for</u> them. They do not represent the people of the Southland.

And may we take note of one other fact, with all trouble with communists that some sections of this country have . . . there are not enough native communists in the South to fill up a telephone booth . . . and THAT is a matter of public FBI record.

We remind all within hearing of this Southland that a <u>Southerner</u>, Peyton Randolph, presided over the Continental Congress in our nation's beginning . . . that a <u>Southerner</u>, Thomas Jefferson, wrote the Declaration of Independence, that a <u>Southerner</u>, George Washington, is the Father of our country . . . that a <u>Southerner</u>, James Madison, authored our Constitution, that a <u>Southerner</u>, George Mason, authored the Bill of Rights and it was a Southerner who said, "Give me liberty . . . . . or give me death," Patrick Henry.

Southerners played a most magnificent part in erecting this great divinely inspired system of freedom . . and as God is our witnesses, Southerners will save it.

Let us, as Alabamians, grasp the hand of destiny and walk out of the shadow of fear . . . and fill our divine destination. Let us not simply defend . . but let us assume the leadership of the fight and carry our leadership across this nation. God has placed us here in this crisis . . . let is not fail in this . . our most historical moment.

You are here today, present in this audience, and to you over this great state, wherever you are in sound of my voice, I want to humbly and with all sincerity, thank you for your faith in me.

I promise you that I will try to make you a good governor. I promise you that, as God gives me the wisdom and the strength, I will be sincere with you. I will be honest with you.

I will apply the old sound rule of our fathers, that anything worthy of our defense is worthy of one hundred percent of our defense. I have been taught that freedom meant freedom from any threat or fear of government. I was born in that freedom, I was raised in that freedom . . . I intend to live live in that freedom . . . and God willing, when I die, I shall leave that freedom to my children . . . as my father left it to me.

My pledge to you . . . to "Stand up for Alabama," is a stronger pledge today than it was the first day I made that pledge. I shall "Stand up for Alabama," as Governor of our State . . . you stand with me . . . and we, together, can give courageous leadership to millions of people throughout this nation who look to the South for their hope in this fight to win and preserve our freedoms and liberties.

So help me God.

And my prayer is that the Father who reigns above us will bless all the people of this great sovereign State and nation, both white and black.

I thank you.

Statement by Alabama Clergymen, April 12, 1963

We the undersigned clergymen are among those who, in January, issued "An Appeal for Law and Order and Common Sense," in dealing with racial problems in Alabama. We expressed understanding that honest convictions in racial matters could properly be pursued in the courts, but urged that decisions of those courts should in the meantime be peacefully obeyed.

Since that time there had been some evidence of increased forbearance and a willingness to face facts. Responsible citizens have undertaken to work on various problems which cause racial friction and unrest. In Birmingham, recent public events have given indication that we will have opportunity for a new constructive and realistic approach to racial problems.

However, we are now confronted by a series of demonstrations by some of our Negro citizens, directed and led in part by outsiders. We recognize the natural impatience of people who feel that their hopes are slow in being realized. But we are convinced that these demonstrations are unwise and untimely.

We agree rather with certain local Negro leadership which has called for honest and open negotiation of racial issues in our area. And we believe this kind of facing of issues can best be accomplished by citizens of our own metropolitan area, white and Negro, meeting with their knowledge and experience of the local situation. All of us need to face that responsibility and find proper channels for its accomplishment.

Just as we formerly pointed out that "hatred and violence have no sanction in our religious and political traditions," we also point out that such actions as incite to hatred and violence, however technically peaceful those actions may be, have not contributed to the resolution of our local problems. We do not believe that these days of new hope are days when extreme measures are justified in Birmingham.

We commend the community as a whole, and the local news media and law enforcement officials in particular, on the calm manner in which these demonstrations have been handled. We urge the public to continue to show restraint should the demonstrations continue, and the law enforcement officials to remain calm and continue to protect our city from violence.

We further strongly urge our own Negro community to withdraw support from these demonstrations, and to unite locally in working peacefully for a better Birmingham. When rights are consistently denied, a cause should be pressed in the courts and in negotiations among local leaders, and not in the streets. We appeal to both our white and Negro citizenry to observe the principles of law and order and common sense.

Signed by:

C.C.J. Carpenter, D.D., LL.D., Bishop of Alabama

Joseph A. Durick, D.D., Auxiliary Bishop, Diocese of Mobile-Birmingham

Rabbi Milton L. Grafman, Temple Emanu-El, Birmingham, Alabama

Bishop Paul Hardin, Bishop of the Alabama-West Florida Conference of the Methodist Church

Bishop Nolan B. Harmon, Bishop of the North Alabama Conference of the Methodist Church

George M. Murray, D.D., LL.D., Bishop Coadjutor, Episcopal Diocese of Alabama

Edward V. Ramage, Moderator, Synod of the Alabama Presbyterian Church in the United States

Earl Stallings, Pastor, First Baptist Church, Birmingham, Alabama

Letter From Birmingham Jail, April 16, 1963
By Martin Luther King, Jr.

My Dear Fellow Clergymen:

(1) While confined here in the Birmingham city jail, I came across your recent statement calling my present activities "unwise and untimely." Seldom do I pause to answer criticism of my work and ideas. If I sought to answer all the criticisms that cross my desk, my secretaries would have little time for anything other than such correspondence in the course of the day, and I would have no time for constructive work. But since I feel that you are men of genuine good will and that your criticisms are sincerely set forth, I want to try to answer your statements in what I hope will be patient and reasonable terms.

(2) I think I should indicate why I am here In Birmingham, since you have been influenced by the view which argues against "outsiders coming in." I have the honor of serving as president of the Southern Christian Leadership Conference, an organization operating in every southern state, with headquarters in Atlanta, Georgia. We have some eighty-five affiliated organizations across the South, and one of them is the Alabama Christian Movement for Human Rights. Frequently we share staff, educational and financial resources with our affiliates. Several months ago the affiliate here in Birmingham asked us to be on call to engage in a nonviolent direct-action program if such were deemed necessary. We readily consented, and when the hour came we lived up to our promise. So I, along with several members of my staff, am here because I was invited here. I am here because I have organizational ties here.

(3) But more basically, I am in Birmingham because injustice is here. Just as the prophets of the eighth century B.C. left their villages and carried their "thus saith the Lord" far beyond the boundaries of their home towns, and just as the Apostle Paul left his village of Tarsus

and carried the gospel of Jesus Christ to the far corners of the Greco-Roman world, so am I compelled to carry the gospel of freedom beyond my own home town. Like Paul, I must constantly respond to the Macedonian call for aid. Moreover, I am cognizant of the interrelatedness of all communities and states. I cannot sit idly by in Atlanta and not be concerned about what happens in Birmingham. Injustice anywhere is a threat to justice everywhere. We are caught in an inescapable network of mutuality, tied in a single garment of destiny. Whatever affects one directly, affects all indirectly. Never again can we afford to live with the narrow, provincial "outside agitator" idea. Anyone who lives inside the United States can never be considered an outsider anywhere within its bounds.

(4) You deplore the demonstrations taking place in Birmingham. But your statement, I am sorry to say, fails to express a similar concern for the conditions that brought about the demonstrations. I am sure that none of you would want to rest content with the superficial kind of social analysis that deals merely with effects and does not grapple with underlying causes. It is unfortunate that demonstrations are taking place in Birmingham, but it is even more unfortunate that the city's white power structure left the Negro community with no alternative.

(5) In any nonviolent campaign there are four basic steps: collection of the facts to determine whether injustices exist; negotiation; self-purification; and direct action. We have gone through all of these steps in Birmingham. There can be no gainsaying the fact that racial injustice engulfs this community. Birmingham is probably the most thoroughly segregated city in the United States. Its ugly record of brutality is widely known. Negroes have experienced grossly unjust treatment in the courts. There have been more unsolved bombings of Negro homes and churches in Birmingham than in any other city in the nation. These are the hard, brutal facts of the case. On the basis of these conditions, Negro leaders sought to negotiate with the city fathers. But the latter consistently refused to engage in good-faith negotiation.

(6) Then, last September, came the opportunity to talk with leaders of Birmingham's economic community. In the course of the negotiations, certain promises were made by the merchants--for example, to remove the stores humiliating racial signs. On the basis of these promises, the Reverend Fred Shuttlesworth and the leaders of the Alabama Christian Movement for Human Rights agreed to a moratorium on all demonstrations. As the weeks and months went by, we realized that we were the victims of a broken promise. A few signs, briefly removed, returned; the others remained. As in so many past experiences, our hopes had been blasted, and the shadow of deep disappointment settled upon us. We had no alternative except to prepare for direct action, whereby we would present our very bodies as a means of laying our case before the conscience of the local and the national community. Mindful of the difficulties involved, we decided to undertake a process of self-purification. We began a series of workshops on nonviolence, and we repeatedly asked ourselves: "Are you able to accept blows without retaliating?" "Are you able to endure the ordeal of jail?" We decided to schedule our direct-action program for the Easter season, realizing that except for Christmas, this is the main shopping period of the year. Knowing that a strong economic withdrawal program would be the by-product of direct action, we felt that this would be the best time to bring pressure to bear on the merchants for the needed change.

(7) Then it occurred to us that Birmingham's mayoralty election was coming up in March, and we speedily decided to postpone action until after election day. When we discovered that the Commissioner of Public Safety, Eugene "Bull" Connor, had piled up enough votes to be in the run-off we decided again to postpone action until the day after the run-off so that the demonstrations could not be used to cloud the issues. Like many others, we waited to see Mr. Connor defeated, and to this end we endured postponement after postponement. Having aided in this community need, we felt that our direct-action program could be delayed no longer.

(8) You may well ask: "Why direct action? Why sit-ins, marches and so forth? Isn't negotiation a better path?" You are quite right in calling for negotiation. Indeed, this is the very purpose of direct action. Nonviolent direct action seeks to create such a crisis and foster such a tension that a community which has constantly refused to negotiate is forced to confront the issue. It seeks to so dramatize the issue that it can no longer be ignored. My citing the creation of tension as part of the work of the nonviolent-resister may sound rather shocking. But I must confess that I am not afraid of the word "tension." I have earnestly opposed violent tension, but there is a type of constructive, nonviolent tension which is necessary for growth. Just as Socrates felt that it was necessary to create a tension in the mind so that individuals could rise from the bondage of myths and half-truths to the unfettered realm of creative analysis and objective appraisal, we must we see the need for nonviolent gadflies to create the kind of tension in society that will help men rise from the dark depths of prejudice and racism to the majestic heights of understanding and brotherhood.

(9) The purpose of our direct-action program is to create a situation so crisis-packed that it will inevitably open the door to negotiation. I therefore concur with you in your call for negotiation. Too long has our beloved Southland been bogged down in a tragic effort to live in monologue rather than dialogue.

(10) One of the basic points in your statement is that the action that I and my associates have taken in Birmingham is untimely. Some have asked: "Why didn't you give the new city administration time to act?" The only answer that I can give to this query is that the new Birmingham administration must be prodded about as much as the outgoing one, before it will act. We are sadly mistaken if we feel that the election of Albert Boutwell as mayor will bring the millennium to Birmingham. While Mr. Boutwell is a much more gentle person than Mr. Connor, they are both segregationists, dedicated to maintenance of the status quo. I have hope that Mr. Boutwell will be reasonable enough to see the futility of massive resistance to desegregation. But he will not see this without pressure from devotees of civil rights. My

friends, I must say to you that we have not made a single civil rights gain without determined legal and nonviolent pressure. Lamentably, it is an historical fact that privileged groups seldom give up their privileges voluntarily. Individuals may see the moral light and voluntarily give up their unjust posture; but, as Reinhold Niebuhr has reminded us, groups tend to be more immoral than individuals.

(11) We know through painful experience that freedom is never voluntarily given by the oppressor; it must be demanded by the oppressed. Frankly, I have yet to engage in a direct-action campaign that was "well timed" in the view of those who have not suffered unduly from the disease of segregation. For years now I have heard the word "Wait!" It rings in the ear of every Negro with piercing familiarity. This "Wait" has almost always meant "Never." We must come to see, with one of our distinguished jurists, that "justice too long delayed is justice denied."

(12) We have waited for more than 340 years for our constitutional and God-given rights. The nations of Asia and Africa are moving with jetlike speed toward gaining political independence, but we stiff creep at horse-and-buggy pace toward gaining a cup of coffee at a lunch counter. Perhaps it is easy for those who have never felt the stinging dark of segregation to say, "Wait." But when you have seen vicious mobs lynch your mothers and fathers at will and drown your sisters and brothers at whim; when you have seen hate-filled policemen curse, kick and even kill your black brothers and sisters; when you see the vast majority of your twenty million Negro brothers smothering in an airtight cage of poverty in the midst of an affluent society; when you suddenly find your tongue twisted and your speech stammering as you seek to explain to your six-year-old daughter why she can't go to the public amusement park that has just been advertised on television, and see tears welling up in her eyes when she is told that Funtown is closed to colored children, and see ominous clouds of inferiority beginning to form in her little mental sky, and see her beginning to distort her personality by developing an unconscious bitterness toward white people; when you have to concoct an answer

268

for a five-year-old son who is asking: "Daddy, why do white people treat colored people so mean?"; when you take a cross-country drive and find it necessary to sleep night after night in the uncomfortable corners of your automobile because no motel will accept you; when you are humiliated day in and day out by nagging signs reading "white" and "colored"; when your first name becomes "nigger," your middle name becomes "boy" (however old you are) and your last name becomes "John," and your wife and mother are never given the respected title "Mrs."; when you are harried by day and haunted by night by the fact that you are a Negro, living constantly at tiptoe stance, never quite knowing what to expect next, and are plagued with inner fears and outer resentments; when you go forever fighting a degenerating sense of "nobodiness" then you will understand why we find it difficult to wait. There comes a time when the cup of endurance runs over, and men are no longer willing to be plunged into the abyss of despair. I hope, sirs, you can understand our legitimate and unavoidable impatience.

(13) You express a great deal of anxiety over our willingness to break laws. This is certainly a legitimate concern. Since we so diligently urge people to obey the Supreme Court's decision of 1954 outlawing segregation in the public schools, at first glance it may seem rather paradoxical for us consciously to break laws. One may want to ask: "How can you advocate breaking some laws and obeying others?" The answer lies in the fact that there are two types of laws: just and unjust. I would be the first to advocate obeying just laws. One has not only a legal but a moral responsibility to obey just laws. Conversely, one has a moral responsibility to disobey unjust laws. I would agree with St. Augustine that "an unjust law is no law at all"

(14) Now, what is the difference between the two? How does one determine whether a law is just or unjust? A just law is a man-made code that squares with the moral law or the law of God. An unjust law is a code that is out of harmony with the moral law. To put it in the terms of St. Thomas Aquinas: An unjust law is a human law that is not rooted in eternal law and natural law. Any law that uplifts human

personality is just. Any law that degrades human personality is unjust. All segregation statutes are unjust because segregation distorts the soul and damages the personality. It gives the segregator a false sense of superiority and the segregated a false sense of inferiority. Segregation, to use the terminology of the Jewish philosopher Martin Buber, substitutes an "I-it" relationship for an "I-thou" relationship and ends up relegating persons to the status of things. Hence segregation is not only politically, economically and sociologically unsound, it is morally wrong and awful. Paul Tillich said that sin is separation. Is not segregation an existential expression 'of man's tragic separation, his awful estrangement, his terrible sinfulness? Thus it is that I can urge men to obey the 1954 decision of the Supreme Court, for it is morally right; and I can urge them to disobey segregation ordinances, for they are morally wrong.

(15) Let us consider a more concrete example of just and unjust laws. An unjust law is a code that a numerical or power majority group compels a minority group to obey but does not make binding on itself. This is difference made legal. By the same token, a just law is a code that a majority compels a minority to follow and that it is willing to follow itself. This is sameness made legal.

(16) Let me give another explanation. A law is unjust if it is inflicted on a minority that, as a result of being denied the right to vote, had no part in enacting or devising the law. Who can say that the legislature of Alabama which set up that state's segregation laws was democratically elected? Throughout Alabama all sorts of devious methods are used to prevent Negroes from becoming registered voters, and there are some counties in which, even though Negroes constitute a majority of the population, not a single Negro is registered. Can any law enacted under such circumstances be considered democratically structured?

(17) Sometimes a law is just on its face and unjust in its application. For instance, I have been arrested on a charge of parading without a permit. Now, there is nothing wrong in having an ordinance which requires a permit for a parade. But such an ordinance becomes

unjust when it is used to maintain segregation and to deny citizens the First Amendment privilege of peaceful assembly and protest.

(18) I hope you are able to see the distinction I am trying to point out. In no sense do I advocate evading or defying the law, as would the rabid segregationist. That would lead to anarchy. One who breaks an unjust law must do so openly, lovingly, and with a willingness to accept the penalty. I submit that an individual who breaks a law that conscience tells him is unjust and who willingly accepts the penalty of imprisonment in order to arouse the conscience of the community over its injustice, is in reality expressing the highest respect for law.

(19) Of course, there is nothing new about this kind of civil disobedience. It was evidenced sublimely in the refusal of Shadrach, Meshach and Abednego to obey the laws of Nebuchadnezzar, on the ground that a higher moral law was at stake. It was practiced superbly by the early Christians, who were willing to face hungry lions and the excruciating pain of chopping blocks rather than submit to certain unjust laws of the Roman Empire. To a degree, academic freedom is a reality today because Socrates practiced civil disobedience. In our own nation, the Boston Tea Party represented a massive act of civil disobedience.

(20) We should never forget that everything Adolf Hitler did in Germany was "legal" and everything the Hungarian freedom fighters did in Hungary was "illegal." It was "illegal" to aid and comfort a Jew in Hitler's Germany. Even so, I am sure that, had I lived in Germany at the time, I would have aided and comforted my Jewish brothers. If today I lived in a Communist country where certain principles dear to the Christian faith are suppressed, I would openly advocate disobeying that country's antireligious laws.

(21) I must make two honest confessions to you, my Christian and Jewish brothers. First, I must confess that over the past few years I have been gravely disappointed with the white moderate. I have almost reached the regrettable conclusion that the Negro's great stumbling block in his stride toward freedom is not the White Citizen's Counciler or the Ku Klux Klanner, but the white moderate, who is more devoted

to "order" than to justice; who prefers a negative peace which is the absence of tension to a positive peace which is the presence of justice; who constantly says: "I agree with you in the goal you seek, but I cannot agree with your methods of direct action"; who paternalistically believes he can set the timetable for another man's freedom; who lives by a mythical concept of time and who constantly advises the Negro to wait for a "more convenient season." Shallow understanding from people of good will is more frustrating than absolute misunderstanding from people of ill will. Lukewarm acceptance is much more bewildering than outright rejection.

(22) I had hoped that the white moderate would understand that law and order exist for the purpose of establishing justice and that when they fail in this purpose they become the dangerously structured dams that block the flow of social progress. I had hoped that the white moderate would understand that the present tension in the South is a necessary phase of the transition from an obnoxious negative peace, in which the Negro passively accepted his unjust plight, to a substantive and positive peace, in which all men will respect the dignity and worth of human personality. Actually, we who engage in nonviolent direct action are not the creators of tension. We merely bring to the surface the hidden tension that is already alive. We bring it out in the open, where it can be seen and dealt with. Like a boil that can never be cured so long as it is covered up but must be opened with an its ugliness to the natural medicines of air and light, injustice must be exposed, with all the tension its exposure creates, to the light of human conscience and the air of national opinion before it can be cured.

(23) In your statement you assert that our actions, even though peaceful, must be condemned because they precipitate violence. But is this a logical assertion? Isn't this like condemning a robbed man because his possession of money precipitated the evil act of robbery? Isn't this like condemning Socrates because his unswerving commitment to truth and his philosophical inquiries precipitated the act by the misguided populace in which they made him drink hemlock? Isn't this like condemning Jesus because his unique God-

consciousness and never-ceasing devotion to God's will precipitated the evil act of crucifixion? We must come to see that, as the federal courts have consistently affirmed, it is wrong to urge an individual to cease his efforts to gain his basic constitutional rights because the quest may precipitate violence. Society must protect the robbed and punish the robber.

(24) I had also hoped that the white moderate would reject the myth concerning time in relation to the struggle for freedom. I have just received a letter from a white brother in Texas. He writes: "All Christians know that the colored people will receive equal rights eventually, but it is possible that you are in too great a religious hurry. It has taken Christianity almost two thousand years to accomplish what it has. The teachings of Christ take time to come to earth." Such an attitude stems from a tragic misconception of time, from the strangely rational notion that there is something in the very flow of time that will inevitably cure all ills. Actually, time itself is neutral; it can be used either destructively or constructively. More and more I feel that the people of ill will have used time much more effectively than have the people of good will. We will have to repent in this generation not merely for the hateful words and actions of the bad people but for the appalling silence of the good people. Human progress never rolls in on wheels of inevitability; it comes through the tireless efforts of men willing to be co-workers with God, and without this hard work, time itself becomes an ally of the forces of social stagnation. We must use time creatively, in the knowledge that the time is always ripe to do right. Now is the time to make real the promise of democracy and transform our pending national elegy into a creative psalm of brotherhood. Now is the time to lift our national policy from the quicksand of racial injustice to the solid rock of human dignity.

(25) You speak of our activity in Birmingham as extreme. At fist I was rather disappointed that fellow clergymen would see my nonviolent efforts as those of an extremist. I began thinking about the fact that I stand in the middle of two opposing forces in the Negro community. One is a force of complacency, made up in part of

Negroes who, as a result of long years of oppression, are so drained of self-respect and a sense of "somebodiness" that they have adjusted to segregation; and in part of a few middle class Negroes who, because of a degree of academic and economic security and because in some ways they profit by segregation, have become insensitive to the problems of the masses. The other force is one of bitterness and hatred, and it comes perilously close to advocating violence. It is expressed in the various black nationalist groups that are springing up across the nation, the largest and best-known being Elijah Muhammad's Muslim movement. Nourished by the Negro's frustration over the continued existence of racial discrimination, this movement is made up of people who have lost faith in America, who have absolutely repudiated Christianity, and who have concluded that the white man is an incorrigible "devil."

(26) I have tried to stand between these two forces, saying that we need emulate neither the "do-nothingism" of the complacent nor the hatred and despair of the black nationalist. For there is the more excellent way of love and nonviolent protest. I am grateful to God that, through the influence of the Negro church, the way of nonviolence became an integral part of our struggle.

(27) If this philosophy had not emerged, by now many streets of the South would, I am convinced, be flowing with blood. And I am further convinced that if our white brothers dismiss as "rabble-rousers" and "outside agitators" those of us who employ nonviolent direct action, and if they refuse to support our nonviolent efforts, millions of Negroes will, out of frustration and despair, seek solace and security in black-nationalist ideologies a development that would inevitably lead to a frightening racial nightmare.

(28) Oppressed people cannot remain oppressed forever. The yearning for freedom eventually manifests itself, and that is what has happened to the American Negro. Something within has reminded him of his birthright of freedom, and something without has reminded him that it can be gained. Consciously or unconsciously, he has been caught up by the Zeitgeist, and with his black brothers of Africa and

his brown and yellow brothers of Asia, South America and the Caribbean, the United States Negro is moving with a sense of great urgency toward the promised land of racial justice. If one recognizes this vital urge that has engulfed the Negro community, one should readily understand why public demonstrations are taking place. The Negro has many pent-up resentments and latent frustrations, and he must release them. So let him march; let him make prayer pilgrimages to the city hall; let him go on freedom rides--and try to understand why he must do so. If his repressed emotions are not released in nonviolent ways, they will seek expression through violence; this is not a threat but a fact of history. So I have not said to my people: "Get rid of your discontent." Rather, I have tried to say that this normal and healthy discontent can be channeled into the creative outlet of nonviolent direct action. And now this approach is being termed extremist.

(29) But though I was initially disappointed at being categorized as an extremist, as I continued to think about the matter I gradually gained a measure of satisfaction from the label. Was not Jesus an extremist for love: "Love your enemies, bless them that curse you, do good to them that hate you, and pray for them which despitefully use you, and persecute you." Was not Amos an extremist for justice: "Let justice roll down like waters and righteousness like an ever-flowing stream." Was not Paul an extremist for the Christian gospel: "I bear in my body the marks of the Lord Jesus." Was not Martin Luther an extremist: "Here I stand; I cannot do otherwise, so help me God." And John Bunyan: "I will stay in jail to the end of my days before I make a butchery of my conscience." And Abraham Lincoln: "This nation cannot survive half slave and half free." And Thomas Jefferson: "We hold these truths to be self-evident, that all men are created equal ..." So the question is not whether we will be extremists, but what kind of extremists we will be. Will we be extremists for hate or for love? Will we be extremists for the preservation of injustice or for the extension of justice? In that dramatic scene on Calvary's hill three men were crucified. We must never forget that all three were crucified for the same crime--the crime of extremism. Two were extremists for

immorality, and thus fell below their environment. The other, Jesus Christ, was an extremist for love, truth and goodness, and thereby rose above his environment. Perhaps the South, the nation and the world are in dire need of creative extremists.

(30) I had hoped that the white moderate would see this need. Perhaps I was too optimistic; perhaps I expected too much. I suppose I should have realized that few members of the oppressor race can understand the deep groans and passionate yearnings of the oppressed race, and still fewer have the vision to see that injustice must be rooted out by strong, persistent and determined action. I am thankful, however, that some of our white brothers in the South have grasped the meaning of this social revolution and committed themselves to it. They are still too few in quantity, but they are big in quality. Some-- such as Ralph McGill, Lillian Smith, Harry Golden, James McBride Dabbs, Ann Braden and Sarah Patton Boyle--have written about our struggle in eloquent and prophetic terms. Others have marched with us down nameless streets of the South. They have languished in filthy, roach-infested jails, suffering the abuse and brutality of policemen who view them as "dirty nigger lovers." Unlike so many of their moderate brothers and sisters, they have recognized the urgency of the moment and sensed the need for powerful "action" antidotes to combat the disease of segregation.

(31) Let me take note of my other major disappointment. I have been so greatly disappointed with the white church and its leadership. Of course, there are some notable exceptions. I am not unmindful of the fact that each of you has taken some significant stands on this issue. I commend you, Reverend Stallings, for your Christian stand on this past Sunday, in welcoming Negroes to your worship service on a non segregated basis. I commend the Catholic leaders of this state for integrating Spring Hill College several years ago.

(32) But despite these notable exceptions, I must honestly reiterate that I have been disappointed with the church. I do not say this as one of those negative critics who can always find something wrong with the church. I say this as a minister of the gospel, who loves

the church; who was nurtured in its bosom; who has been sustained by its spiritual blessings and who will remain true to it as long as the cord of Rio shall lengthen.

(33) When I was suddenly catapulted into the leadership of the bus protest in Montgomery, Alabama, a few years ago, I felt we would be supported by the white church. I felt that the white ministers, priests and rabbis of the South would be among our strongest allies. Instead, some have been outright opponents, refusing to understand the freedom movement and misrepresenting its leader era; all too many others have been more cautious than courageous and have remained silent behind the anesthetizing security of stained-glass windows.

(34) In spite of my shattered dreams, I came to Birmingham with the hope that the white religious leadership of this community would see the justice of our cause and, with deep moral concern, would serve as the channel through which our just grievances could reach the power structure. I had hoped that each of you would understand. But again I have been disappointed.

(35) I have heard numerous southern religious leaders admonish their worshipers to comply with a desegregation decision because it is the law, but I have longed to hear white ministers declare: "Follow this decree because integration is morally right and because the Negro is your brother." In the midst of blatant injustices inflicted upon the Negro, I have watched white churchmen stand on the sideline and mouth pious irrelevancies and sanctimonious trivialities. In the midst of a mighty struggle to rid our nation of racial and economic injustice, I have heard many ministers say: "Those are social issues, with which the gospel has no real concern." And I have watched many churches commit themselves to a completely other worldly religion which makes a strange, un-Biblical distinction between body and soul, between the sacred and the secular.

(36) I have traveled the length and breadth of Alabama, Mississippi and all the other southern states. On sweltering summer days and crisp autumn mornings I have looked at the South's beautiful churches with their lofty spires pointing heavenward. I have beheld the

impressive outlines of her massive religious-education buildings. Over and over I have found myself asking: "What kind of people worship here? Who is their God? Where were their voices when the lips of Governor Barnett dripped with words of interposition and nullification? Where were they when Governor Wallace gave a clarion call for defiance and hatred? Where were their voices of support when bruised and weary Negro men and women decided to rise from the dark dungeons of complacency to the bright hills of creative protest?"

(37) Yes, these questions are still in my mind. In deep disappointment I have wept over the laxity of the church. But be assured that my tears have been tears of love. There can be no deep disappointment where there is not deep love. Yes, I love the church. How could I do otherwise? I am in the rather unique position of being the son, the grandson and the great-grandson of preachers. Yes, I see the church as the body of Christ. But, oh! How we have blemished and scarred that body through social neglect and through fear of being nonconformists.

(38) There was a time when the church was very powerful in the time when the early Christians rejoiced at being deemed worthy to suffer for what they believed. In those days the church was not merely a thermometer that recorded the ideas and principles of popular opinion; it was a thermostat that transformed the mores of society. Whenever the early Christians entered a town, the people in power became disturbed and immediately sought to convict the Christians for being "disturbers of the peace" and "outside agitators"' But the Christians pressed on, in the conviction that they were "a colony of heaven," called to obey God rather than man. Small in number, they were big in commitment. They were too God intoxicated to be "astronomically intimidated." By their effort and example they brought an end to such ancient evils as infanticide and gladiatorial contests.

(39) Things are different now. So often the contemporary church is a weak, ineffectual voice with an uncertain sound. So often it is an archdefender of the status quo. Far from being disturbed by the

presence of the church, the power structure of the average community is consoled by the church's silent and often even vocal sanction of things as they are.

(40) But the judgment of God is upon the church as never before. If today's church does not recapture the sacrificial spirit of the early church, it will lose its authenticity, forfeit the loyalty of millions, and be dismissed as an irrelevant social club with no meaning for the twentieth century. Every day I meet young people whose disappointment with the church has turned into outright disgust.

(41) Perhaps I have once again been too optimistic. Is organized religion too inextricably bound to the status quo to save our nation and the world? Perhaps I must turn my faith to the inner spiritual church, the church within the church, as the true ecclesia and the hope of the world. But again I am thankful to God that some noble souls from the ranks of organized religion have broken loose from the paralyzing chains of conformity and joined us as active partners in the struggle for freedom, They have left their secure congregations and walked the streets of Albany, Georgia, with us. They have gone down the highways of the South on tortuous rides for freedom. Yes, they have gone to jai with us. Some have been dismissed from their churches, have lost the support of their bishops and fellow ministers. But they have acted in the faith that right defeated is stronger than evil triumphant. Their witness has been the spiritual salt that has preserved the true meaning of the gospel in these troubled times. They have carved a tunnel of hope through the dark mountain of disappointment.

(42) I hope the church as a whole will meet the challenge of this decisive hour. But even if the church does not come to the aid of justice, I have no despair about the future. I have no fear about the outcome of our struggle in Birmingham, even if our motives are at present misunderstood. We will reach the goal of freedom in Birmingham and all over the nation, because the goal of America is freedom. Abused and scorned though we may be, our destiny is tied up with America's destiny. Before the pilgrims landed at Plymouth, we were here. Before the pen of Jefferson etched the majestic words of the

Declaration of Independence across the pages of history, we were here. For more than two centuries our forebears labored in this country without wages; they made cotton king; they built the homes of their masters while suffering gross injustice and shameful humiliation--and yet out of a bottomless vitality they continued to thrive and develop. If the inexpressible cruelties of slavery could not stop us, the opposition we now face will surely fail. We will win our freedom because the sacred heritage of our nation and the eternal will of God are embodied in our echoing demands.

(43) Before closing I feel impelled to mention one other point in your statement that has troubled me profoundly. You warmly commended the Birmingham police force for keeping "order" and "preventing violence." I doubt that you would have so warmly commended the police force if you had seen its dogs sinking their teeth into unarmed, nonviolent Negroes. I doubt that you would so quickly commend the policemen if you were to observe their ugly and inhumane treatment of Negroes here in the city jail; if you were to watch them push and curse old Negro women and young Negro girls; if you were to see them slap and kick old Negro men and young boys; if you were to observe them, as they did on two occasions, refuse to give us food because we wanted to sing our grace together. I cannot join you in your praise of the Birmingham police department.

(44) It is true that the police have exercised a degree of discipline in handing the demonstrators. In this sense they have conducted themselves rather "nonviolently" in public. But for what purpose? To preserve the evil system of segregation. Over the past few years I have consistently preached that nonviolence demands that the means we use must be as pure as the ends we seek. I have tried to make clear that it is wrong to use immoral means to attain moral ends. But now I must affirm that it is just as wrong, or perhaps even more so, to use moral means to preserve immoral ends. Perhaps Mr. Connor and his policemen have been rather nonviolent in public, as was Chief Pritchett in Albany, Georgia but they have used the moral means of nonviolence to maintain the immoral end of racial injustice. As T. S.

Eliot has said: "The last temptation is the greatest treason: To do the right deed for the wrong reason."

(45) I wish you had commended the Negro sit-inners and demonstrators of Birmingham for their sublime courage, their willingness to suffer and their amazing discipline in the midst of great provocation. One day the South will recognize its real heroes. There will be the James Merediths, with the noble sense of purpose that enables them to face jeering and hostile mobs, and with the agonizing loneliness that characterizes the life of the pioneer. There will be the old, oppressed, battered Negro women, symbolized in a seventy-two-year-old woman in Montgomery, Alabama, who rose up with a sense of dignity and with her people decided not to ride segregated buses, and who responded with ungrammatical profundity to one who inquired about her weariness: "My feets is tired, but my soul is at rest." There will be the young high school and college students, the young ministers of the gospel and a host of their elders, courageously and nonviolently sitting in at lunch counters and willingly going to jail for conscience' sake. One day the South will know that when these disinherited children of God sat down at lunch counters, they were in reality standing up for what is best in the American dream and for the most sacred values in our Judaeo-Christian heritage, thereby bringing our nation back to those great wells of democracy which were dug deep by the founding fathers in their formulation of the Constitution and the Declaration of Independence.

(46) Never before have I written so long a letter. I'm afraid it is much too long to take your precious time. I can assure you that it would have been much shorter if I had been writing from a comfortable desk, but what else can one do when he is alone in a narrow jail cell, other than write long letters, think long thoughts and pray long prayers?

(47) If I have said anything in this letter that overstates the truth and indicates an unreasonable impatience, I beg you to forgive me. If I have said anything that understates the truth and indicates my having a

patience that allows me to settle for anything less than brotherhood, I beg God to forgive me.

(48) I hope this letter finds you strong in the faith. I also hope that circumstances will soon make it possible for me to meet each of you, not as an integrationist or a civil rights leader but as a fellow clergyman and a Christian brother. Let us all hope that the dark clouds of racial prejudice will soon pass away and the deep fog of misunderstanding will be lifted from our fear-drenched communities, and in some not too distant tomorrow the radiant stars of love and brotherhood will shine over our great nation with all their scintillating beauty.

Yours for the cause of Peace and Brotherhood,
Martin Luther King, Jr.

John F. Kennedy
American University Commencement Address
Delivered 10 June 1963

President Anderson, members of the faculty, board of trustees, distinguished guests, my old colleague, Senator Bob Byrd, who has earned his degree through many years of attending night law school, while I am earning mine in the next 30 minutes, distinguished guests, ladies and gentlemen:

It is with great pride that I participate in this ceremony of the American University, sponsored by the Methodist Church, founded by Bishop John Fletcher Hurst, and first opened by President Woodrow Wilson in 1914. This is a young and growing university, but it has already fulfilled Bishop Hurst's enlightened hope for the study of history and public affairs in a city devoted to the making of history and to the conduct of the public's business. By sponsoring this institution of higher learning for all who wish to learn, whatever their color or their creed, the Methodists of this area and the Nation deserve the Nation's thanks, and I commend all those who are today graduating.

Professor Woodrow Wilson once said that every man sent out from a university should be a man of his nation as well as a man of his time, and I am confident that the men and women who carry the honor of graduating from this institution will continue to give from their lives, from their talents, a high measure of public service and public support. "There are few earthly things more beautiful than a university," wrote John Masefield in his tribute to English universities -- and his words are equally true today. He did not refer to towers or to campuses. He admired the splendid beauty of a university, because it was, he said, "a place where those who hate ignorance may strive to know, where those who perceive truth may strive to make others see."

I have, therefore, chosen this time and place to discuss a topic on which ignorance too often abounds and the truth too rarely perceived. And that is the most important topic on earth: peace. What kind of peace do I mean and what kind of a peace do we seek? Not a Pax Americana enforced on the world by American weapons of war. Not the peace of the grave or the security of the slave. I am talking about genuine peace, the kind of peace that makes life on earth worth living, and the kind that enables men and nations to grow, and to hope, and build a better life for their children -- not merely peace for Americans but peace for all men and women, not merely peace in our time but peace in all time.

I speak of peace because of the new face of war. Total war makes no sense in an age where great powers can maintain large and relatively invulnerable nuclear forces and refuse to surrender without resort to those forces. It makes no sense in an age where a single nuclear weapon contains almost ten times the explosive force delivered by all the allied air forces in the Second World War. It makes no sense in an age when the deadly poisons produced by a nuclear exchange would be carried by wind and water and soil and seed to the far corners of the globe and to generations yet unborn.

Today the expenditure of billions of dollars every year on weapons acquired for the purpose of making sure we never need them is essential to the keeping of peace. But surely the acquisition of such idle stockpiles -- which can only destroy and never create -- is not the only, much less the most efficient, means of assuring peace. I speak of peace, therefore, as the necessary, rational end of rational men. I realize the pursuit of peace is not as dramatic as the pursuit of war, and frequently the words of the pursuers fall on deaf ears. But we have no more urgent task.

Some say that it is useless to speak of peace or world law or world disarmament, and that it will be useless until the leaders of the Soviet Union adopt a more enlightened attitude. I hope they do. I believe we can help them do it. But I also believe that we must reexamine our own attitudes, as individuals and as a Nation, for our attitude is as essential as theirs. And every graduate of this school, every thoughtful citizen who despairs of war and wishes to bring peace, should begin by looking inward, by examining his own attitude

284

towards the possibilities of peace, towards the Soviet Union, towards the course of the cold war and towards freedom and peace here at home.

First examine our attitude towards peace itself. Too many of us think it is impossible. Too many think it is unreal. But that is a dangerous, defeatist belief. It leads to the conclusion that war is inevitable, that mankind is doomed, that we are gripped by forces we cannot control. We need not accept that view. Our problems are manmade; therefore, they can be solved by man. And man can be as big as he wants. No problem of human destiny is beyond human beings. Man's reason and spirit have often solved the seemingly unsolvable, and we believe they can do it again. I am not referring to the absolute, infinite concept of universal peace and good will of which some fantasies and fanatics dream. I do not deny the value of hopes and dreams but we merely invite discouragement and incredulity by making that our only and immediate goal.

Let us focus instead on a more practical, more attainable peace, based not on a sudden revolution in human nature but on a gradual evolution in human institutions -- on a series of concrete actions and effective agreements which are in the interest of all concerned. There is no single, simple key to this peace; no grand or magic formula to be adopted by one or two powers. Genuine peace must be the product of many nations, the sum of many acts. It must be dynamic, not static, changing to meet the challenge of each new generation. For peace is a process -- a way of solving problems.

With such a peace, there will still be quarrels and conflicting interests, as there are within families and nations. World peace, like community peace, does not require that each man love his neighbor, it requires only that they live together in mutual tolerance, submitting their disputes to a just and peaceful settlement. And history teaches us that enmities between nations, as between individuals, do not last forever. However fixed our likes and dislikes may seem, the tide of time and events will often bring surprising changes in the relations between nations and neighbors. So let us persevere. Peace need not be impracticable, and war need not be inevitable. By defining our goal more clearly, by making it seem more manageable and less remote, we can help all people to see it, to draw hope from it, and to move irresistibly towards it.

And second, let us reexamine our attitude towards the Soviet Union. It is discouraging to think that their leaders may actually believe what their propagandists write. It is discouraging to read a recent, authoritative Soviet text on military strategy and find, on page after page, wholly baseless and incredible claims, such as the allegation that American imperialist circles are preparing to unleash different types of war, that there is a very real threat of a preventive war being unleashed by American imperialists against the Soviet Union, and that the political aims -- and I quote -- "of the American imperialists are to enslave economically and politically the European and other capitalist countries and to achieve world domination by means of aggressive war."

Truly, as it was written long ago: "The wicked flee when no man pursueth."

Yet it is sad to read these Soviet statements, to realize the extent of the gulf between us. But it is also a warning, a warning to the American people not to fall into the same trap as the Soviets, not to see only a distorted and desperate view of the other side, not to see conflict as inevitable, accommodation as impossible, and communication as nothing more than an exchange of threats.

No government or social system is so evil that its people must be considered as lacking in virtue. As Americans, we find communism profoundly repugnant as a negation of personal freedom and dignity. But we can still hail the Russian people for their many achievements in science and space, in economic and industrial growth, in culture, in acts of courage.

Among the many traits the peoples of our two countries have in common, none is stronger than our mutual abhorrence of war. Almost unique among the major world powers, we have never been at war with each other. And no nation in the history of battle ever suffered more than the Soviet Union in the Second World War. At least 20 million lost their lives. Countless millions of homes and families were burned or sacked. A third of the nation's territory, including two thirds of its industrial base, was turned into a wasteland -- a loss equivalent to the destruction of this country east of Chicago.

Today, should total war ever break out again -- no matter how -- our two countries will be the primary target. It is an ironic but accurate fact that the two strongest powers are the two in the most danger of devastation. All we have built, all we have worked for, would be destroyed in the first 24 hours. And even in the cold war, which brings burdens and dangers to so many countries, including this Nation's closest allies, our two countries bear the heaviest burdens. For we are both devoting massive sums of money to weapons that could be better devoted to combat ignorance, poverty, and disease. We are both caught up in a vicious and dangerous cycle, with suspicion on one side breeding suspicion on the other, and new weapons begetting counter-weapons. In short, both the United States and its allies, and the Soviet Union and its allies, have a mutually deep interest in a just and genuine peace and in halting the arms race. Agreements to this end are in the interests of the Soviet Union as well as ours. And even the most hostile nations can be relied upon to accept and keep those treaty obligations, and only those treaty obligations, which are in their own interest.

So let us not be blind to our differences, but let us also direct attention to our common interests and the means by which those differences can be resolved. And if we cannot end now our differences, at least we can help make the world safe for diversity. For in the final analysis, our most basic common link is that we all inhabit this small planet. We all breathe the same air. We all cherish our children's futures. And we are all mortal.

Third, let us reexamine our attitude towards the cold war, remembering we're not engaged in a debate, seeking to pile up debating points. We are not here distributing blame or pointing the finger of judgment. We must deal with the world as it is, and not as it might have been had the history of the last 18 years been different. We must, therefore, persevere in the search for peace in the hope that constructive changes within the Communist bloc might bring within reach solutions which now seem beyond us. We must conduct our affairs in such a way that it becomes in the Communists' interest to agree on a genuine peace. And above all, while defending our own vital interests, nuclear powers must avert those confrontations which bring an adversary to a choice of either a humiliating retreat or a nuclear war. To adopt that kind of course in the nuclear age would be evidence only of the bankruptcy of our policy -- or of a collective death-wish for the world.

To secure these ends, America's weapons are nonprovocative, carefully controlled, designed to deter, and capable of selective use. Our military forces are committed to peace and disciplined in self-restraint. Our diplomats are instructed to avoid unnecessary irritants and purely rhetorical hostility. For we can seek a relaxation of tensions without relaxing our guard. And, for our part, we do not need to use threats to prove we are resolute. We do not need to jam foreign broadcasts out of fear our faith will be eroded. We are unwilling to impose our system on any unwilling people, but we are willing and able to engage in peaceful competition with any people on earth.

Meanwhile, we seek to strengthen the United Nations, to help solve its financial problems, to make it a more effective instrument for peace, to develop it into a genuine world security system -- a system capable of resolving disputes on the basis of law, of insuring the security of the large and the small, and of creating conditions under which arms can finally be abolished. At the same time we seek to keep peace inside the non-Communist world, where many nations, all of them our friends, are divided over issues which weaken Western unity, which invite Communist intervention, or which threaten to erupt into war. Our efforts in West New Guinea, in the Congo, in the Middle East, and the Indian subcontinent, have been persistent and patient despite criticism from both sides. We have also tried to set an example for others, by seeking to adjust small but significant differences with our own closest neighbors in Mexico and Canada.

Speaking of other nations, I wish to make one point clear. We are bound to many nations by alliances. Those alliances exist because our concern and theirs substantially overlap. Our commitment to defend Western Europe and West Berlin, for example, stands undiminished because of the identity of our vital interests. The United States will make no deal with the Soviet Union at the expense of other nations and other peoples, not merely because they are our partners, but also because their interests and ours converge. Our interests converge, however, not only in defending the frontiers of freedom, but in pursuing the paths of peace. It is our hope, and the purpose of allied policy, to convince the Soviet Union that she, too, should let each nation choose its own future, so long as that choice does not interfere with the choices of others. The Communist drive to impose their political and economic system on others is the primary cause of world tension today. For there can be no doubt that if all nations could refrain from interfering in the self-determination of others, the peace would be much more assured.

This will require a new effort to achieve world law, a new context for world discussions. It will require increased understanding between the Soviets and ourselves. And increased understanding will require increased contact and communication. One step in this direction is the proposed arrangement for a direct line between Moscow and Washington, to avoid on each side the dangerous delays, misunderstandings, and misreadings of others' actions which might occur at a time of crisis.

We have also been talking in Geneva about our first-step measures of arm[s] controls designed to limit the intensity of the arms race and reduce the risk of accidental war. Our primary long range interest in Geneva, however, is general and complete disarmament, designed to take place by stages, permitting parallel political developments to build the new institutions of peace which would take the place of arms. The pursuit of disarmament has been an effort of this Government since the 1920's. It has been urgently sought by the past three administrations. And however dim the prospects are today, we intend to continue this effort -- to continue it in order that all countries, including our own, can better grasp what the problems and possibilities of disarmament are.

The only major area of these negotiations where the end is in sight, yet where a fresh start is badly needed, is in a treaty to outlaw nuclear tests. The conclusion of such a treaty, so near and yet so far, would check the spiraling arms race in one of its most dangerous areas. It would place the nuclear powers in a position to deal more effectively with one of the greatest hazards which man faces in 1963, the further spread of nuclear arms. It would increase our security; it would decrease the prospects of war. Surely this goal is sufficiently important to require our steady pursuit, yielding neither to the temptation to give up the whole effort nor the temptation to give up our insistence on vital and responsible safeguards.

I'm taking this opportunity, therefore, to announce two important decisions in this regard. First, Chairman Khrushchev, Prime Minister Macmillan, and I have agreed that high-level discussions will shortly begin in Moscow looking towards early agreement on a comprehensive test ban treaty. Our hope must be tempered -- Our hopes must be tempered with the caution of history; but with our hopes go the hopes of all mankind. Second, to make clear our good faith and solemn convictions on this matter, I now declare that the United States does not propose to conduct nuclear tests in the atmosphere so long as other states do not do so. We will not -- We will not be the first to resume. Such a declaration is no substitute for a formal binding treaty, but I hope it will help us achieve one. Nor would such a treaty be a substitute for disarmament, but I hope it will help us achieve it.

Finally, my fellow Americans, let us examine our attitude towards peace and freedom here at home. The quality and spirit of our own society must justify and support our efforts abroad. We must show it in the dedication of our own lives -- as many of you who are graduating today will have an opportunity to do, by serving without pay in the Peace Corps abroad or in the proposed National Service Corps here at home. But wherever we are, we must all, in our daily lives, live up to the age-old faith that peace and freedom walk together. In too many of our cities today, the peace is not secure because freedom is incomplete. It is the responsibility of the executive branch at all levels of government -- local, State, and National -- to provide and protect that freedom for all of our citizens by all means within our authority. It is the responsibility of the legislative branch at all levels, wherever the authority is not now adequate, to make it adequate. And it is the responsibility of all citizens in all sections of this country to respect the rights of others and respect the law of the land.

All this -- All this is not unrelated to world peace. "When a man's way[s] please the Lord," the Scriptures tell us, "He maketh even his enemies to be at peace with him." And is not peace, in the last analysis, basically a matter of human rights: the right to live out our lives without fear of devastation; the right to breathe air as nature provided it; the right of future generations to a healthy existence?

While we proceed to safeguard our national interests, let us also safeguard human interests. And the elimination of war and arms is clearly in the interest of both. No treaty, however much it may be to the advantage of all, however tightly it may be worded, can provide absolute security against the risks of deception and evasion. But it can, if it is sufficiently effective in its enforcement, and it is sufficiently in the interests of its signers, offer far more security and far fewer risks than an unabated, uncontrolled, unpredictable arms race.

The United States, as the world knows, will never start a war. We do not want a war. We do not now expect a war. This generation of Americans has already had enough -- more than enough -- of war and hate and oppression.

We shall be prepared if others wish it. We shall be alert to try to stop it. But we shall also do our part to build a world of peace where the weak are safe and the strong are just. We are not helpless before that task or hopeless of its success. Confident and unafraid, we must labor on--not towards a strategy of annihilation but towards a strategy of peace.

John F. Kennedy
Civil Rights Address
Delivered 11 June 1963

Good evening, my fellow citizens:

This afternoon, following a series of threats and defiant statements, the presence of Alabama National Guardsmen was required on the University of Alabama to carry out the final and unequivocal order of the United States District Court of the Northern District of Alabama. That order called for the admission of two clearly qualified young Alabama residents who happened to have been born Negro. That they were admitted peacefully on the campus is due in good measure to the conduct of the students of the University of Alabama, who met their responsibilities in a constructive way.

I hope that every American, regardless of where he lives, will stop and examine his conscience about this and other related incidents. This Nation was founded by men of many nations and backgrounds. It was founded on the principle that all men are created equal, and that the rights of every man are diminished when the rights of one man are threatened.

Today, we are committed to a worldwide struggle to promote and protect the rights of all who wish to be free. And when Americans are sent to Vietnam or West Berlin, we do not ask for whites only. It ought to be possible, therefore, for American students of any color to attend any public institution they select without having to be backed up by troops. It ought to to be possible for American consumers of any color to receive equal service in places of public accommodation, such as hotels and restaurants and theaters and retail stores, without being forced to resort to demonstrations in the street, and it ought to be possible for American citizens of any color to register and to vote in a free election without interference or fear of reprisal. It ought to to be possible, in short, for every American to enjoy the privileges of being American without regard to his race or his color. In short, every

American ought to have the right to be treated as he would wish to be treated, as one would wish his children to be treated. But this is not the case.

The Negro baby born in America today, regardless of the section of the State in which he is born, has about one-half as much chance of completing a high school as a white baby born in the same place on the same day, one-third as much chance of completing college, one-third as much chance of becoming a professional man, twice as much chance of becoming unemployed, about one-seventh as much chance of earning $10,000 a year, a life expectancy which is 7 years shorter, and the prospects of earning only half as much.

This is not a sectional issue. Difficulties over segregation and discrimination exist in every city, in every State of the Union, producing in many cities a rising tide of discontent that threatens the public safety. Nor is this a partisan issue. In a time of domestic crisis men of good will and generosity should be able to unite regardless of party or politics. This is not even a legal or legislative issue alone. It is better to settle these matters in the courts than on the streets, and new laws are needed at every level, but law alone cannot make men see right. We are confronted primarily with a moral issue. It is as old as the Scriptures and is as clear as the American Constitution.

The heart of the question is whether all Americans are to be afforded equal rights and equal opportunities, whether we are going to treat our fellow Americans as we want to be treated. If an American, because his skin is dark, cannot eat lunch in a restaurant open to the public, if he cannot send his children to the best public school available, if he cannot vote for the public officials who will represent him, if, in short, he cannot enjoy the full and free life which all of us want, then who among us would be content to have the color of his skin changed and stand in his place? Who among us would then be content with the counsels of patience and delay?

One hundred years of delay have passed since President Lincoln freed the slaves, yet their heirs, their grandsons, are not fully free. They are not yet freed from the bonds of injustice. They are not yet freed from social and economic oppression. And this Nation, for all its hopes and all its boasts, will not be fully free until all its citizens are free.

We preach freedom around the world, and we mean it, and we cherish our freedom here at home, but are we to say to the world, and much more importantly, to each other that this is the land of the free except for the Negroes; that we have no second-class citizens except Negroes; that we have no class or caste system, no ghettoes, no master race except with respect to Negroes?

Now the time has come for this Nation to fulfill its promise. The events in Birmingham and elsewhere have so increased the cries for equality that no city or State or legislative body can prudently choose to ignore them. The fires of frustration and discord are burning in every city, North and South, where legal remedies are not at hand. Redress is sought in the streets, in demonstrations, parades, and protests which create tensions and threaten violence and threaten lives.

We face, therefore, a moral crisis as a country and a people. It cannot be met by repressive police action. It cannot be left to increased demonstrations in the streets. It cannot be quieted by token moves or talk. It is a time to act in the Congress, in your State and local legislative body and, above all, in all of our daily lives. It is not enough to pin the blame on others, to say this a problem of one section of the country or another, or deplore the facts that we face. A great change is at hand, and our task, our obligation, is to make that revolution, that change, peaceful and constructive for all. Those who do nothing are inviting shame, as well as violence. Those who act boldly are recognizing right, as well as reality.

Next week I shall ask the Congress of the United States to act, to make a commitment it has not fully made in this century to the proposition that race has no place in American life or law. The Federal judiciary has upheld that proposition in a series of forthright cases. The Executive Branch has adopted that proposition in the conduct of its affairs, including the employment of Federal personnel, the use of Federal facilities, and the sale of federally financed housing. But there are other necessary measures which only the Congress can provide, and they must be provided at this session. The old code of equity law under which we live commands for every wrong a remedy, but in too many communities, in too many parts of the country, wrongs are inflicted on Negro citizens and there are no remedies at law. Unless the Congress acts, their only remedy is the street.

I am, therefore, asking the Congress to enact legislation giving all Americans the right to be served in facilities which are open to the public -- hotels, restaurants, theaters, retail stores, and similar establishments. This seems to me to be an elementary right. Its denial is an arbitrary indignity that no American in 1963 should have to endure, but many do.

I have recently met with scores of business leaders urging them to take voluntary action to end this discrimination, and I have been encouraged by their response, and in the last two weeks over 75 cities have seen progress made in desegregating these kinds of facilities. But many are unwilling to act alone, and for this reason, nationwide legislation is needed if we are to move this problem from the streets to the courts.

I'm also asking the Congress to authorize the Federal Government to participate more fully in lawsuits designed to end segregation in public education. We have succeeded in persuading many districts to desegregate voluntarily. Dozens have admitted Negroes without violence. Today, a Negro is attending a State-supported institution in every one of our 50 States, but the pace is very slow.

Too many Negro children entering segregated grade schools at the time of the Supreme Court's decision nine years ago will enter segregated high schools this fall, having suffered a loss which can never be restored. The lack of an adequate education denies the Negro a chance to get a decent job.

The orderly implementation of the Supreme Court decision, therefore, cannot be left solely to those who may not have the economic resources to carry the legal action or who may be subject to harassment.

Other features will be also requested, including greater protection for the right to vote. But legislation, I repeat, cannot solve this problem alone. It must be solved in the homes of every American in every community across our country. In this respect I wanna pay tribute to those citizens North and South who've been working in their communities to make life better for all. They are acting not out of sense of legal duty but out of a sense of human decency. Like our soldiers and sailors in all parts of the world they are meeting freedom's challenge on the firing line, and I salute them for their honor and their courage.

My fellow Americans, this is a problem which faces us all -- in every city of the North as well as the South. Today, there are Negroes unemployed, two or three times as many compared to whites, inadequate education, moving into the large cities, unable to find work, young people particularly out of work without hope, denied equal rights, denied the opportunity to eat at a restaurant or a lunch counter or go to a movie theater, denied the right to a decent education, denied almost today the right to attend a State university even though qualified. It seems to me that these are matters which concern us all, not merely Presidents or Congressmen or Governors, but every citizen of the United States.

This is one country. It has become one country because all of us and all the people who came here had an equal chance to develop their talents. We cannot say to ten percent of the population that you can't have that right; that your children cannot have the chance to develop whatever talents they have; that the only way that they are going to get their rights is to go in the street and demonstrate. I think we owe them and we owe ourselves a better country than that.

Therefore, I'm asking for your help in making it easier for us to move ahead and to provide the kind of equality of treatment which we would want ourselves; to give a chance for every child to be educated to the limit of his talents.

As I've said before, not every child has an equal talent or an equal ability or equal motivation, but they should have the equal right to develop their talent and their ability and their motivation, to make something of themselves.

We have a right to expect that the Negro community will be responsible, will uphold the law, but they have a right to expect that the law will be fair, that the Constitution will be color blind, as Justice Harlan said at the turn of the century.

This is what we're talking about and this is a matter which concerns this country and what it stands for, and in meeting it I ask the support of all our citizens.

Thank you very much.

John F. Kennedy
Ich bin ein Berliner ("I am a 'Berliner'")
Delivered 26 June 1963, West Berlin

I am proud to come to this city as the guest of your distinguished Mayor, who has symbolized throughout the world the fighting spirit of West Berlin. And I am proud -- And I am proud to visit the Federal Republic with your distinguished Chancellor who for so many years has committed Germany to democracy and freedom and progress, and to come here in the company of my fellow American, General Clay, who -- -- who has been in this city during its great moments of crisis and will come again if ever needed.

Two thousand years ago -- Two thousand years ago, the proudest boast was "civis Romanus sum."[1] Today, in the world of freedom, the proudest boast is "Ich bin ein Berliner."

(I appreciate my interpreter translating my German.)

There are many people in the world who really don't understand, or say they don't, what is the great issue between the free world and the Communist world.

Let them come to Berlin.

There are some who say -- There are some who say that communism is the wave of the future.

Let them come to Berlin.

And there are some who say, in Europe and elsewhere, we can work with the Communists.

Let them come to Berlin.

And there are even a few who say that it is true that communism is an evil system, but it permits us to make economic progress.

Lass' sie nach Berlin kommen.

Let them come to Berlin.

Freedom has many difficulties and democracy is not perfect. But we have never had to put a wall up to keep our people in -- to prevent them from leaving us. I want to say on behalf of my countrymen who live many miles away on the other side of the Atlantic, who are far distant from you, that they take the greatest pride, that they have been able to share with you, even from a distance, the story of the last 18 years. I know of no town, no city, that has been besieged for 18 years that still lives with the vitality and the force, and the hope, and the determination of the city of West Berlin.

While the wall is the most obvious and vivid demonstration of the failures of the Communist system -- for all the world to see -- we take no satisfaction in it; for it is, as your Mayor has said, an offense not only against history but an offense against humanity, separating families, dividing husbands and wives and brothers and sisters, and dividing a people who wish to be joined together.

What is -- What is true of this city is true of Germany: Real, lasting peace in Europe can never be assured as long as one German out of four is denied the elementary right of free men, and that is to make a free choice. In 18 years of peace and good faith, this generation of Germans has earned the right to be free, including the right to unite their families and their nation in lasting peace, with good will to all people.

You live in a defended island of freedom, but your life is part of the main. So let me ask you, as I close, to lift your eyes beyond the dangers of today, to the hopes of tomorrow, beyond the freedom merely of this city of Berlin, or your country of Germany, to the advance of freedom everywhere, beyond the wall to the day of peace with justice, beyond yourselves and ourselves to all mankind.

Freedom is indivisible, and when one man is enslaved, all are not free. When all are free, then we look -- can look forward to that day when this city will be joined as one and this country and this great Continent of Europe in a peaceful and hopeful globe. When that day finally comes, as it will, the people of West Berlin can take sober satisfaction in the fact that they were in the front lines for almost two decades.

All -- All free men, wherever they may live, are citizens of Berlin.

And, therefore, as a free man, I take pride in the words "Ich bin ein Berliner."

Martin Luther King's Keynote Address at the March on Washing
(Commonly referred as "I Have a Dream")
Delivered August 28, 1963 Washington DC

I am happy to join with you today in what will go down in history as the greatest demonstration for freedom in the history of our nation.

Five score years ago, a great American, in whose symbolic shadow we stand today, signed the Emancipation Proclamation. This momentous decree came as a great beacon light of hope to millions of Negro slaves who had been seared in the flames of withering injustice. It came as a joyous daybreak to end the long night of their captivity.

But one hundred years later, the Negro still is not free. One hundred years later, the life of the Negro is still sadly crippled by the manacles of segregation and the chains of discrimination. One hundred years later, the Negro lives on a lonely island of poverty in the midst of a vast ocean of material prosperity. One hundred years later, the Negro is still languishing in the corners of American society and finds himself an exile in his own land. So we have come here today to dramatize a shameful condition.

In a sense we have come to our nation's capital to cash a check. When the architects of our republic wrote the magnificent words of the Constitution and the Declaration of Independence, they were signing a promissory note to which every American was to fall heir. This note was a promise that all men, yes, black men as well as white men, would be guaranteed the unalienable rights of life, liberty, and the pursuit of happiness.

It is obvious today that America has defaulted on this promissory note insofar as her citizens of color are concerned. Instead of honoring this sacred obligation, America has given the Negro people a bad check, a check which has come back marked "insufficient funds." But we refuse to believe that the bank of justice is bankrupt. We refuse to believe that there are insufficient funds in the great vaults of opportunity of this nation. So we have come to cash this check — a check that will give us upon demand the riches of freedom and the security of justice. We have also come to this hallowed spot to remind America of the fierce urgency of now. This is no time to engage in the luxury of cooling off or to take the tranquilizing drug of gradualism. Now is the time to make real the promises of democracy. Now is the time to rise from the dark and desolate valley of segregation to the sunlit path of racial justice. Now is the time to lift our nation from the quick sands of racial injustice to the solid rock of brotherhood. Now is the time to make justice a reality for all of God's children.

It would be fatal for the nation to overlook the urgency of the moment. This sweltering summer of the Negro's legitimate discontent will not pass until there is an invigorating autumn of freedom and equality. Nineteen sixty-three is not an end, but a beginning. Those who hope that the Negro needed to blow off steam and will now be content will have a rude awakening if the nation returns to business as usual. There will be neither rest nor tranquility in America until the Negro is granted his citizenship rights. The whirlwinds of revolt will continue to shake the foundations of our nation until the bright day of justice emerges.

But there is something that I must say to my people who stand on the warm threshold which leads into the palace of justice. In the process of gaining our rightful place we must not be guilty of wrongful deeds. Let us not seek to satisfy our thirst for freedom by drinking from the cup of bitterness and hatred.

We must forever conduct our struggle on the high plane of dignity and discipline. We must not allow our creative protest to degenerate into physical violence. Again and again we must rise to the majestic heights of meeting physical force with soul force. The marvelous new militancy which has engulfed the Negro community must not lead us to a distrust of all white people, for many of our white brothers, as evidenced by their presence here today, have come to realize that their destiny is tied up with our destiny. They have come to realize that their freedom is inextricably bound to our freedom. We cannot walk alone.

As we walk, we must make the pledge that we shall always march ahead. We cannot turn back. There are those who are asking the devotees of civil rights, "When will you be satisfied?" We can never be satisfied as long as the Negro is the victim of the unspeakable horrors of police brutality. We can never be satisfied, as long as our bodies, heavy with the fatigue of travel, cannot gain lodging in the motels of the highways and the hotels of the cities. We cannot be satisfied as long as the Negro's basic mobility is from a smaller ghetto to a larger one. We can never be satisfied as long as our children are stripped of their selfhood and robbed of their dignity by signs stating "For Whites Only". We cannot be satisfied as long as a Negro in Mississippi cannot vote and a Negro in New York believes he has nothing for which to vote. No, no, we are not satisfied, and we will not be satisfied until justice rolls down like waters and righteousness like a mighty stream.

I am not unmindful that some of you have come here out of great trials and tribulations. Some of you have come fresh from narrow jail cells. Some of you have come from areas where your quest for freedom left you battered by the storms of persecution and staggered by the winds of police brutality. You have been the veterans of creative suffering. Continue to work with the faith that unearned suffering is redemptive.

Go back to Mississippi, go back to Alabama, go back to South Carolina, go back to Georgia, go back to Louisiana, go back to the slums and ghettos of our northern cities, knowing that somehow this situation can and will be changed. Let us not wallow in the valley of despair.

I say to you today, my friends, so even though we face the difficulties of today and tomorrow, I still have a dream. It is a dream deeply rooted in the American dream.

I have a dream that one day this nation will rise up and live out the true meaning of its creed: "We hold these truths to be self-evident: that all men are created equal."

302

I have a dream that one day on the red hills of Georgia the sons of former slaves and the sons of former slave owners will be able to sit down together at the table of brotherhood.

I have a dream that one day even the state of Mississippi, a state sweltering with the heat of injustice, sweltering with the heat of oppression, will be transformed into an oasis of freedom and justice.

I have a dream that my four little children will one day live in a nation where they will not be judged by the color of their skin but by the content of their character.

I have a dream today.

I have a dream that one day, down in Alabama, with its vicious racists, with its governor having his lips dripping with the words of interposition and nullification; one day right there in Alabama, little black boys and black girls will be able to join hands with little white boys and white girls as sisters and brothers.

I have a dream today.

I have a dream that one day every valley shall be exalted, every hill and mountain shall be made low, the rough places will be made plain, and the crooked places will be made straight, and the glory of the Lord shall be revealed, and all flesh shall see it together.

This is our hope. This is the faith that I go back to the South with. With this faith we will be able to hew out of the mountain of despair a stone of hope. With this faith we will be able to transform the jangling discords of our nation into a beautiful symphony of brotherhood. With this faith we will be able to work together, to pray together, to struggle together, to go to jail together, to stand up for freedom together, knowing that we will be free one day.

This will be the day when all of God's children will be able to sing with a new meaning, "My country, 'tis of thee, sweet land of liberty, of thee I sing. Land where my fathers died, land of the pilgrim's pride, from every mountainside, let freedom ring."

And if America is to be a great nation this must become true. So let freedom ring from the prodigious hilltops of New Hampshire. Let freedom ring from the mighty mountains of New York. Let freedom ring from the heightening Alleghenies of Pennsylvania!

Let freedom ring from the snowcapped Rockies of Colorado!

Let freedom ring from the curvaceous slopes of California!

But not only that; let freedom ring from Stone Mountain of Georgia!

Let freedom ring from Lookout Mountain of Tennessee!

Let freedom ring from every hill and molehill of Mississippi. From every mountainside, let freedom ring.

And when this happens, when we allow freedom to ring, when we let it ring from every village and every hamlet, from every state and every city, we will be able to speed up that day when all of God's children, black men and white men, Jews and Gentiles, Protestants and Catholics, will be able to join hands and sing in the words of the old Negro spiritual, "Free at last! free at last! thank God Almighty, we are free at last!"